ABANDONED
AND SACRIFICED

KATHRYN SPURLING

ABANDONED AND SACRIFICED

THE TRAGEDY OF MONTEVIDEO MARU

To the citizens and families of New Britain and New Ireland 1942.
Your loss was great yet your Government deserted you.
May the lessons of the past be learnt and not repeated.

Published in 2022 by New Holland Publishers
First published in Australia in 2017 by New Holland Publishers
Sydney • Auckland

Level 1, 178 Fox Valley Road, Wahroonga, NSW 2076, Australia
5/39 Woodside Ave, Northcote, Auckland 0627, New Zealand

newhollandpublishers.com

A record of this book is held at the National Library of Australia.

ISBN 9781760794774

Group Managing Director: Fiona Schultz
Project Editor: Jess Cox
Designer: Andrew Davies
Production Director: Arlene Gippert
Printed in Australia by SOS Print + Media Group

10 9 8 7 6 5 4 3 2 1

Keep up with New Holland Publishers:

 NewHollandPublishers
 @newhollandpublishers

CONTENTS

Foreword 7

Preface 9

Chapter One Too Young 11

Chapter Two Brothers and Brothers at Arms 24

Chapter Three An Inviolate Enclave of the British Empire 42

Chapter Four Tropical Paradise, Tropical Discord 58

Chapter Five Ill-Prepared for War 77

Chapter Six The Beginning of the End 96

Chapter Seven Sacrificed And Abandoned 114

Chapter Eight Situation Hopeless 135

Chapter Nine Escape or Perish 157

Chapter Ten Gruesome Death 176

Chapter Eleven Desperate 193

Chapter Twelve Any Means of Escape 212

Chapter Thirteen Prisoners-Of-War 232

Chapter Fourteen Down to the Sea in Ships 254

Chapter Fifteen Subterfuge and Denial 279

Bibliography 303

Acknowledgements 308

About the Author 311

FOREWORD

I write this foreword in the recent shadow of the 75th anniversary of the Battle of Rabaul. With that context, it is with particular pride that I introduce Dr Kathryn Spurling's seventh book, *Abandoned and Sacrificed: The Tragedy of the* Montevideo Maru.

Through the engaging personal stories of the Australian soldiers and nurses who served in New Britain, the hauntingly beautiful account of pre-war Rabaul and its local inhabitants, and analysis of the decisions made by the military leadership of the day, Dr Spurling crafts a compelling narrative and commentary. Together the stories and observations build inexorably to their heartbreaking conclusion – the defeat of Rabaul, the massacre of Australian soldiers and local volunteers and other civilians, and the terrible loss of over 1000 souls on the Japanese POW ship, *Montevideo Maru*, at the hands of a US submarine.

It is a story of youthful, naive optimism pitted against flawed and stubborn leadership. It is a story of both bravery and brutality in war, a story of resilience and resourcefulness in the face of defeat and despair. And, finally, it is a story of painful silence for families, of the struggle for justice for the survivors, and of late recognition for those lost in a hopeless battle and to the ocean depths.

This is yet another engaging, meticulously researched account by Dr Spurling of an Australian military tragedy – one which weaves together first-person memoirs, historical military documents, and analysis made possible by the passing of time and lifting of the veil of secrecy. It asks the hard questions about why the lives of the inhabitants and the defenders of New Britain were so readily sacrificed and why justice and recognition were so long in coming. It is both easy to read and yet difficult and confronting to consider.

It is a piece of Australian history of which too few people are aware.

Dr Spurling assists us as a nation, and you as a reader, to remedy that gap.

– Gordon Ramsay MLA.

PREFACE

Australians who made their homes in New Britain, New Ireland and surrounding New Guinea islands at the beginning of World War II, and those deployed as *Lark Force* – who faced overwhelming Japanese forces in January 1942 – have been almost forgotten in Australian history.

Growing up in the Witu Islands and Rabaul I knew of the occupation and the disappearance of 1053, including my grandfather Philip Coote and my great uncle, onboard the *Montevideo Maru* on 1 July 1942 – but I knew very little. The 40th anniversary in Rabaul in 1982 had a profound effect. My father, Peter Coote, introduced me to survivors. There was the Wirraway pilot, the Tol Massacre survivor and the one who escaped hundreds of kilometres via the New Britain north coast with nothing but the clothes on his back, surviving the rugged terrain, ferocious river crossings and hostile villages – to eventually meet up with Keith McCarthy, and Gladys Baker on whose plantation my family would later live. I thought about my father's family – my grandmother and how she had coped after being evacuated to Australia and having no home to go to. How she and other families were left to wonder what happened to their husbands and fathers for nearly four years. I thought about the grandfather I hadn't known and what my grandfather was thinking as he heard and felt the Japanese bombs destroy the family home. I knew of the ramifications which transcended generations. Yes – abandoned and sacrificed indeed! The stories mesmerized me and I never ceased to wonder why this extraordinary chapter in our history was not better known and widely commemorated.

The entire, complex story has not been told until *Abandoned and Sacrificed: The Tragedy of the* Montevideo Maru. Kathryn Spurling is to be congratulated. With impeccable research, honour and compassion, and a tremendous understanding of the circumstances, Kathryn has managed to successfully bring the diverse aspects together, portraying the complexities in an easy to read manner. It is a powerful, significant, important story and a great tribute to the men and women who experienced so much in the New Guinea islands at the start of the Pacific War.

— Andrea Williams

CHAPTER ONE

TOO YOUNG

*'Being a coast defence battery,
we won't be in the field.*

In 1941 war raged in Europe, boots goosestepped past stunned civilians and the burning remnants of their destroyed militaries. A rapid German offensive, too, in the deserts of the Middle East, negated Allied victories against Italian forces in Libya. Royal Australian Navy (RAN) warships fought desperate sea battles in the Mediterranean, bombarding enemy shore positions when they could, while being subjected to unrelenting air attacks. Royal Australian Air Force (RAAF) personnel struggled to clear their aircraft of invasive desert sands and watched pilots disappear, never to return. At Tobruk, it was vital for the defence of Egypt and the Suez Canal for a garrison, mostly Australian, to hold the town with its harbour.[1] From April 1941, around 14,000 Australian soldiers were besieged in Tobruk by a German-Italian army commanded by General Erwin Rommel. Their tenacity and bravery ensured their lasting fame as 'The Rats of Tobruk'. Their exploits echoed those of their predecessors in 1914–18, with iconic rising sun badges adorning battered slouch hats. It was the stuff of legend and the Australian media grandly trumpeted that theme.

On 13 June 1941, the editorial in Tasmania's Hobart *Mercury* exalted 'the superb fighting spirit of the British race':

> *To the Empire the moment of need was the testing hour, and in that hour it rose to supreme heights to prove for all time that empires are built not on violence and force, but on the rights that freedom confers.*[2]

The editorial praised leaders and warriors: 'our fighting efficiency not only unimpaired, but increased and increasing', and concluded with the prediction that while June 1940 could be considered by some as a 'disaster', June 1941 meant 'hope', and June 1942 would likely mean 'victory'.[3] The prediction was myopic and the ensuing year was anything but victorious for the Australians enticed to enlist by the 1941 nationalistic rhetoric.

The Hobart *Mercury* editorial, like others throughout Australia, made soldiering and war noble and adventurous – an opportunity to leave behind a mundane civilian world with few prospects and to travel to a mysterious, exciting, distant world. Young men besieged recruiting offices, anxious for something so much more. Those who crowded into Hobart's army recruiting office in February 1941 could never foresee where this eagerness would take them.

Left Gerald McShane and right John Carr. Australian War Memorial AWM

They arrived from Nubeena, Sorell and Penguin, pretty temperate climate towns known for their close-knit farming and fishing communities. Many came from working class comfortable homes in the southern state's capital, such as brothers Alfred Johnson Crawford and Harold Maxwell Crawford. Recruiters in Hobart struggled to cope, the influx was overwhelming and enlisters were subsequently processed with great haste. Authentication of ages and parental consent received only cursory consideration. According to their declarations, the Crawford brothers were less than six months apart in age, but this fact went unchallenged. John Eshott Carr was possibly not even 18. He certainly wasn't when he first attempted to enlist on 25 June 1940. Carr decided to return to the enlistment office on 22 February 1941, when recruiting officers were grappling with a long line of youthful faces. This time he was enlisted, regardless of the vague details concerning place of birth and residence, no parental consent and his audacity to write occupation as 'soldier'. Carr was delighted because he had enlisted with his best mate, Gerald John McShane, who also 'might' have been 18. Military numbers were stamped on files as quickly as humanly possible – temporary ones. Those who enlisted in Hobart in February 1941 were advised to join the coast artillery. Many were too young to join the Australian Imperial Force (AIF) for overseas service.[4] They were told they could then volunteer to go overseas in 'the belief that they would be reinforcements for the AIF in the Middle East.'[5] With only obsolete weaponry available, training was brief and inadequate. In less than two months, 40 Tasmanians boarded a ship bound northwards; all but two had enlisted in February. Alan James Batchler (TX16308) barely had time to grab his toothbrush, having enlisted in March. The 20-year-old was designated 'L' Heavy Battery, Signalman. He felt confident he would become proficient in his duties and he was just pleased he was on the ship. Laurence 'Laurie' William Sawford had enlisted in the military forces in July 1940. A strapping lad of 6ft (180cm) and 178lb (81kg), the carpenter's labourer wrote his birthday as 11 January 1922, and signed the oath to 'resist His Majesty's enemies and cause His Majesty's peace to be kept and maintained.' The 1922 was really 1923. He became Gunner (TX16392). Their enlistment papers were not entirely clear or accurate but their youth was obvious. Nineteen of the 40 Tasmanians were too young to vote, 17 were 21–25 years old. The old men of their number were Gunner Aubrey Thomas Trail (TX4427), 27, Bombardier John

Laurie Ramsay (TX4384), 28, Lance Bombardier James Samuel Priestly (TX5226), 31, and their Staff Sergeant, William Warhurst (TX4358), 40. Warhurst was army through and through, having enlisted in Victoria in January 1919 as an 18-year-old. After maturing during the grim days of the last war and an era of unbridled imperial loyalty, the military was for Warhurst a natural fit. Warhurst was transferred to the Tasmanian detachment in 1941. He was an experienced non-commissioned officer (NCO), seasoned enough to realize there was going to be much work to turn this group of ebullient Tasmanians into fighting artillerymen. Four of the 40 assumed the duties of fortress engineers.[6]

Regardless of the enthusiasm of the volunteers, the Australian Government and military bureaucracy were stifled by indecision and a lack of preparation. In 1940, attention was firmly focused on the Northern Hemisphere, and the Australian forces committed to a European war in the Middle East. For years, authorities had adopted a 'hear no evil, see no evil' attitude to the rise of Japanese military nationalism, known as Bushido, the 'Way of the Warrior', and were largely unconcerned by Japanese aggression through Asia, which had commenced as early as 1931 with Japan's invasion of Manchuria. In September 1940, Japan invaded Indochina. Western Allies responded by freezing Japan's assets and imposing an oil embargo. The aggression continued under the 'Three Alls' – kill all, burn all, destroy all – policy towards China. However, serene in its belief of racial superiority (resulting in a severe underestimation of the ambition, audacity and capability of the Japanese), the British Empire continued to prioritise defence of the motherland.

In a hastily improvised strategy, grandly titled 'The Malay Barrier', the decision was made to send two brigades of the AIF 8th Division to Malaya. One brigade, the 23rd, was split into three battalion-sized garrison military forces to protect the northern approaches to Australia and airfields that linked Australia to South-East Asian Allied territory. These small forces were named, ominously, after non-predatory species of birds. Sparrow Force was destined for Timor, Gull Force for Ambon Island in the Dutch East Indies and *Lark Force* for New Britain and New Ireland in New Guinea. Typically, the garrisons were formed around an infantry battalion, supported by other Australian Defence Force (ADF) units. On Ambon and Timor, Netherlands East Indies (NEI) troops supplemented the garrison; in New Guinea, members of the New Guinea Volunteer Rifles (NGVR) supported the garrison.

The *Lark Force* advance party of eight officers and 33 other ranks disembarked from SS *Neptuna* on 16 March 1941 at Rabaul, New Britain, the capital of Australian New Guinea. Over ensuing months, the number of Australians rose to around 1400. The AIF 2/22nd Battalion, Australian Infantry, formed on 17 July 1940 and commanded by Lieutenant Colonel Howard Hammer Carr (VX41567) from Ballarat, Victoria, which was 938 strong, centred the garrison. Attached also were engineers; anti-tank and artillery batteries; signals corps; army ordnance corps; members of the 2/10 Field Ambulance, accompanied by six Australian Army nurses; and 150 officer and men of the 1st Independent Company, who were to be based on nearby New Ireland and outlying islands. A detachment of RAAF 24 Squadron personnel with Wirraway fighters and Hudson bombers, arrived during December 1941.

As with the Tasmanians, artillery volunteers from mainland states, who were attached to heavy and Anti-Aircraft (AA) units, dragged their military kit and a few personal belongings down the gangway of Zealandia in March and April 1941 at Rabaul and were stunned by this foreign and exotic place. They had been led to believe that they were to be AIF reinforcements, but this most definitely was not the Middle East. Commanding Officer (CO) of the Anti-Aircraft unit was Lieutenant (Lt) David Mayer Selby, whose physical appearance seemed more at home in the courtroom from which he had come. A graduate of Sydney's Shore School, he graduated from Sydney University in Arts in 1924, and Law in 1927, before entering the bar the following year. In March 1939, he married Barbara Phillips, and in 1940 their first daughter, Alison, was born. Slight, fair and outwardly serious, he too saw how young his recruits were.

Gunners Harley Douglas McCallum, Ernest George Tucker, Alfred Henry Herron and Ivan Leo Hatcher were four of the Victorians who for official purposes were 18. Gnr Henry Porter filled out his enlistment form in May 1940 and wrote his date of birth as 19 February 1921. He also mentioned that he had served with the militia artillery since 1939. Porter was in fact born in 1923. Another, Gunner Keith Reginald James McIntosh, posed proudly with siblings on pre-embarkation leave – he did look older than 18. Gunner Earl James Arrow however, did not.

Arrow was one of Selby's boys, a member of the Anti-Aircraft detachment. Selby was totally impressed with the 'keenness' exhibited, but with the 'great majority under nineteen years of age'[7] he had concerns, and not just about their age – the words 'trained, experienced and well-equipped' came to mind. Their equipment consisted of two ancient 3-inch Anti-Aircraft guns. His 52 artillerymen had never fired a shot.

The 1941 recruiting drive had enticed these young men with the promise that they would become members of the legendary AIF. They were then informed that they were too young to become Anzacs; instead, they remained militiamen, members of the Coast Defence Command. They were promised that with age and training there may be a transfer to the AIF. Lt David Selby was clearly frustrated:

They were not told that once in the Coast Defence Command they would be held there as firmly as though chained by leg irons.[8]

LEFT: *Gunner (Gnr) Keith McIntosh.* RIGHT: *Gnr Earl Arrow.* AWM

The draft to 1 Anti-Aircraft (AA) Battery Unit was viewed by the volunteers as a stepping stone, particularly as an Australian AA regiment had travelled to the Middle East 'with all the glory of greybacked colour patches and Australian badges on their shoulders.'[9]

On behalf of his gunners, Selby continued to pass 'requests, petitions and representations' to senior officers, but these were met 'with a discreet silence', especially when his men were told they were off to Rabaul, New Britain, and not the Middle East.[10] The recriminations did not stop when the AA boys disembarked. There was a huge demarcation between militia and regular AIF. The AIF referred to militiamen by the uncomplimentary name of 'chocos', short for 'chocolate soldiers', soldiers who would melt away in action. Militia could only be stationed on Australian soil. Even though these volunteers were now overseas, they were still technicially on Australian soil. Members of the AIF proudly wore metal 'Australia' shoulder badges and were known to point to these and taunt militiamen, saying: 'Get a bit of weight on your shoulders.' An even more derisive name for militiamen was 'koalos', meaning 'not to be exported or shot at.' The division between the artillery militiamen and infantry soldiers of the 2/22nd AIF created unnecessary tension and disciplinary problems when cohesion was desirable.

More artillerymen arrived on Zealandia on 29 September. Commanded by Captain Gwynne Matheson (VX45210), a former insurance inspector, the 17th Anti-Tank Battery, Royal Australian Artillery (RAA), looked impressive as they alighted, six officers and 104 men with a battery of eight 2-pounder guns. This unit had previously been the 23rd Anti-Tank Company and was redesignated 17th Anti-Tank Battery (less C Troop) on 9 August 1941. It was only in 1940 that AIF infantry brigades began forming anti-tank companies, 'with the establishment of three platoons each equipped with three-pounders.'[11] Then, in August 1941, three anti-tank companies of the Australian 8th Division were reformed into the 17th and 18th Anti-Tank Batteries, and the 17th was sent to New Guinea. The 17th Anti-Tank was supposed to be 'composed mainly of men who had previously served in AIF infantry anti-tank companies.'[12]

LEFT: *Gnr Keith Trigg (alias Eric Triggs);* MIDDLE: *Gnr George Thornton;* RIGHT: *Sgt Victor Wainwright.* AWM

Clearly, this was far from universal. Anti-tank Gunner (Gnr) Eric Kenneth Triggs (NX53269) from Tuggerah, New South Wales, wrote on his enlistment paper that he had previous artillery training and was nearly 23. Only too late was his name discovered to be Keith Alwyn Trigg and that he was underage. The expression on the face of anti-tank Gnr George Henry Thornton (NX55060) was one of sheer pride. He was wearing an AIF uniform, resplendent with the artillery leather ammunition bandolier across his chest. Thornton was unconcerned that the enlistment form cited the warning that, should details be untruthful he was 'liable to heavy penalties under the Defence Act', and wrote his date of birth as 3 February 1919. Nor did Thornton have any artillery experience, which was unsurprising for a 17-year-old.

Furthermore, early training had left a lot to be desired. Archibald Norman 'Arch' Taylor (NX51929) joined the 36th Battalion militia at

the age of 17. He impatiently waited until June 1940, when he was allowed to transfer to the AIF at 18.

There was no equipment available so we were called 'day boys'. We were sent home and we had to report to the local oval to learn military drill until such time as we could get rifles and

Gnr Arch Taylor. UNSW   *uniform.*[13]

18

At last Taylor was transferred from the 'day boys' to the 2/18th Battalion at Wallgrove, and finally began preliminary training. The battalion moved to Bathurst and Taylor became a member of the 22nd Anti-Tank Battery. There were no guns.

Allegedly they had a two pounder. We had the dashboard of an old motor car with an axle and a clothes prop sticking out the back. And that was our gun that we did our anti-tank training on.[14]

There was another change of number when they became the 17th Anti-Tank battery, and 'we thought we were going to the Middle East.'[15]

To this youth and inexperience was entrusted the protection of airfields, seaplane anchorages and the aerial gateway to Australian territory by senior and war-seasoned military official in faraway Melbourne, Victoria – something not lost on their Sergeant, Victor Ernest Ross Wainwright (NX54267). Wainwright had married Winifred Scott just four months before his deployment. As a memento for his bride, he visited a photographic studio. The photographer posed him in front of a fine European vista, now as amusing as it was incongruous.

The trip to the Middle East may have stalled, but they were still overseas and Rabaul was stunning. Blanche Bay and its purple-blue waters stretched to St George's Channel and numerous coral atolls. Simpson Harbour was one of the finest in the South Pacific, capable of holding 300,000 tons of shipping. In 1914, these waters held a mighty Royal Australian Navy (RAN) fleet and members of the Australian Naval and Military Expedition Force (AN&MEF). Australia's first submarine AE1, disappeared with 35 crew on 14 September 1914 off Rabaul, the first ustralian military unit lost in war. In 2016 it was yet to be found.[16]

The entire length of New Britain, a crescent-shaped island 370 miles (595km) long and 50 miles (80km) wide, was transversed by the rugged Baining mountain range. Entering the harbour it was impossible not to be impressed by the rugged ridge, which rose at Raluana Point to a height of 1,500 feet (457m). The Rabaul skyline was dominated dramatically by the island's highest mountain, Ulawun, 'The Father' and

Left to right: Sgt Bruce Macintosh Gilchrist (NX191442), Lt Peter Fisher,
Chaplain John Lovett May (TX6004), Lt David Selby, Sgt Ernest Green
(NX191434) and Sgt Hamilton John Frederick Peters (NX191443).
"Frisbee Ridge" AWM

volcanic peaks Toyanumbatir, 'North Daughter', Kombiu, 'The Mother' and Turanguna, 'South Daughter'. Lakunai airfield was set in one of the few flat stretches of ground, between the slopes of 'North Daughter' and 'The Mother'.[17] Looming over the township was Mount Tavurvur (Matupi Crater), its barren and pummelled appearance a 'reminder of Rabaul's volcanic past'.[18]

To Lt David Selby, describing his unit as 'AA Battery, Rabaul', was a 'flattering title of the two officers and fifty-two other ranks and their two 3-inch guns and obsolete ring-sight telescope.'[19] It took him 'considerable research' to discover that the title was actually the 'Anti-Aircraft and Anti-Military Landing Craft' Battery – the second part of the name was rather ironic given his unit was positioned high on Observation Point.[20] The elevated position offered a spectacular panorama but his battery was in a very 'unpromising gun position, silhouetted as it was against both northern and southern skylines.'[21]

The AA position was 'painfully conspicuous from land, sea, and air', so cramped that his gunners were liable to trip over each other or slip down the slope while manning their guns. In short this battery was, according to its CO, 'everything an AA battery position should not be.'[22]

The 'L' Heavy Battery, to which the 40 Tasmanians were attached, was commanded by Major James Rowland Purcell Clark (TX6041) a Hobart-born 38-year-old. He had similar misgivings. Many of these young men he was responsible for, such as Gnr Gordon Abel (TX15429), already had difficult lives and they weren't getting any easier. Abel was another kid whose life had been severely deprived by a father who struggled to re-adjust after being wounded in France during World War I (WWI). Abel's mother died when he was six and the boy was fostered by different people. The Depression saw him leave school at 11 to work on the Jane River goldfields in south-west Tasmania. At 14 he worked on a fishing boat and then cut timber for the mines, before going underground in the mines of Mount Lyell. Joining the military meant many things to Abel, most of all to finally be part of a large, close family. In Hobart, he visited RAN, RAAF and AIF recruiters and received the same response: he was too young at 17 and needed a parent's signature. But there were no parents, no guardian. The militia were happy for him to join them and he became part of *Lark Force* in Rabaul, with the suggestion that a rising sun badge would follow.

On arrival the battery unit faced further challenges Battery artillery consisted of two 6-inch WWI coast guns taken from Fort Wallace at Stockton near Newcastle, New South Wales, which they had yet to fire. They unloaded the guns and were left to move them eight miles (13km) from the town to be installed at Praed Point. First they built a road, and then built equipment that allowed them to roll

Gnr John Haywood 'Jack' Pearce (TX4393), from Lindisfarne, Tasmania, of the Heavy Battery Unit, is farewelled by his widowed mother Ethel. He did not return, dying on 1 July 1942, aged 19.

11 tons of guns the eight miles (13km) up an incline to a place where the battery could cover the St George's Channel and Blanche Bay approaches, also set precariously on the southern slopes of 'South Daughter'. Then concrete emplacements were needed, accommodation prepared, a command post built and trenches dug. They felt more like construction workers than artillerymen. Gnr Ronald Parker Robb (NX191433) had written to his family before leaving Australia: 'don't know where we are going but ... being a coast defence battery we won't be in the field '[23] As a postscript he was looking forward to his next birthday: 'Just think when I come home I'll be 26, gosh that's awful. I'm getting old.'[24]

Topography required the 6-inch guns to be placed on different levels – less than ideal. The artillerymen could only look out over the horizon from their elevated positions and wonder what awaited them.

In early 1941, New Britain, New Guinea, was a beautiful tropical paradise, but between January and July 1942, it became a tragic and terrifying place. Hundreds of civilians and members of the 1,400-strong *Lark Force* were massacred by invading Japanese forces. On 22 June 1942, more than a thousand more were forced into the squalid holds of the *Montevideo Maru*, and perished on 1 July, in Australia's worst maritime disaster. Of the 40 Tasmanians who enlisted in February 1941, half of whom still too young to vote, only 2 returned to Australia. For decades afterwards, the Australian Government and Australian military leaders who abandoned them denied what had occurred in Rabaul, denied responsibility for their senseless sacrifice and denied resolution for the families that waited.

Endnotes

1. The garrison was commanded by Lieutenant General Leslie Morshead and consisted of the 9th Division (20th, 24th and 26th Brigades), the 18th Brigade of the 7th Division, along with four regiments of British artillery and some Indian troops.

2. *Mercury* (Hobart), 13 June 1941.

3. Ibid.

4. Horner, D. *The Gunners: A History of Australian Artillery*, Allen & Unwin, 1995, p.233.

5. Selby, D. *Hell and High Fever*, Currawong Publishing, 1956, p.5.

6. Corporal Rowland Ernest Domeney, Corporal John Leonard Rodway, Sapper Henry Harold Taylor, and Sapper Francis Gordon Williams.

7. Selby, p 5

8. Ibid.

9. Ibid.

10. Ibid.

11. Horner, p.233.

12. Ibid.

13. australiansatwarfilmar hive.unsw. edu.au/archive/113-archibald-taylor accessed 19 June 2016.

14. Ibid.

15. Ibid.

16. Spurling, K. *The Mystery of AE1: Australia's Lost Submarine and Crew*, Missing Pages Books, 2014.

17. Rabaul derived its name from the large but idle crater of Rabalanakaia.

18. Gill, J.C.H. 'The last days of Rabaul: (December 13, 1941 to January 23, 1942)' *Journal of the Royal Historical Society of Queensland*, vol 6, 1961, Royal Historical Society of Queensland, p.643. espace. library.uq.edu.au/view/UQ:212613/ s00855804_1960_1961_6_3_635 accessed 11 May 2016.

19. Selby, p.4.

20. Ibid.

21. Ibid.

22. Ibid.

23. Robb, R.P. PR01219, AWM, Canberra.

24. Ibid.

CHAPTER TWO

BROTHERS AND BROTHERS AT ARMS

'When you're eighteen ...
you just think you're invincible.'

The lessons of the previous world war were too quickly forgotten by authorities and young men alike. So many Australians falsified enlistment forms then and Australian military forces turned a blind eye in those heady, naive, uninitiated days; in 1940 the same occurred. Norm Furness was part of a generation of battlers, used to surviving through their own initiative and hard work. Norm was born on 15 January 1922 in the Melbourne suburb of Prahran and, as a young child growing up in the Depression, he went with his father to collect council handouts.

> *You'd go up with your bag and they'd give you a loaf of bread and some potatoes, and possibly a tin of golden syrup or treacle. And we used to do that every week ... Everything was tough, and my brothers were out of work.*[1]

Norm had started delivering newspapers at eight years old, first the morning round, then the evening round, earning 3d for every dozen he

Trench warfare training. Johnson[2]

sold. His father died and his mother failed to cope. Norm left school at 13, and at 15 was pleased to land a job in a furniture factory, sanding timber 48 hours a week. Then there was shift work in a paper mill. At 16 he joined the militia as an 18-year-old, because it paid and the once-a-week training and twice-a-year camps sounded adventurous.

When war was declared, Norm Furness was ordered to report to camp. Part of his new training consisted of a 'replica of the trenches from France from the First War.'

They used to pour water down the trenches, and we used to have to go in there and it was, sort of, re-enacting what they did in the trenches in France. And as it turned out it was absolutely useless.[3]

Norm Furness. australians-atwarfilmarchive.unsw.edu.au

Enlisting in the regular army seemed the best fit: 'I thought I could look after myself.'

You don't worry about that you might get killed. When you're eighteen that never enters your head. You just think you're invincible.[4]

The new volunteer had a sister sign the form.

I wasn't twenty-one, I was eighteen. But according to the army records I was twenty ... it shows that I was born in 1920. In actual fact I was born in '22.[5]

The medical examination caused some tilt at the confidence. They asked him to strip naked with around 100 other recruits.

Well, the first thing they do ... they hold you by the whatnots, and ask you to cough to see whether you've got a hernia or anything else ... it's quite a shock to the system.[6]

Private (Pte) Norman Furness was now VX23557, 2/22nd Infantry Battalion. The 2/22nd Battalion, part of the 23rd Brigade of the 8th Division, was raised on 1 July 1940, at Melbourne's Victoria Barracks. On 11 July, the Battalion moved to the central Victorian town of Trawool, near Seymour. Trawool was uninviting, 'one of those flat boggy corners of ground that always seem colder and more miserable than anywhere else nearby', described Pte Henry Robert Mitchell (VX19233).[7]

At the base of a steep, large, treeless hill, the campsite was spartan. Previously the 46th Militia camp, Trawool consisted of '109 tents, 4 marquees, 2 store tents, 5 mess tents, 1 HQ tent, 1 PO tent, 1 CWA tent and 1 YMCA marquee.' The only buildings were at either end, one housing the kitchen and the other the shower block.[8] It rained one day in three and many soldiers became ill. The physical training and route march regime was relieved by the odd concert in the YMCA marquee.

With more recruits arriving, in September the 2/22nd relocated to Bonegilla, near Wodonga, on the New South Wales–Victoria border. The term 'hard

Members of the 2/22nd training at Bonegilla.

www.jje.info/lostlives/places/2-22

26

slog' was quickly applied by the soldiers for their 146-mile (235km) week-long journey on foot, after receiving their live vaccine injections. They were nonetheless buoyed along the route with community fanfare. Nightly bonfires with local donations of food and drink eased the pain. For the army it was a useful recruiting drive, reminiscent of the WWI marches that proceeded through country towns, collecting volunteers to the sound of the beating drum. Their arrival at the new camp on 4 October was welcome, though barely had the blisters and fatigue abated when training resumed.

While the enthusiasm and belief in the immortality of youth was inevitable, less understandable was the view that it was suitable, even preferable, for the cohesiveness of a unit that brothers and mates should serve together. The wisdom of this policy had proven costly to many families and districts in WWI but it did not die with the soldiers on those battlefields.

It was a legacy that Pte Norman 'Les' Leslie Keid (QX64902) could speak of with authority. His father Leonard was killed in WWI – so too were his uncles, Bill, Walter and Ted Keid. Bill died at Quinn's Post on the Turkish Peninsula in June 1915. Leonard and Walter were killed in France within a day of each other in September 1916, during the battle for Mouquet Farm. Ted Keid died of wounds after the Passchendaele offensive in Ypres, Belgium, in November 1917.[9] The family had paid a huge price in the last war, but Les Keid still believed it was his duty to volunteer in this one. The 28-year-old mechanic, who had done his apprenticeship on Brisbane trams, probably persuaded his family that because he served with Army Ordnance, and not infantry, he would not be on the front line. In March 1941, Les Keid found himself on a ship bound for New Britain, one of the few Queenslanders attached to *Lark Force*.

Just as the army believed that the posting of brothers to the same battalion was useful, so too did it appeal to the brothers themselves. They harboured the belief that if they stayed together they could look after each other, rarely appreciating the indiscriminate risks in war and the ensuing family grief should they die. The Lambton family had been enticed to leave England under the assisted passage scheme and the promise of a better life and plentiful employment. Unfortunately, upon arrival in the late 1920s they found an Australia that was falling into a recession, with the promise of employment hollow. Their first days were a struggle for survival. Lawrence 'Laurie' Lambton moved his young family to Melbourne to take up a position as chauffeur and gardener to a wealthy family – somewhat ironic for a young man who believed he had moved around the world to a supposedly classless society. His employers invited his wife Maggie to work as cook, and her sister Mary to be housekeeper. The stable employment enabled the family to save for their own home and gave the opportunity for their boys, Lawrence 'Laurie' and Richard 'Dick', to flourish [10]

When war broke out in Europe, the younger Laurie and Richard saw the opportunity not only to protect the 'mother country' but possibly to get a sea passage to England. Richard filled out his enlistment papers on 22 July 1940 with a flourish, his fine handwriting vowing that he was '21yrs 10mths', a 'Grocer Assistant', and had 'three months' militia experience. His papers were stamped VX38273. Laurie had not displayed the same flair and confidence when he beat Dick to the recruiting office in June 1940. He simply wrote his occupation as 'store' and was a tad confused; his age, 20, did not tally with his date of birth. His file was stamped VX25979.

They found many brothers in the 2/22nd. John 'Jack' Skelton Russell (VX26521) was two years senior to brother Robert 'Bob' William Russell (VX26518). Born in the Australian Rules Football (AFL) stronghold of Essendon, Melbourne, John had trained as an analytical chemist and had just married before he was sent into camp. Bob was establishing a career in process engraving and graphic arts when he and John enlisted on the same day in June 1940. They were delighted when long-time mate Ormond 'Orm' Frederick Clarke Copas (VX27001) joined them.[11]

Parents throughout Victoria suffered mixed emotions as their sons turned, smiled, waved for the last time and marched off to war. There was pride, but also a deeply unsettling fear. Joseph and Eileen Dalton may have been consoled that their son Bernard (VX24210), at 21 was at least serving with his older brother Francis (VX129336), 26. Oliver and Elizabeth Smith, from their Central Goldfields town of Dunolly, 117 miles

LEFT: *Richard Lambton*. RIGHT: *Laurie Lambton*. www.jje.info/lostlives/people/lambton/
Lindsey Weightman

(188km) north-west of Melbourne, watched as sons David (VX44521), 30, and Donald (VX38091), 34, departed to enlist in July 1940. It was a vast distance from Dunolly to Warrnambool, a port on the Victorian shipwreck coastline 165 miles (266 km) south-west of Melbourne, but the Vinnell brothers, Albert (VX47739), 30, and Arthur (VX47742), 22, soon trained alongside the Daltons. Hamilton, 186 miles (299 km) from Melbourne in the Southern Grampians, prided itself as being the 'Wool Capital of the World'. It was also the home of Basil and Rex Wythe, both 23, when they were caught in the recruiting drive and became privates VX24187 and VX18861. The Yench brothers, Henry Charles (VX24121), 23, Raymond (VX24130), 21, and George Andrew (VX35948), 27, were born in Wagga Wagga, New South Wales, but lived in Victoria.

Leslie Charles Whittle (VX24045), 25, and brother Walter Frederick Whittle (VX24036), 21, enlisted together on 7 June 1940 with their best mates Hugh 'Nipper' Joseph Webster (VX23821), 20, and Norman Wickham Walkley (VX23167), 20. As a symbol of mateship, perhaps aided by intoxication of a different kind, they each had a 'W' tattooed on their arms and were known in the 2/22nd henceforth as 'the four W's'.

Unlike their artillery counterparts, the 2/22nd included a great

LEFT TO RIGHT: *Bob Russell, John 'Jack' Russell, Bob Russell and Orm Copas.*
www.jje.info/lostlives/people/russelljs

number of men who could be designated as 'mature'. Private (Pte) Cecil Howard Toms (VX37531), 37, served with his 35-year-old brother Pte Claude Hector Toms (VX33107); similarly, Pte Clarence Thomas Bellingham (VX28007), 33, served with Pte William Henry Bellingham (VX28017), 34. Privates Charles Stuart Roy (VX28997) and Colin Campbell Roy (VX28980) were 32-year-old twins.

In an era of large families, the Burnett boys, from Collingwood, Melbourne, were not unusual – seven enlisted. Private (Pte) Angus William Burnett (VX24203) and Pte Edward Joseph Burnett (VX16483) served with the 2/22 Battalion and could debate at length with the Russell brothers about which was the better AFL team, Collingwood or Essendon.[12] Angus was the elder by 12 years and the expectation was that he could keep his 20-year-old brother in check and safe, something Angus soon found challenging. Many were country lads. On leaving school, Jack Moyle worked on his family's Spring Creek property near Tallangatta. Typical of his generation and country upbringing, Jack believed 'war seemed inevitable' and, 'determined to be ready for it', he joined the local Light Horse Regiment and trained part-time.[13] Nonetheless 'It became obvious that there was no place for Light Horse troops in modern warfare',[14] so Jack, with mates Alexander George Cardwell (VX20534) and Peter Joseph 'Joe' Kelleher (VX19573), travelled to Melbourne to enlist. Another local lad, John 'Jack' Price Sutherland (VX42440), caught up with them when they arrived at Trawool; all became privates in the 2/22nd.

Angus Burnett. AWM *Edward Burnett.* AWM *Pte Jack Moyle.* Moyle

Bonegilla camp was a marked improvement on the congested tent city of Trawool but the training soon became monotonous – square bashing (marching on a parade ground), doubling with full pack, and target practice with .303-calibre Lee Enfield rifles. The soldiers were unimpressed with their equipment. Pte Norm Furness was not alone in believing:

> *Most of the stuff we were getting was old stuff from the First World War that had been stacked away in grease for twenty years. It was pretty ancient the stuff that we got.*[15]

There were now around 3,000 in the 23rd Brigade of the 8th Division AIF. Friendships were forged among men with dissimilar backgrounds who now banded together in squads and troops, such as the 38 soldiers in 12 Platoon B Company. Pte John Andrew Edward Cameron (VX26803) was the youngest of a family of five boys and three girls to James and Margaret Cameron of Fife, Scotland. James and his extended family worked as coal miners, as labourers or in domestic service. John migrated to Australia in pursuit of greater opportunities. He needed to work as a labourer, but life started improving when he became co-owner of an orchard. With a large family in Scotland, a war endangering Britain was personal and John lost no time in enlisting. It was also the only way a man of his means stood any chance of visiting his extended family.

In 12 Platoon B Company, there was another Cameron – Stanley

Back left to right: Bill Smith, Stan Cameron, Eric Firmstone, Sydney McGregor. Front left to right: John Cameron, Horace Newman, Russell Kelly, Ronald Long.

Allan Cameron (VX26283), but they were not related, and Stanley was born in North Sydney. The Scottish theme continued, in name only, with Harold Stewart (VX47709) a 37-year-old from Wallacedale, Victoria, and Sydney McGregor (VX24423). McGregor was 39 and married to Elinor 'Madge' Marjorie with three daughters, Marjorie, 9, Mattie, 7, and Helen, 3. He was a tennis player of some note and a chess devotee. Horace George Newman (VX24138), 30, was born in England; Eric Douglas Firmstone (VX23936), 28, was a Victorian, as were William Allan Geoffrey 'Bill' Smith (VX37739), 40, and Ronald Long (VX24223), 37. Arnold William Woodhead (VX26446), 33, was from New South Wales, as was Sgt Russell Kelly (VX33979) whose parents had given him the impressive middle name of 'Livingstone'. As Kelly, at 41, was older than most and outranked them, it was best not to

Sydney McGregor. www.jje.info/lostlives/people/mcgregors

Farewell parade in Melbourne. Johnson

make fun of the name. Besides if a name was a point of mirth few could beat Neville Curtis (VX42144), 24, who had been a bank clerk living in St Kilda, Melbourne, and who snatched enough leave in December 1940 to marry Jean. It was tedious enough filling out forms when you had two names, but though Neville Edward Curtis was okay, Neville Edward Hercules Curtis caused a few smiles. By May 1941, the brothers-in-arms were part of the 2/22nd deployed in Rabaul, New Guinea.

For these men, who enlisted in the first six months of WWII, an overriding motivation was loyalty to Britain and her empire. School textbooks were dominated by British history, industry, trade, politics and culture, and by world maps stained with red, representative of the British Commonwealth. Few students were taught the geography and history of any other part of the globe, particularly Asia. It was widely accepted that:

Britain was our ideal, if it was British it was best: the substantial red shadings on any world map seemed ample proof of this and gave us great confidence [16]

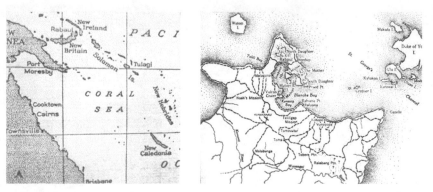

LEFT: *Rabaul*. RIGHT: *Blanche Bay*. The Japanese Thrust, Australia in the War 1939–1945[18]

The buzzes around the 2/22nd camp had been rife but confusing: deployment where? the Middle East or Europe? It was with some misgivings that the 23rd Brigade was not included when the 8th Division shipped out early in 1941 for destinations unknown. The disappointment at being left behind was short lived; the 23rd, now broken into the 2/21st, 2/40th and the 2/22nd, were transported to Sydney for deployment as the 'bird forces', bound for Ambon, Timor and New Britain respectively, from March 1941.

The place names were completely foreign: 'Rabaul, never heard of it'[17] the youthful Norm Furness said, and it was an unusually educated soldier who could tell you where any of the islands were. The other question on most lips was, why?

As HMAS *Katoomba* sailed into Blanche Bay, Pte Norm Furness was astonished.

I thought it was the most beautiful spot I'd ever seen in my life. It was absolutely beautiful. This massive great bay surrounded by greenery and the mountains. Surrounded by mountains. And it's hard to describe how nice it looked. Absolutely beautiful ... we thought this is going to be marvellous ... it was a beautiful harbour and a beautiful town, Rabaul.[19]

Rabaul before 1937 was beautiful, with broad, carefully laid-out avenues, lush green parks and gardens highlighted with prodigious

LEFT: *Rabaul in the 1930s.* RIGHT: *Main Street, Rabaul.* NGVR Museum

bougainvillea in strong splashes of red, purple, pink, yellow and white; nature offering a more glorious display than any artist's palette. It was very much a British outpost. In 'its heyday', Rabaul was 'an inviolate enclave of the British Empire'.[20] Life for Europeans was 'self-indulgent and privileged'.[21]

It was a racially divided society, physically and socially.

The colonial 'masters' were the 700 Caucasians, mainly
Australian and German. Next in line, came the 1,000 Asians,
mainly Chinese and a few Malays and last about 8,000 New
Guineans, including many indentured laborers [sic].[22]

Europeans were scattered throughout New Britain and nearby New Ireland as missionaries, plantation owners and managers, business leaders and administrators. With cheap labour in abundance, European women socialized and shopped, and their husbands regularly returned for lunch and a two-hour rest. At night it was cocktails at the local Rabaul and New Guinea clubs, where membership was restricted.

LEFT: *New Guinea Club.* RIGHT: *Rabaul Club.* NGVR Museum

LEFT: *Tavurvur exploding.* RIGHT: *Kathleen Bignell, owner of the Rabaul Hotel, outside her damaged hotel.* Johnson, R.W. & Threlfall, N.A. Volcano Town: The 1937–43 Eruptions at Rabaul

This idyllic setting was shattered in 1937, when the Tavurvur and Vulcan volcanoes erupted simultaneously, hurtling lava, pumice and ash over vast distances, burying Rabaul and the surrounding region in a heavy, suffocating blanket of grey. Boats were left stranded on the Rabaul foreshore from ensuing tsunamis. More than 200 people were killed and Rabaul was never the same.

For the men of *Lark Force*, the Rabaul of 1941 was still a tropical paradise but a shock to Australian men who came predominantly

The 2/22nd marching into Rabaul. Johnson

Gnr Gordon Abel. Johnson

from cool, temperate places. Everything was so very different, not just the climate and vegetation, but a population of ethnically diverse peoples – it all required considerable assimilation.

For working class youngsters such as Norm Furness, observing the lives of the white citizenry was a revelation.

They lived the good life. They all had two or three servants each, every white family there. They did no work, basically. All the physical work was done by natives. They ran the offices and things like that. But no physical work there. The women did no physical work.[23]

The soldiers were briefed on how they should behave; of particular importance was that they were not to fraternize with the indigenous people, particularly the women. At 17, Tasmanian Gnr Gordon Abel wasn't exactly experienced with women, he was actually 'scared of girls' so it was disturbing when he was told 'don't touch the native women,

Cameron, front left, with mates. www.jje.info/lostlives/people/cameronjae

37

you might catch a disease that could make your little Willie fall off.'[24]

There was still much to explore and, for Pte John Cameron, many a photo to send home. Chinatown, consisting of four streets of stores, was popular with the troops and an exotic place to spend their pay, according to Lieutenant David Selby.

On a multitudinous variety of goods imported from Hong Kong – the silks, ivory ornaments, perfumes, satin slippers and a host of knick-knacks to tempt the eyes of the homesick soldiery. In the centre of the town was the Bung, the native marker where the coons displayed and noisily proclaimed the excellence of their luscious papaws, bananas, pineapples, tomatoes and vegetables.[25]

For Norm Furness and his fellow privates, the Chinese tailors offered better-fitting uniforms than the army issue, which was 'usually too big or it doesn't match the colours, you know, shirt and trousers.'[26] For

relatively little cost, 'you could get a beautifully made, tailored shorts and shirts.'[27]

Soldiers, particularly the married ones, became increasingly homesick. Sapper (Spr) John 'Jack' Mervyn Render (VX129387), of the Royal Australian Engineers (RAE), was attached to the Fortress Engineers. He was another born in England whose family migrated to Australia to the pleasant seaside township of Frankston, Victoria. Jack became a stonemason like his father, and in 1931 married Doris Fleming. By 1941 the couple had two daughters, Joan and Jennifer, and had purchased a small weatherboard house. Jack was

TOP: *Cameron in front of Rabaul church.* BOTTOM: *Cameron and friend in a native outrigger.*

Sapper John 'Jack' Render. www.jje info/lostlives/ people/renderjm

a gentle man who enjoyed growing flowers. At the Frankston Autumn Flower Show in 1937 he won four times, with three roses and a bowl of dahlias. A bowl of zinnias and a vase of gladioli won him two second-place cards.[28] In May 1939 the National Registration Act was introduced, requiring all men aged 18 to 65 to register or be fined or imprisoned. Recruiting for the 6th Division of the 2nd AIF took place in November 1940 in Frankston and all men, aged 20 to 35, not in reserved occupations, were required to attend. Jack was not accepted in November but was enlisted on 12 March 1941. He embarked for Rabaul the following month. Between March 1941 and January 1942, Spr Jack Render wrote 35 letters to his wife. In the beginning he marvelled, and from his battery position above Rabaul wrote:

View from the hill, members of Lark Force. AWM P02395.001

It is beautiful and moonlight at night time up here at present
and the weather is very pleasant. At the new site there is
always a breeze blowing and we are right on the sea. So we
can have a swim any time we get a chance.[29]

Tavurvur continued to tremble ominously and belch a column of smoke, fumes and pumice dust, as if a portent of the destruction that would soon engulf the region. In June 1941, Tavurvur erupted again with a devastating blast. Once more Rabaul and surrounds were enveloped in a sickening poisonous haze of dust and sulphur. In letter no. 22, Jack Render, who had been ill from the dust and sulphur fumes, wrote of the volcano, 'making a bit of a mess down the town', as this adventure was losing its lustre.

I myself rue the day I left the old battalion as I would not
condemn my worst enemy to this deadly existence.[30]

But the situation went from bad to worse, and on 4 January 1942 the war became personal when bombs began to fall. Letter no. 35 was Jack Render's last. With further attacks imminent and the knowledge that there will be 'no withdrawal', Jack wrote:

Well sweetheart I will close now with my dearest wishes to
you & children and all my to you all & hoping to see you in the
near future & if by any chance that God wills I do not make the
grade in a tough spot remember I tried to do my duty & I will
meet you again but be of good cheer & God go with you all,
Yours for ever & ever Love Jack.[31]

Endnotes

1. australiansatwarfilmar hive.unsw. edu.au/archive/464-norman-furness accessed 2 June 2106.
2. Johnson, C. *Little Hell: the Story of the 2/22nd Battalion and Lark Force*, History House, 2004.
3. australiansatwarfilmar hive.unsw. edu.au/archive/464-norman-furness accessed 2 June 2016.
4. Ibid.
5. Ibid.
6. Ibid.
7. Mitchell, R.A. *One Bloke's Story 1937 to 1946: Henry Mitchell's MM Escape from Rabaul*, NSW Development and Advisory Publications Australia, 1998, p.21.
8. Ibid.
9. Trooper William Keid (170), 29, Australian Light Horse, died 23/06/1915, Lone Pine Memorial wall. Lt Leonard Keid, AIF 49th Battalion, killed 03/09/1916, and Sergeant Bennett Walter Keid (3909) killed 04/09/1916, A.I.F. 49th Battalion, graves unknown, memoralized on Villers-Bretonneux memorial. Sgt Edward Alexander Keid (1153) AIF 9th Battalion, died 02/11/1917, buried Lijooenthoek Military Cemetery, Belgium. Sons of Charles George and Mary Elizabeth Keid, of Molonga Terrace, Graceville, Brisbane. Two other brothers, Guy and Harry Keid survived the war – Harry was returned to Australia on compassionate grounds.
10. www.jje.info/lostlives/people/lambtonl. html Lindsey Weightman, accessed 28 May 2016.
11. www.jje.info/lostlives/people/russelljs. html Robert Ditterich, accessed 28 May 2016.
12. VX6703 Corporal Patrick Alfonsus Burnett, 2/6 Battalion, VX60088

Pte Harold Burnett, 2/29 Battalion, VX115736 Pte Victor Burnett, 2/6 Battalion and 147019 Leading Aircraftsman John James Burnett, RAAF.
13. Moyle, Jack. T. *Escape from Rabaul and The Moyles of Spring Creek*, self-published, 1999, p.4.
14. Ibid.
15. australiansatwarfilmar hive.unsw. edu.au/archive/464-norman-furness accessed 2 June 2106.
16. West, F.J. *Hubert Murray: The Australian Pro-consul*, Oxford University Press, 1968, p.125.
17. australiansatwarfilmar hive.unsw.edu. au/archive/464-norman-furness
18. Wigmore, L. *The Japanese Thrust, Australia in the War of 1939–1945*, Series One, Army, Vol. 1V, Australian War Memorial, Canberra, 1957, p.394.
19. Ibid.
20. Nikakis, G. *He's Not Coming Home*, Lothian, 2005, p.37.
21. Ibid., p.39.
22. Ibid., p.37.
23. australiansatwarfilmar hive.unsw.edu. au/archive/464-norman-furness
24. Abel, G. MSS1623, AWM
25. Selby, p.2.
26. australiansatwarfilmar hive.unsw.edu. au/archive/464-norman-furness
27. Ibid.
28. www.jje.info/lostlives/exhib/chocojack/ index.html Jenny Evans, accessed 4 June2016.
29. www.jje.info/lostlives/people/renderjm. html Jenny Evans, accessed 4 June 2016.
30. Ibid.
31. Ibid.

CHAPTER THREE

AN INVIOLATE ENCLAVE OF THE BRITISH EMPIRE

*'Well aware of what was happening in Europe ...
[we] did not suspect we would have problems in
the Pacific.*

George Oakes

The day was dazzling, filled with the laughter of children enjoying the sights, sounds, and play. There were rides, cold drinks, animals, treats to eat and parents were happy to hand over 6d for a lemonade or 6d for a treasured child's opportunity to pet the ducks. Adults were also pleased to have an opportunity to socialize with friends and partake of something stronger than lemonade. Government officials wore the favoured pristine long whites and sun helmets; their wives in fashionable floral dresses and hats to match. Bunting draped from tree to tree added to the tropical vibrancy in the grounds of the BP (British Petroleum) Club, Rabaul, on Friday and Saturday 27 and 28 September 1941. High on the main flagpole the Union Jack moved languidly, as if in keeping with the tempo of the region. The London Relief Fete, instigated by the Administrator of the Mandated Territory of New Guinea, Brigadier-General Sir Walter Ramsay McNicoll, KBE, CB, CMG, DSO,[1] was held to raise money for the citizens of London, a people and city damaged by relentless German bombing between September 1940 and May 1941.

This was a welcome opportunity for residents to mingle socially,

The September London blitz fete – the Administrator, Sir Walter McNicoll, centre, facing camera. AWM

particularly those from outlying plantations and missions. Wide-eyed mission children, in their best outfits, observed the pomp and circumstance of another culture – patronizing and segregated by race and class division, but generous in other ways, introducing education, better medical care and improving the quality of lives.

At the Paris Peace Conference of 1919, Australian Prime Minister

Mission children enjoying the London Relief Fete. AWM

43

William Morris Hughes had argued for the annexation of former German New Guinea. This mandate was granted to Australia under Article 22 of the Covenant of the League of Nations[2] and it became the Territory of New Guinea (TNG). The mandate obliged Australia to take charge of the 'spiritual interests of the natives and their development to the higher level of culture'.[3]

'Rabaul' in the local Kuanua language means 'mangrove swamp' – a depressing name – and those who called New Britain and nearby New Ireland home had to become accustomed to the many hazards of island life. Dealing with heat and humidity, the very real risk of volcanic eruption, the ever-present danger of malaria and other debilitating tropical diseases, volatile economic conditions and a society made up of dissimilar ethnicities, required bravery and stoicism. This was unmistakably an 'inviolate enclave of the British Empire', a 'racially stratified society' in which 'the colonial masters' were the Caucasians.[4] Another description was 'a brotherhood of whiteness'.[5]

Society was based on race and position. Loyalty to the British Empire was common and the vestiges of British colonial life, its strengths and oversights, were strongly evident. Rank and status were the basis of respect. The Administrator of the TNG, Sir Ramsay Walter McNicoll, headed the social order. Another with a distinguished military career was retired Major General Gerald George Hogan, MC. Awarded a Military Cross in WWI, Hogan became the Australian Crown Law Officer in Rabaul. The Deputy Administrator came with distinguished family connections. Harold Harris Page was the brother of Dr Earle Christmas Grafton Page, MHR, founder of Australia's Country Party, Deputy Prime Minister, 1923–29, and again in 1934–39, and Australia's 11th Prime Minister, from 7 April 1939, for 19 days. In September 1941 Earle Page was the Australian Minister Resident in London and, from December 1941, he attended British war cabinet committee meetings.[6]

Many of those holding senior positions in Rabaul were born in England, which reinforced the British character of the district: Judge Frederick William Mantell; Chief Administrator Medical, Dr Herbert Champion Hosking; Chief Administrator Dispensary, John Bertrand Cruise; District Officer Henry Anthony Gregory; Eric Clive Duckett, the agricultural Superintendent at Kerevat; the Medical Practitioners Robert William Cooper and Arthur Hay; and X-ray technician Roger Davies.

By June 1941, Europeans in New Britain numbered 4,100, some 400 of whom were employed in administration positions. Around 600 served as missionaries or on mission stations – half were of German descent.[7] As the community grew, so too did the need for government and private infrastructure. Some newcomers were transient as their occupations required, some were wanting to escape their past and cherish a new life, still more had realized that a remote posting was prerequisite for promotion. Albert Grant Herron was a Commonwealth Bank officer. He and Barbara Ann Veronica Hatherell married in Rabaul and were expecting their first child. Anthony John King, 22, lived on Mango Ave. An audit clerk, he moved between Rabaul and his home in Brighton-le-Sands, Sydney.

Septimus Henry Filan was 30, a clerk who for eight years had split his time between his hometown, Murrurundi, NSW, and Rabaul. Thomas Evan Evans 38 was Senior Technical Officer at the Medical Experimental Station, and had resided in the territory for 15 years. He and Grace Lansley married in Rabaul, resided in Central Avenue, had a two-year old son, Thomas David, and were expecting their second child.

The Australian Administration had given the Asian population the same legal status as European descent residents. By June 1941 there were 2,200 Chinese in New Britain[8] but the galvanized-iron shacks and shops of Rabaul's Chinatown and its residents were physically and socially detached. Merchants, craftsmen and entrepreneurs, the Chinese became a quasi-middle class between the colonists and the native New Guineans. One observer wrote:

When the day's work is done each race retires to its own
distinct world, the Asiatic having no time for the Kanakas –
the European having no time for neither [sic].[9]

There were separate hospitals, and other facilities, for European, Chinese and indigenous New Guineans. Only white children attended

Rabaul Primary School children 1941. Reeson[10]

Rabaul Primary School. In communal areas and events, each citizen was aware of where they stood and how they should behave – fraternisation was considered inappropriate.

Though conditions and separation from the Australian mainland were harsh, for the European population the rewards could be seductive. Rabaul houses were relatively comfortable bungalows, built on six foot-high piles and surrounded with spacious verandahs, decorated by ornate balustrades. The town boasted wide tree-lined roads, like Malaguna and Mango, lush tropical vegetation, elegant colonial buildings and Government House perched on Namanula Hill. Good recreation facilities were available, including turfed tennis courts and the town swimming pool, which connected to the waters of Simpson Harbour at high tide. Grand social clubs with restricted membership, a close-knit community and easy access to cheap labour accorded many expats a lifestyle few could afford in urban Australia.

The major industry in Rabaul was shipping, with the companies Burns Philp, Colyer Watson and Carpenters dominating the two wharves, numerous warehouses and Pacific trade. Though in competition, Philip Coote, the manager of Burns Philp, and William 'Bill' Spensley, manager of Colyer Watson, were friends, and at the end of the day when they retired to the club, the banter was easy. William

TOP: *Very much a gentleman's club – Rabaul Club 1936.*

BOTTOM: *Government House 1930.* sites.google.com/site/rabaulhistory

Maynard Yarrington was private secretary to Coote. Bill Yarrington, 54, was by nature a restless man and had spent much of his life on the move, enjoying his postings to tropical islands and feeling unsettled whenever he was returned to an Australian capital city.[11] Henry Fulton was a recent arrival to Rabaul and an employee with Burns Philip. Henry's life had not been easy after being crippled with childhood polio. Because of his disability, he was unable to enlist with his three brothers – Ted, Jack and Frank. Moving to New Britain meant the 30-year-old might have some adventures of his own.

Adventure was a common motivation for those who elected to live in New Guinea. Following WWI, returned soldiers found little solace in quiet suburban lifestyles. Australian boys who had travelled overseas to fight in Europe struggled to accept life as they had previously known it, particularly as the Depression limited employment options. Their belief that the war and sacrifice of so many lives would lead to a better world had been trampled in the mud of the Western Front. As the demand for copra, timber, cocoa and marine products accelerated, the Australian Government offered soldier-settlement opportunities to WWI veterans in New Guinea and this held some appeal – it quenched the desire for a new adventure and offered greater prosperity.

Australians and Europeans who accepted the challenge to own or manage plantations throughout New Britain and New Ireland were hardy souls; the demands were multifarious for men and women. Not only did families suffer the same hazards of tropical living as those living in Rabaul or New Ireland's capital, Kavieng, but they also struggled with isolation. Ernest and Audrey Stanfield moved from India to Queensland, then to New Guinea. For the Stanfield children, James,

TOP: *A typical plantation home, with New Ireland resident Myra Ashby.*
BOTTOM: *The white community of New Ireland at the Kavieng Club c.1930s.*
Reeson

then seven, and Patricia, then five, it meant a move to Bolegila Plantation in New Ireland, in 1927. Electricity and running water were luxuries not enjoyed by families on the smaller plantations. Two more children were born – challenging, in a place with so few services. The children were unaware of the struggles their parents navigated, particularly during the Depression when Ernest fossicked for gold on Tabar Island. The two eldest children worked hard and were awarded high school scholarships at Australian boarding schools. When war broke out, James joined the RAAF and father Ernest re-joined the army. With a shortage of civilian workers, Pat, at 19, became the Post Mistress of Kavieng and Secretary for the District Officer, and lived in the Kavieng Club, only returning to Bolegila on weekends.[12]

Frank Holland was a typical young Englishman of the 1920s. Captive in a nation that classified an individual by his birthright, with limited family influence and wealth, his life's trajectory was set to be average. Having left school at 14 to work in his brother's grocery shop, he realized that this was likely to be his lot in life and it was depressing. Frank Holland yearned for excitement and this came in the form of the Empire Settlement Scheme and the opportunity to be an assisted migrant to Australia. It seemed like an adventure for the bravest and hardiest with the possibilities limited only by one's imagination. He was 16 when he climbed the gangway of SS *Orvieto* at London's Tilbury docks in July 1924.

Frank's journey took him to one of Australia's remotest regions, Atherton in northern Queensland. He was a tall and sturdy teenager, and the ensuing years of farm labouring saw his independence increase. He 'courted' Mabel Clark-Kennedy, a diminutive woman whose size belied her enduring pioneering spirit. They married on 23 June 1938 and the following morning boarded Burns Philp steamer SS *Montoro* for New Guinea. Port Moresby was not to Mabel's liking so they reboarded the ship. The beauty of Rabaul captivated the couple and Frank quickly found a position with Pacific Timbers Ltd. The following years were unsettled due to the Mokolkols, a fierce band of indigenous people. This, plus the arrival of their son John, meant Mabel spent more time than she wished in Australia separated from Frank. Frank had built a home for them in

TOP: *Home in New Britain.*

BOTTOM: *The Holland family.* John Holland

The Oakes family. George Oakes

49

Methodist mission staff 1939. Left to right: Carl Vasey, Bill Huntley, Laurie Linggood, Helen Pearson, Howard Pearson, Nellie Simpson, Jean Christopher, Mary Jenkins, Laurie McArthur, Jessie March, Tom Simpson, Dorothy Beale, Margaret Harris, Ben Chenoweth, Con Mannering, Herbert Shelton, Syd Beazley, Dan Oakes, Percy Clark. Eight men died on 1 July 1942, two women became Japanese prisoners. Reeson

Wide Bay, south of Rabaul, and 'isolation' took on new meaning for the young family. John was the first white baby in the district and this resulted in much attention from the workers his father supervized.[13] In April 1941 a daughter, Ann, was born.

Tom and Nellie Simpson boarding the mission pinnace Kanai. Henderson

The pioneering spirit was also prominent in the Methodist, Catholic and Seventh Day Adventist missionaries spread throughout New Britain and New Ireland, intent on bringing God's word to, and improving the lives of indigenous people. In 1941, there were eight ordained and

TOP: *Parishioners and the Oakes mission home.* BOTTOM: *Parker and George Oakes with playmates.* Oakes

two lay Methodist missionaries: Laurence Archie McArthur, Herbert Bolus Shelton, William Lawrence Irving Linggood, William Daniel Oakes, Thomas Nevison Simpson, Howard James Pearson, John William Poole, Jack William Trevitt, Ernest Wilfred Pearce and Sydney Colin Beazley.

Sydney Colin Beazley was born in 1909 to Alfred and Mary, in Northam, 60 miles (97km) north-east of the Western Australian capital, Perth. A carpenter, he volunteered to become a Methodist Missionary Trainer and carpenter at Malakuna, Rabaul. Arriving in 1937, he selected four New Guineans as his first trainees. 'They were a travelling school moving from job to job and based at the Malakuna workshop.'[14] By 1938, he was married to Beryl and became father to Pauline.

Thomas 'Tom' Nevison Simpson was born in London in 1909 – to a life full of hardship. His father, William, died of consumption when Tom was five, and his mother Maria struggled to support her four children on her wage, earned by making light bulbs in the Osram factory. Tom was accepted by a charity boarding school, the Royal Caledonian Asylum (the 'Cally') at six, because his father had served with a Scottish Regiment. Then 'Maria died of influenza and consumption in 1918 and Tom was an orphan at eight years of age.'[15] The 'Cally' educated boys for domestic service or a trade. Tom was sent to South Australia, at 15, under the Barwell Boys Scheme to become a farm apprentice. His treatment was as harsh as the Mallee region itself; his only respite came from the companionship and support he found within local Christian church communities. It made his decision to become a Methodist minister an easy one. Tom met Nellie Sudlow, 'an extroverted, ebullient young woman', and the same time he decided to become a missionary. In August 1936, they sailed for New Guinea. On 7 September 1937, the couple were married in Rabaul. Their responsibilities, from education to health care in the outlying islands, were challenging. In May 1941, their daughter Margaret was born in Kavieng, and the supportive and social relationships between missionary and plantation families became increasingly important.[16]

Children and family life were a delight for the Reverend (Rev.) William Daniel 'Dan' Oakes. Born in Liverpool, England, at school Dan 'did not distinguish himself as very clever but he certainly was a persistent lad with a definite will.'[17] He developed a love of scouting and religion. In 1927, the Rev. D.C. Hughes visited England, hoping to find young men interested in becoming ministers in the NSW Methodist Church. Dan and 11 other young men, soon referred to as 'The Twelve Apostles', sailed to Australia in 1928. On arrival at Melbourne, Dan

The Administrator of the Mandated Territory of New Guinea, Sir Walter McNicoll, inspecting the NGVR Guard. NGVR Museum

The NGVR on parade in Rabaul. NGVR Museum

was sent to Braidwood, a small town 53 miles (85km) from the newly established Australian capital city, Canberra. As Home Missionary, travel was extensive and in his first six months he 'Travelled 1270 miles by pony; 1420 by car; held 89 services; paid 472 visits and baptized six children.'[18] Following three years at the NSW Methodist Training Centre for Ministers, and an appointment on the NSW south coast, he volunteered for overseas mission work and was appointed to the Ulu Circuit in New Britain. On 19 April 1933, he married Marion Lilian Johnson, the daughter of Rev. George E. Johnson.

By the time their son George was 15 months old, the family had moved to Pinikidu Mission station in New Ireland, to assist the Lelet Plateau people in the centre of the island and the Lihir and Tabar Island groups. The missionary home at Pinikidu was a comfortable, raised, four-room timber dwelling surrounded by verandahs. Mosquito proofin made life that much more pleasant. The separate kitchen was joined to the house, and a bathroom was positioned near the water tanks at ground level.

The large mango tree provided a natural climbing frame and there was a swing suspended from one branch. Playmates were local children, and George and his younger brother Parker saw them simply as that. It was a happy and carefree existence for the children, except when the occasional python slithered into a cooler place and needed to be dispensed with. The family travelled frequently to Sydney, but more often the 112 miles (180km) to Kavieng, or from Namatanai to Rabaul, by pinnace. In July 1941, it was decided that the boys and Marion should return to Australia for the boys' education. Dan intended to remain in New Guinea for another few months to finish 10 years' missionary service. A poignant memory for George Oakes was that, although his father 'was well aware of what was happening in Europe, he did not suspect we would have problems in the Pacific.'[19] In July 1941 'we left Kavieng on the Macdhui and waved goodbye to Dad. I never saw Dad again.'[20]

The Rev. Dan Oakes was not alone in believing war unlikely in the Pacific – his belief was shared by those in government, the military hierarchy and much of the general population. The Australian consciousness was squarely focused on Britain's war against European powers and, in Rabaul, on a fête to raise funds for blitz-affected London. A guard of honour for the Administrator of the Mandated Territory of New Guinea, Brigadier General Sir Walter McNicoll, by the New Guinea Volunteer Rifles (NGVR), added some pomp and spectacle.

The soldier resettlement program had brought a decidedly military orientation to the region, so much so that Rabaul was sometimes referred to as 'a suburb of ANZAC'.[21] On a visit to the township in 1937, former Prime Minister William 'Billy' Hughes, dubbed in WWI as 'The Little Digger', had emphatically declared that German aggression would not reclaim the territory: 'All hell is not going to take it [New Guinea)] away.'[22] The local residents agreed – in this war with Germany, repossession of the TNG could not happen.

When the Australian Army ordered the raising of the militia in September 1939, the response was overwhelming. The Superintendent of Police in Rabaul, Lieutenant Colonel (Lt Col) John Walstab, DSO, VD (VX17626), initiated the formation of the New Guinea Volunteer Rifles (NGVR). Between September 1939 and July 1940, there was little difficulty in finding recruits on whom to pin the brass 'NGVR' shoulder badges; in all 226 men enlisted in the NGVR in Rabaul and Kokopo.[23] There was a wealth of military experience to establish

Papuan Infantry Battalion (PIB). NGVR Museum

an officer corps. Among the appointments in December 1939 were: Commanding Officer: Maj Charles Ross-Field, the Director of Public Works, Rabaul; 2nd-in-Command (2IC): Capt Harold Taylour; and Adjutant: Lt John Charles Mullaly. Battalion Headquarters (HQ) was a small bungalow at the corner of Casuarina Avenue and Kamerere Street, Rabaul, and a parade ground with training huts was established in the botanical gardens. Fit men between the ages of 18 and 50 were accepted. Enlistment was for two years, with 20 full days training a year. There was no pay, and an allowance failed to cover the cost of the khaki uniform and embellishments. Leather boots, belts, bandoliers, felt hats and puttees were supplied from Australia. Weaponry consisted of WWI era .303 rifles and some equally aged Vickers and Lewis machine guns.

Originally, the strength of the battalion was limited to 20 officers and 400 other ranks but this was increased in June 1940 to 23 officers and 482 other ranks. The NGVR was a whites-only battalion but, from June 1940, indigenous volunteers were allowed to serve in the Papuan Infantry Battalion (PIB). Chinese volunteers were attached to the NGVR as medical assistants.

An initial NGVR duty was the armed escort of German and Austrian residents, now deemed 'aliens', by ship to Australian internment camps.[24] The celebrated cosmopolitan fabric of New Britain and New

Ireland was fraying as wartime security regulations required neighbour to turn on neighbour. The 'small white community, [was] always rich ground for gossip and rumour, but now the suspicions of wartime were added', wrote Assistant District Officer John McCarthy.[25] Initially, people of German descent were placed under night curfew; then they were forcibly removed. Many had lived in Rabaul for a quarter of a century, working as businessmen, planters and missionaries. Several were outspoken supporters of Nazi Germany, but harmonious past residency now meant little. 'Now suddenly their nationality was important. Whether they supported Hitler didn't matter: they were different from other men.'[26]

The initial enthusiasm for joining the NGVR came from WWI returned servicemen, but with the remoteness of many members, and with men returning to Australia to enlist in regular military forces, by December 1941 only 80 men attended the Rabaul training parades regularly. Their varied backgrounds and occupations, from plantation manager to mechanic to public servant, reflected New Britain's European population and made for a truly unique military force. While NGVR numbers were small, the standard of marksmanship was very high. Their numbers may have diminished by January 1942 but the NGVR's exceptional knowledge of local people and terrain would prove indispensable, and would save the lives of hundreds of Australian troops.

The September fête was successful in raising £3,000 for Londoners. The official focus remained very much on Europe. The arrival of 1,400 troops from the Australian mainland throughout 1941 was unnerving and disruptive, and there was increasing disquiet within the Rabaul community. Questions were being raised with no clear consensus – no one in authority was willing to take responsibility for the lives of people in New Britain and New Ireland.

Endnotes

1. 1st AIF 7 Battalion and CO 6 Battalion; CO 10 Infantry Brigade, 1916–1918; MHR 1931–34.
2. *Montevideo Maru* Memorial Committee, 'The Tragedy of the *Montevideo Maru*. Time for Recognition', Submission to the Commonwealth Government, 2009, p.9.
3. Ibid.
4. Johnson, R.W., and Threlfall, N.A. *Volcano Town*, p.10.
5. Winter, C. 'A Good-Will Ship: The Light Cruiser *Koln* Visits Rabaul (1933)'. *Australian Journal of Politics and History*, 54(1), 44–54, 2008.
6. A1200, L69705, National Archives, Canberra.
7. Sweeting, A.J. 'Civilian Wartime Experience in the Territories of Papua and New Guinea', in Hasluck, P. *The Government and the People 1942–1945*, Australia in the War of 1939–1945, series 4 – Civil, vol. 2 (1st edition), AWM, 1970, p.668.
8. Ibid.
9. asopa.typepad.com/asopa_people/2013/04/a-story-of-brutality-depravity-triumph-over-adversity.html Keith Jackson, accessed 14 July 2016.
10. Reeson, M. *A Very Long War: The Families Who Waited*, Melbourne University Press, 2000.
11. www.jje.info/lostlives/exhib/yarringtonwm/index.html Ruth Woodward.
12. www.pngaa.net/Library/PatMurray.htm Anne Peters, accessed 14 July 2016.
13. Stone, P., with Holland, M and Holland, J. *El Tigre: Frank Holland, MBE., Commando, Coastwatcher*, Oceans Enterprise, 1999, pp.6–8. Also Holland, J., Interview, 18 May 2016.
14. australianchristianmartyrs.blogspot.com.au/2011/08/martyrs-of-montevideo-maru.html accessed 11 July 2016.
15. www.jje.info/lostlives/exhib/simpsontn/index.html Margaret Henderson.
16. Ibid. see also; Henderson, M.L. *Yours sincerely, Tom: A Lost child of the Empire*, self-published, 2000.
17. www.jje.info/lostlives/exhib/oakeswd/index.html George Daniel Oakes.
18. Ibid.
19. Ibid.
20. Ibid.
21. *Montevideo Maru* Memorial Committee, 'The Tragedy of the *Montevideo Maru*', p.10.
22. Ibid.
23. Downs, I. *The New Guinea Volunteer Rifles 1939– 943 – A History*, Pacific Press, 1999, p.33.
24. Ibid., p.35.
25. McCarthy, J.K. *Patrol Into Yesterday: My New Guinea Years*, Cheshire, 1963, p.179.
26. Ibid.

CHAPTER FOUR

TROPICAL PARADISE, TROPICAL DISCORD

*'I had begged for permission to fire a couple of
rounds into the sky ... but this was always refused.'*

Lieutenant David Selby

Lt David Selby watched his youthful AA battery gunners with increasing concern; their morale was dropping fast. He continued to argue with authorities that his men were entitled to AIF enlistment, but there was no positive reaction. He was pleased at how these young men had taken pride in their own unit. 'Their difference in status kept the A.A. boys to a certain extent apart' but they soon 'developed a very strongly marked esprit de corps.'[1] Boredom, however, set in over the months spent 'sweating under the daily monotony of gun drill ... No aircraft co-operation', and the numerous occasions when Selby 'had begged for permission to fire a couple of rounds into the sky ... but this was always refused.'[2] There was a hairline fracture in one of the guns' breechblocks and command HQ did not wish to risk further damage. There was also a shortage of ammunition. The south easterly blew incessantly, sometimes at gale force, bringing with it dense clouds of black pumice dust and choking sulphur fumes from Matupi Crater. Throats and eyes were irritated and all metal was blackened. Twice daily, gun firing mechanisms needed to be dismantled, wiped clean of the invasive grit, re-oiled and re-assembled, and the slightest scratch painted with bituminous paint to avoid corrosion.

For many personnel, assimilation had not been easy. Rabaul was a shock for young men like Gnr Gordon Abel:

We were mostly eighteen-year-olds from Tasmania,
everything was a new experience, the climate, the birds,
the insects and the heat ... and sometimes frightening earth
tremors ... the caste system of living was still proving offensive,
we had been given no information or local knowledge of the
people or their lifestyle and customs.[3]

There was a clash of cultures between the army way and the Rabaul way, and invariably this was over work and status. As soldiers built camps, roads and fortifications they were criticized by local administrators. 2/22nd Pte Norm Furness witnessed:

One of the public servants came out and said 'Good God,
what are you doing there?' and I said, 'Well, you can see what
we're doing,' and he said, 'But you can't work like that, put
your shirts back on. You'll ruin the image of the white man.
No white man up here strips to the waist to work.' That was
a bit of a shock to the system, so you can imagine some of the
answers he got told that day. So that put a bit of an edge on.
That continued. Not in the evenings, once they finished work
they were different altogether, but during work, there was a
clash of the two personalities.[4]

Leisure pursuits provided a more relaxed atmosphere and *Lark Force* sporting teams staged friendly matches against resident teams. The Rabaul swimming pool provided a wonderful reprieve from the omnipresent heat and humidity. Rabaul's pubs were popular. The Cosmopolitan was a favourite with artillerymen because of the friendly owner, Bert Gaskin. Sometimes, however, the pubs were a little too popular. Many Absent Without Leave (AWOL) charges resulted from

2/22nd mates enjoying Rabaul swimming pool. Back row (left to right): H. Cooling, A. Robinson, W. Aspey. Front row (left to right): W. Maher, R. Yench, B. Gleeson and Norm Furness. Johnson

2/22nd enjoying a beer at the New Guinea Hotel. Left to right: Cpl Noel Barley, A/Sgt Tony Watson, Sgt E. A. Blaby, Cpl Alf Cock. Johnson

enjoying a night at the pub to excess. Selby struggled to keep his young gunners on the straight and narrow as 'they got drunk on payday', went AWOL 'if they thought they would not be caught', and if a fight broke out he knew, 'like as not an A.A. man was at the bottom of it.'[5] For the youngest troops, freedom from parental attention and money in their pockets resulted in over-exuberance. Pte Angus Burnett set a good example for his much younger brother but he could do only so much. Pte Edward Burnett was struggling with the free spirit he could be in New Britain and the discipline of the army. Various charges were added to his file, including 'drunk and disorderly'. The drunken and boisterous behaviour of the soldiers was not lost on Rabaul citizens, who lamented the loss of their once quiet and orderly town and who believed the soldiers should be better disciplined. For soldiers less inclined to drink, a good meal at Chinatown and a trip to the picture theatre at the aerated waters factory, owned by Bert Renton, was the most popular outing. Bert Renton asked Gnr David Maurice

Soldiers enjoyed the company of the Tolai people, particularly the children.
Johnson

Bloomfield (N109549) to a home-cooked meal, because he had met David's father in Sydney. The publican drove him to Kokopo to meet planter Vic Pennyfather, through whom the 17-year-old gunner met

Pte Clyde Vincent Reynalds. National Library

more civilians. The Lambton brothers, Richard and Laurie, were also fortunate. The wealthy Melbourne family for whom their parents worked had friends who owned a plantation outside of Rabaul and invited the boys to visit. They greatly enjoyed the outings, especially when their hosts took them hunting and sailing. This experience was unusual; the sheer numbers of the military overwhelmed Rabaul's citizens. While most did their best to entertain *Lark Force* members, there were simply too many. Consequently, it was a minority of soldiers who were treated to what they missed most – family interaction and home cooking.

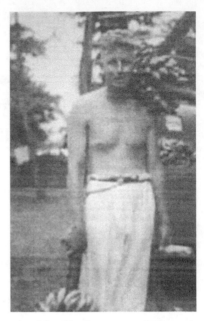

Climbing Matupi Crater.
National Archives

Gnr Keith Alfred Newman (TX4399) collecting bananas. National Archives

Lark Force officers were welcome at the New Guinea Club but their troops were not. Soldiers were left to make the best of the situation, and non-European interaction disturbed the social harmony of Rabaul. Gnr Gordon Abel:

I was never invited into a white person's home, so we made friends with the Chinese community. One of our favourite pastimes was trying to take the Chinese shopkeepers daughters out to the movies. I never got one to go with me but I sure had a lot of happy hours trying.[6]

On market days, the soldiers found it fascinating to watch the procession of colour and vibrancy as the indigenous population arrived with a wide range of food and handmade products.

'The kids in particular were beautiful, they always seemed to have a huge smile,' recalled Abel.[7] Soldiers purchased handicrafts and were entertained by 'what they called a sing-sing ... special dances and

Idyllic tropical paradise. Furness

they dressed up for it.'[8] Friendships formed between the native boys and men, and the soldiers: 'we used to treat them as equals whereas everybody else used to treat them as inferiors,' Abel believed; 'we didn't know any different, we just thought they were coloured but they were decent blokes.'[9]

Pte Norm Furness was very impressed with the local Tolai people, who he believed were 'a very calm, pleasant type of native people … gentle people, and very loving people.'[10] Furness's opinion was undoubtedly influenced by what happened when he went swimming at a particular beach. Several Tolai people ran to the water's edge and excitedly pleaded for Furness to come out of the water. It was a favourite haunt of crocodiles – Norm 'got out very smartly.'[11]

Curiosity and increasing boredom meant that the troops were constantly exploring the vicinity of Rabaul from volcano to coastline. It was easy to get tired of standard army food, canned chopped-up meat in gelatine, better known as 'bully beef'. This made little sense given they were in a fresh food paradise, and every opportunity was thus taken to fish and hunt to supplement diets.

Pte William John 'Jock' Olney (VX30074), a member of D Company, 2/22nd, and a couple of mates were fortunate, thanks to another publican, Gilmore, who owned the Rabaul Hotel. Gilmore had invited

Happy times, New Britain, 1941. Taylor

four soldiers to stay at his plantation at Put Put. The soldiers had no idea what to expect but wanted a change to the boring routine, so accepted. The trip by land in a vehicle and driver provided by Gilmore took most of a day, broken by a stop at the memorial stone 'for the Aussies who were killed capturing' the German radio station at Pita Baka 'in the last war.' It was a sobering reminder. Upon their arrival at the homestead, after being rowed across the Warangoi River, which was 'alive with crocodiles', the boys from Victoria were 'staggered by its beauty.' Olney wrote to sister Marion: 'it was like the tropics you read about, with the beautiful blue waters and lovely cool nights.' It was pure luxury to have a bedroom overlooking the open ocean, surrounded by trees full of frangipani, 'which would be worth a small fortune in Melbourne', and the house had a large enough refrigerator to keep 'our beer cool'. After a glorious week, Gilmore sent his boat down to collect them to make trip back to Rabaul shorter. The soldiers were 'very sorry the trip was over' but 'much fitter than when we left.'[12]

Photographs that the soldiers sent home probably raised eyebrows in all-white Australian households; in the same way, soldier and indigenous interaction caused consternation further north.

If the exuberant behaviour of *Lark Force* troops annoyed and disrupted the sleepy, genteel Rabaul at times, two *Lark Force* units had the opposite effect. The Regimental Band and a contingent of the Australian Army Medical Corps provided joy and nurturing to the locals.

Of the 15,000-strong 8th Division of the 2nd AIF, 292 who served overseas were members of the 2/10 Field Ambulance, 27th Brigade.[13] Their story during the war was particularly tragic. Out of 292 non-combatants, only 131 returned to Australia. The unit was formed in June 1940, under the command of Lt Col. Edmund MacArthur Sheppard (NX34665), a general practitioner from Newcastle, NSW. Having seen service with the Army Medical Corps Reserve, Sheppard recruited the unit's nucleus from fellow serving members, and the remainder from Newcastle and Sydney recruiting depots.

They were 'a mixed bag, including farmers from the far North Coast and Hunter Valley', and 'workmen from the industrial city of Newcastle.'[14]

Pte Billy Cook. NGVR Museum

Twin brothers Richard and Cecil Buck of 2/10 Field Ambulance. Johnson

Many were surprized at being designated medical rather than combat corps. William 'Billy' Cook (NX56978) enlisted through the Paddington recruiting office on 9 July 1940, and found himself placed with the 2/10. Cook was not exactly the tall, bronzed Aussie lifesaver type, nor at 32 was he as young as many lining up, so he was not entirely upset at being declared a non-combatant. Perhaps rather than physical appearance, it

Maj Palmer. Connolly, Wilson

Capt 'Sandy' Robertson, photo taken in Japanese POW camp.

www.auspostalhistory.com/articles/435.php

was more to do with the alphabet ... those with surnames starting with A, B, C? Billy Cook was joined in the 2/10 by Ptes Roger Miller Attwater (NX47047), 23, from North Sydney, Ronald Maurice Cantwell (NX46687), 25, and Wilkie Desmond Collins (NX57343), 22, who enlisted the same fortnight as Cook. Ptes Stewart Cameron Caston (NX60008), 23, and Thomas Benjamin Clissold (NX57642), 28, were just two more 'C'-surname volunteers through Paddington in July 1940 who found themselves attached to the 2/10.

Also at the beginning of the alphabet and enlisting at Paddington were the 23-year-old twin sons of Edward and Catherine Buck, of Sydney. Cecil and Richard had always done everything together, so it was fitting that their numbers were NX32404 and NX32405. The 2/10 may not have been their first choice but at least they were in the same unit.

The intensive six weeks of army training was followed by weeks of ambulance driving, stretcher bearing, hygiene, medical and first aid, combined with a fitness regime – undertaken at Bathurst or Dubbo Army Camp Hospital. The medical men were broken into small units and 'many groups of men were separated and the men were boiling mad' that they were not being posted together overseas – there seemed to be a degree of dysfunction in Melbourne Army HQ.[15] When their Colonel complained on their behalf, he was told that 'a further request would be treated as insubordinate', wrote one volunteer.

Of those at Bathurst, two officers, six nurses and 20 soldiers, under the command of Major Edward Charles Palmer (NX35096), were seconded to *Lark Force*. Palmer was a 31-year-old medical practitioner, born in the remote Western Australian gold mining town of Coolgardie. He was practising in NSW when he enlisted in June 1940.

His 2nd-in-command was Captain Edwin John 'Sandy' Robertson (NX35101), also a medical practitioner, who confused recruiters by putting his family properly down as his place of birth – army staff could not fin Collacenalin, NSW, on any map.

After training in heavy coats and long underwear in the winter snow of the NSW Blue Mountains, it was a shock to come off a ship into steamy New Britain. Clothing was at least easily adjusted to lightweight khaki shirts and shorts. For the six members of the Australian Army Nursing Service (AANS), there was no such relief. Their uniform had changed little since WWI, and the heat was unbearable. They wore heavy long-sleeved uniforms made of material that simply did not breathe and heavy regulation stockings. Lieutenant (Lt) Nancy Williamson (WFX23354) wrote:

Most unsuitable uniform for New Guinea. Large veils, starched collars and cuffs etc., had to be put aside. The climate was hot and very humid no protection for mosquitoes to start with. Issued with army boiler suits and boots later, until Safari Suits could be manufactured and issued.[16]

The nurses in Rabaul were not so fortunate; the boiler suits were not available and the 'Safari Suits' were still on their way. They managed to get rid of the long sleeves and stockings, and the long evening gowns,

Three of the six Lark Force *AANS nurses. Left to right: Capt Kathleen
'Kay' Isabel Alice Parker (NFX180287), Lt Daisy Cardin 'Tootie' Keast
(NFX180286) and Lt Marjory Jean 'Jean' Anderson (NFX180285).* AWM

but not the heavy material, veils and stiff collars. A Rabaul civilian nurse
decided the situation was ridiculous and wrote to the Matron-in-Chief
of the AANS in Australia, complaining on their behalf.

> *A hostile letter arrived from Matron chastising the nurses and
> threatening to bring them back to Australia, if they did not
> obey the dress code.*[17]

Captain (Capt) Kay Parker, the sister-in-charge, was known to be 'an
excellent nurse, down to earth, sensible, yet always very professional.
She had a big heart', and 'wasn't scared of showing some feelings if the
situation arose … [to] give the patients a hug.'[18] The arrival of the AANS
nurses was warmly received and not just for their nursing expertise.
There was always a shortage of European women in this British outpost.
The few female Australian Government administration employees
were billeted in houses separate to the others. This cluster of houses
was known by male members of the township as 'Virgins' Retreat'.[19]
Though soldiers were informed that the nurses were off limits, that
only commissioned officers were entitled to ask the nurses out, this

did not prevent a few of the more confident soldiers from trying. The nurses had never had so much attention, but their priority was to set up a good working hospital. Civilian women, particularly those who were pregnant, celebrated this new female medical presence, and the Australian nurses were pleased with having assistance from four Methodist missionary nurses.

The tropics caused conditions rarely treated in Australia, such as tropical ulcers, dysentery and scrub typhus, and medical personnel were busy with seemingly endless admissions for malaria. Pte Jack Groat (VX23647) wrote to an aunt in November 1941 that 'the mosquitoes are very bad and we each have a net under which we have to sleep.' Groat saw others admitted to hospital with malaria and wrote that although 'I have been bitten plenty of times' he had been fortunate. He assured her he was trying to avoid the 'malaria mosquitoes', which 'are much smaller, black and white in colour', but because they 'do not make any noise', that was difficult. He was taking his fire grams of quinine every day but 'it is horrible stuff ... it makes one's head ache and your eyes get rather sore', and he wondered if 'the prevention isn't worse than the disease.'[20]

Those suffering from the physically and mentally debilitating malaria would have argued that its terrible symptoms were much worse than the preventive medication. Pte Jock Olney (VX30074) was diagnosed with tonsillitis, but he believed it was malaria and he was also struggling with the volcanic dust, which 'has been very bad.'[21] Many *Lark Force* troops were admitted to hospital with respiratory illnesses. Between volcanic dust, malaria, the stomach upsets and skin complaints caused by tropical conditions, the 2/22nd Regimental Medical Officer (RMO), Major John Finch Akeroyd (VX18194), and his staff, were kept very busy. Akeroyd was born in Melbourne and educated at Bendigo and Melbourne high schools, where he was an honours student. He graduated in medicine from the University of Melbourne with honours in obstetrics and surgery. While at university, he was actively involved in the Melbourne University Rifles and the 46th Battalion, gaining recognition for his marksmanship. After graduation, Akeroyd was appointed an RMO at the Royal Melbourne Hospital and later the medical superintendent at Ballarat Base Hospital. Following his marriage in 1935 to Barbara Brown, he established a private medical practice in Frankston, Victoria. In June 1940 he enlisted in the AIF. The RMO had the bearing of an officer, but not the physicality. Fortunately, his medical knowledge was first-class and the soldiers warmed to his manner. Akeroyd was to prove indispensable and his devotion to duty admirable.

Arriving in March and April 1941, the medical personnel found Rabaul well served by four very experienced civilian doctors: Herbert Champion Hosking, Robert William Cooper, Maj Norman Bennington Watch and Arthur Hay. Hosking was an Adelaide University graduate who had been with the Territory Health Service since 1936. Cooper was a graduate of Melbourne and had been in the TNG since the mid-1930s. Hay, also a graduate of Melbourne, had moved to Rabaul in 1941 from Madang on the New Guinean mainland. Watch, a WWI veteran, had been in the TNG for nearly two decades and was RMO for the NGVR.[22] There was nonetheless little interaction, the military preferring to operate under their own routines and regimes. As the number of military patients spiralled, friction over duty priorities occurred between Major Akeroyd and members of the Regimental Band – were they musicians or stretcher-bearers? The Regimental Band of the 2/22nd Battalion was particularly popular with the citizens of Rabaul. The band and their music were exceptionally 'heavenly' thanks to Bandmaster Sgt William Arthur Gullidge (VX37499). They entertained young and old in Rabaul, from church to government garden party, leaving everyone smiling. The *Rabaul Times* reported:

Unique and galaxy of entertainment ... so ably furnished by Conductor Gullidge and his talented band. From the opening bars of 'Lilac Time' selection by the Regimental Band, to the closing chorus of 'Land of Hope and Glory' there was not a dull moment.[23]

Salvation Army
Bandmaster,
Arthur Gullidge.

Brunswick Citadel Band, c.1939. Cox

Born in Broken Hill, NSW, on 9 April 1909, Arthur Gullidge was an inspiring and inspired man, and his band was derived from an army of a different kind, the Salvation Army.

In the 1870s, William and Catherine Booth believed that the poor of industrial England were neglected by mainstream churches, and nothing less than an army could save them from poverty and despair. They formed a new church, the Salvation Army, led by ministers, both men and women, known as Majors and Captains. The Salvation Army grew and spread quickly; a socially progressive and creative church, it offered assistance to the most vulnerable. In 1884, a citadel of the church was built in the Melbourne suburb of Brunswick. An early member was

Private Jack Stebbings (VX37505). Cox

John Curtin, who became Labor Party leader, and was Australian Prime Minister during WWII. Another member of the Brunswick Citadel was Arthur Gullidge.

Gullidge was no stranger to hardship. He was a child when his father William was killed in a Broken Hill mine cave-in. His mother Emily, a Salvation Army officer, moved the family to Tasmania where they shifted between her appointments, and Arthur matured in a world of Christian ethics and brass bands. He quickly outgrew

Drew with Salvationist parents
Maj Richard and Hilda Drew. Cox

Private Kenneth Drew.
National Archives

his cornet tutor's proficiency. By 17, he was the Deputy Bandmaster of the Victorian Brunswick Salvation Army Band. From 1933, the year he won the prestigious Australian Broadcasting Commission (ABC) National Composition Award, he was Bandmaster. Three years later he married Mavis Ellen Anderson, an accomplished pianist. The strains of aggressive staccato and highly accented passages, especially in minor keys and stunning lyrical counter melodies, flawed from the Gullidge pen.[24] This was transformed into beautiful music by the 'blend of youth, and maturity, excellent musicians, with a talent for providing magnificent entertainment', who made up the Brunswick Salvation Army Band.[25] With the outbreak of war, Gullidge was faced with the same moral dilemma troubling others with strong religious convictions. Sentiments of pacifism were entrenched in Salvation Army beliefs, but Salvationists were permitted to follow their own conscience. Gullidge was 31, a husband and father, and arguably Australia's 'most prolific composer of brass band music during and between WWI and WWII'.[26] Traditionally, bandsmen acted in war as stretcher-bearers. Not only did the Bandmaster enlist in July 1940, but the bulk of his band did as well. More Salvation Army Band members

The pride of the 2/22nd Battalion on the road to Bonegilla. Cox

changed their blue uniforms for khaki ones – eventually 23 made up the bulk of the 2/22nd Regimental Band.

The chinstrap tightened as Jack Stebbings smiled, which he did frequently enough to unconsciously melt female hearts. Kenneth 'Ken' Rawie Drew (VX37496), nicknamed 'Sonny', was less gregarious. Both were excellent musicians, Stebbings on the trombone and Drew on the tenor horn. Both were clerks in civilian life and on enlistment in July 1940, both were underage for overseas deployment. Jack looked older so writing '21' on his enlistment papers caused no question – but he was at least two years younger. Ken looked 18, so there was a short administrative delay while he convinced authorities he must be accepted.

At Trawool Camp, bandsmen undertook the same basic military, physical and weapons training, as their infantry counterparts. As stretcher-bearers, they learned additional first-aid skills before they took up their instruments to lead the battalion on that long

Pte Frederick 'Fred' William Kollmorgen (VX29061). AWM

march to Bonegilla, much to the enjoyment of townsfolk along the way.

While Jack Stebbing's smile illuminated photographs and he was considered to be a potential 'good catch'[27] by local girls, Frederick William Kollmorgen (VX29061), had little choice but to keep his mouth closed as much as he wanted 'to blow his own trumpet', or euphonium. Born in 1917 to Melbourne market gardeners Albert and Ruby Kollmorgen, who were Salvation Army congregation members, his instrument of choice was the large, conical-bore, baritone-voiced brass euphonium, but

TOP: *Arthur, Mavis and Judith Gullidge.* Cox BOTTOM: *Mavis, Eleanor, Bert and Drew Morgan.* Cox

he also played the tenor horn and trombone. Kollmorgen was already in the army when Gullidge organized the transfer. The band was already well settled at Bonegilla when Kollmorgen arrived, anxious to impress. Unfortunately, army dentists had just extracted three teeth and Kollmorgen was unable to play for weeks. Gullidge accepted his mumbled apology and Fred joined the band. They were impressing everyone who was fortunate to hear the Bandmaster's arrangements of everything from the national anthem – of which a Melbourne Sun journalist wrote, 'everybody is pleased with the beautiful arrangement of the grand melody' – to his joyful arrangement of 'The Wizard of Oz'.[28]

The bandsmen returned home on their final leave before departing for service.

Musician, Pte Bert Morgan. Cox

74

Arthur Gullidge enjoyed his time with wife Mavis and daughter Judith. Ken Drew and Jack Stebbings valued their quality time with family; and Fred Kollmorgen had regained enough ability to open his mouth to say 'I do' and marry. On 14 February 1941, 4,000 23rd Infantry Brigade marched through Melbourne on farewell parade, with an estimated 100,000 'emotionally-charged spectators lining Swanston Street'.[29] It was Gullidge's arrangement of the 'Wizard of Oz' that put bounce in their step and smiles on civilian faces.

As they left their homes, family memories were to become increasingly precious. Bert Morgan's daughter, Eleanor, remembered:

While he was cutting our breakfast toast fingers to dig in our
boiled eggs, he said while he was away Jesus would look after
me and not to forget to say my prayers every night
… My father swung me on his shoulders, his khaki jacket with
special buttons and high neck was scratchy and I did not like it
much…. 'Kiddo,' he said, 'Look after Rex and mummy. Daddy's
going to be fighting for God and the King.'[30]

As the ship was about to head north to Rabaul, Arthur Gullidge posted a few words to wife Mavis.

I feel strangely confident that all is going to turn out well.
I shouldn't use the word strangely for I believe it is the
knowledge that God is caring for me all along the way that
gives me that confidence for a safe return to you, Judith and
Mum again.[31]

From this magnificent band, only one member returned to Australia. From the Rabaul-based 2/10 Field Ambulance contingent of two officers and 20 soldiers, only the two officers and 5 soldiers survived.

Endnotes

1. Selby, p.7.
2. Ibid., p.17.
3. Abel, G. MSS1623, AWM, Canberra.
4. australiansatwarfilmar hive.unsw. edu.au/archive/464-norman-furness accessed 2 June 2106.
5. Selby, p.7.
6. Abel, G. MSS1623, AWM, Canberra.
7. Ibid.
8. Ibid.
9. Ibid.
10. australiansatwarfilmar hive.unsw. edu.au/archive/464-norman-furness accessed 2 June 2106.
11. Ibid.
12. Johnson. P.36.
13. Connolly, R. and Wilson, B. (eds.) *Medical Soldiers: 2/10 Australian Field Ambulance 8 Div., 1940–45*, 2/10 Australian Field Ambulance Association, 1985, p.7.
14. Ibid., p.9.
15. Ibid., p.15.
16. Bassett, J. *Guns and Brooches: Australian Army Nursing from the Boer War to the Gulf War*, Oxford, 1992, p.162.
17. Nikakis, G. *He's Not Coming Home*, Lothian, 2005, p.66.
18. Ibid., p.65.
19. Ibid., p.59.
20. Johnson, p.36.
21. Ibid., p.52.
22. Watters, D.A.K. *Stitches in Time: Two Centuries of Surgery in Papua New Guinea*, Xlibris, 2011.
23. Cox, L.C. *Brave & True: From Blue to Khaki – The Band of the 2/22nd Battalion*, Salvation Army, 2003, p.62.
24. www.abc.net.au/compass/s2768821. htm, 3 January 2010, accessed 21 July 2016.
25. Cox, p.vii.
26. Ibid., p.4.
27. Ibid., p.33.
28. Ibid., p.27.
29. Ibid., p.43.
30. Ibid.
31. Ibid.

CHAPTER FIVE

ILL-PREPARED FOR WAR

*'Australia would never stand our men
being deserted.'*

Sir Earle Page

In an attempt to provide a respite for his men from tinned food, Selby took his better marksmen on a pig shoot in the AA Battery Ford utility truck. His soldiers were bored, restless, and not battle ready. The move to Frisbee Ridge added isolation to the mix. Observation Hill had been renamed Frisbee Ridge in honour of the AA CO whose nickname was 'Frisbee' because of his flowing moustache. To vary the monotony, Selby organized competitions and gave lectures 'on every subject I could think of from International Law to the White Man's Burden.'[1] He even read passages from adventure books.

Chaplain John May became 'an invaluable friend to the whole battery', as each Sunday he drove up to the ridge to conduct Church Parade and then talk casually to the gunners. Selby admired May for his calming effect. 'Young and unsophisticated, his youthful enthusiasm communicated itself to these youngsters', appealing to them in a manner, 'which no older and more experienced man could have done.'[2]

Whereas before it was only the threat of disciplinary action that

Gnr Tom Gordon, Bombadier (Bdr) Jim Heriot, Gnr

ensured that gunners attended Church Parade, now Sunday was a highlight of the week.

Lark Force was neither cohesive nor ready for war. Much of this was due to lack of leadership.

It had not taken the men of the 2/22nd long to realise that Lieutenant Colonel Carr was unequal to the task of running a battalion-size force.[3]

A pleasant man, Carr was more accustomed to being part of a large organization than an effective leader. Australian soldiers were quick to assume the worst of their leaders unless command and respect were earned – they were less than kind in their summation of Carr.

Not until 8 October 1941 did *Lark Force* Command HQ staff arrive. Colonel John Joseph 'Joe' Scanlan DSO and bar had served in WWI with distinction. Born in Melbourne and educated at Christian Brothers College, St Kilda, he started his working life as a shipping clerk with the Customs Department. In 1910, he joined the Citizens Military Force (CMF) and, by 1913, he was a Second Lieutenant in the 58th Infantry (Essendon Rifles). With the outbreak of WWI, he enlisted in the Australian Imperial Force (AIF) and with the 7th Battalion served in

Lt David Selby in the AA Ford. AWM

Egypt. As a Lieutenant he landed at Gallipoli on 25 April 1915.[4]

Thirteen days later he was shot in the chest and evacuated. He spent a year recovering from his wounds. Posted to France with the 57th Battalion, he fought in the battles of Amiens, Mont Saint-Quentin, and St Quentin Canal. Returning to Australia with the DSO and bar, he left the AIF in August 1919.[5] During the interwar years, Scanlan worked as a secretary for the Victorian Prices Commission. He tried farming, before becoming an official with the Sustenance Department. In 1936, Scanlan moved to Tasmania when he was offered the post of Deputy Governor of Hobart Gaol. Called up in the reserve with the outbreak of WWII, he took command of the 6th Garrison Battalion. In September 1940, he was promoted to temporary Colonel and Commanding Officer of *Lark Force*.

It was a Herculean task to turn the *Lark Force* skeleton garrison into a fighting or defensive force. New Britain and New Ireland's inhospitable geography was legendary, with some still unexplored. The 994 miles (1600km) plus coastline of New Britain alone was formidable. *Lark Force* was expected to protect two airfields, Lakunai and Vunakanau (the upper drome), as well as the seaplane base at Sulphur Creek.

Chaplain John May. Johnson

The major volcanic eruption in June 1941 convinced the Australian Minister for External Territories that the TNG Administration must be moved from Rabaul to Lae. This commenced the month that Col Scanlan arrived in Rabaul. The Administrator, Brigadier General Sir Walter McNicoll, departed in November with the Assistant Government Secretary S.A. Lonergan and Edward Taylor, the Acting Director of the Department of District Services and Native

Scanlan as a young officer. AWM

Affairs, along with other senior staff. The Government Secretary, Harold Hillis Page, became Deputy Administrator and the senior government official in Rabaul. Page had served in WWI and achieved the rank of Major, together with the awards of DSO and Military Cross (MC), but he, too, was unused to being in charge, controlling the civilian administration and questioning superiors. When Page asked the Australian Minister when the remaining government staff could leave Rabaul for Lae, the request was rejected outright, because 'the natives might go on a rampage.'[6] Governance of New Britain was in disarray.

On 19 November, the earth again ripped apart as pent-up gasses hurled a thick column of magma and ash more than 100,000 feet (30km) skywards in a terrifying blast from Tavurvur. Boiling hot rocks were jettisoned 100 yards (91m) from the foot of the volcano, and large

Inaugural meeting of the Australian War Cabinet, September 1939. Left to right: Senator George McLeay, Sir Henry Gullett, Hon. Richard Casey, Prime Minister Menzies, Geoffrey Street and Mr Frank Shedden. William Hughes was absent. Hasluck

clumps of glowing pumice were flung still further. The pyroclastic cloud spread, blanketing and choking, and adding further chaos to a township on the edge.

During 1940–1 when the people in Rabaul required strong, united support, the Australian Government lacked stability. Joseph Aloysius Lyons, the first Australian Prime Minister (PM) to win three successive elections, died in office on 7 April 1939. For 19 days, the Country Party leader, Earle Christmas Grafton Page, held the top office, before Robert Gordon Menzies, leader of the minority United Australia Party, was sworn in as PM on 26 April 1939. Animosity between Menzies and Page resulted in Page refusing to serve in the Menzies Government and withdrawing the Country Party from the coalition.

A special War Cabinet was created, initially comprising the Prime Minister and five senior ministers, but Menzies assumed more and more portfolios.

In December 1939, he had added the Department of Defence Co-ordination to his Treasury and Prime Ministerial duties. In February 1940, he assumed the Trade and Customs portfolio.[7] With the election of a new Country Party leader, Archie Cameron, a new coalition party was formed and Menzies relinquished the Treasury and Customs portfolios.

In August 1940, a Royal Australian Air Force (RAAF) plane crashed while attempting to land at Canberra. Included among the 10 passengers and crew were Australia's Chief of the General Staff, General Sir Cyril Brudenell Bingham White, and three senior ministers: James Valentine Fairbairn, Minister for Air and Civil Aviation; Sir Henry Somer Gullett, Vice-President of the Executive Council and Minister in charge of Scientific and Industrial

There was a need for lifesaving but Australia's politicians were not working together. Cartoon: 'Our Emergency Life-Saving Squad'. The Bulletin, 11 September 1940

Election advertisements in 1941 demonstrated the difference in focus – the Coalition for Britain and the Labor Party more for Australia. Hasluck

Research; and Brigadier Geoffrey Austin Street, Minister for the Army and Repatriation. To lose such experienced and influential individuals was a terrible loss to the nation.

A federal election was conducted on 21 September 1940; the result was a hung parliament, with two Independents holding the balance of power. It was a perilous time for Australia but, in late January 1941, Menzies flew to Britain. Towards the end of May 1941, Menzies flew back to Australia via Lisbon and the United States. 'Rumblings about his leadership had grown louder during his absence.'[8] In June 1941, there was a complete reorganisation of the ministry with five new departments being created and the Cabinet increasing to 26 ministers and 15 junior portfolios.[9] In August, Cabinet decided that Menzies should return to Britain to represent Australia's interests in the British War Cabinet. The Labor Caucus disagreed, believing that in a time of crisis the PM should remain in Australia. The Houses of the Australian Parliament erupted.

Australia was at war but its parliament was in disorder.

On 29 August 1941, Robert Menzies resigned as Prime Minister. Former PM, William Morris 'Billy' Hughes, assumed leadership of the

United Australia Party, and the Country Party leader, Arthur William Fadden, was elected PM. His Prime Ministership lasted '40 days and 40 nights'; in October 1941 the two Independents holding the balance of power voted with the Australian Labor Party to defeat the Coalition government.

On 7 October 1941 John Joseph Ambrose Curtin became Australia's 14th Prime Minister.[10] With so much political energy and attention focussed on the Houses of Parliament, strategic awareness and concern for New Guinea and its people were muted by the world of political intrigue.

Eric Augustas Feldt was born on 3 January 1899, at Cardwell in Queensland. Educated locally and at Brisbane Grammar School (BGS), Feldt won Cadet Midshipman selection in the first entry – 1 March 1913 – of 28 boys aged 13–14 to the Royal Australian Naval College (RANC), Geelong. He achieved the position of Chief Cadet Captain before graduating as a Midshipman in January 1917. His navy career was reduced due to government defence cutbacks and he was placed on the Retired List in 1922. Feldt became a government clerk in the TNG in 1923, and a patrol officer the following year.

He served as District Officer in various parts of New Guinea. By 1936

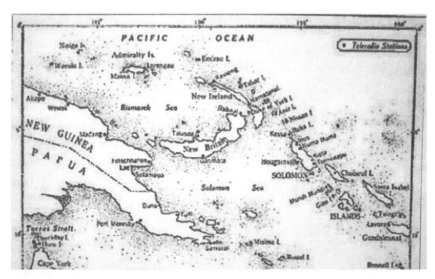

The Coastwatcher network.

Feldt was Warden at Morobe Goldfield [11] – his knowledge of New Guinea was extensive.

With the outbreak of WWII, Lt Cdr Feldt was tasked with installing a screen of Coastwatchers in the Pacific islands, to warn of hostile sea and air incursions. Travelling by air, sea and on foot, he visited New Guinea, the Solomon Islands and the New Hebrides, recruiting individuals with great familiarity

Eric Feldt. Gill

about their districts, and distributing 'teleradio' sets. Codenamed 'Ferdinand' from the children's book, *The Story of Ferdinand, about a bull who refused to fight* – the Coastwatchers were a network of brave men and one woman, in remote Pacific outposts, who watched and reported any suspicious military activity to the Australian Commonwealth Naval Board (ACNB).

Although civilians, they were awarded military rank. The Coastwatchers were hunted throughout the war and, if captured, faced immediate execution. Ably supported by indigenous volunteers, they spent much of the war hiding in jungle camps behind enemy lines, forever on the move to evade capture. Their warnings on enemy movements proved invaluable to Allied forces. By May 1941, Feldt was Supervising

Intelligence Officer, North Eastern Area. His responsibilities were heavy; his advice was being ignored by the highest echelon of authority.

In late 1941, Feldt despatched to Rabaul, calling for intelligence officer Sub Lieutenant (Sub Lt) James Connal Howard Gill (B2518), a 25-year-old lawyer enlisted in the RAN Reserve (RANR), to assist Lt Hugh Alexander McKenzie, RAN. Like Feldt, McKenzie was an original graduate of RANC. Like Feldt, he left the RAN after WWI, moving to New Guinea as a trader and planter. In 1939, McKenzie

Lt Hugh McKenzie. AWM

had a plantation at Megigi on the north coast

84

of New Britain but was brought back into the RAN and was appointed Naval Officer in Charge (NOIC), New Britain, in August 1941.

Prior to his departure, Gill had sat in on a Port Moresby meeting of Australian army officers. He was unsettled by their indecision. 'The Army was divided in its views' with some believing the Japanese were 'cooking up something' but with others dismissing the suggestion and 'the day ended without any positive agreement.'[12] Gill found Rabaul to be in a state of confusion, and McKenzie was clearly frustrated – no one was listening, no one was taking responsibility. The Australian bureaucratic silence was stunning. Feldt, McKenzie and Gill believed that New Britain was not only very vulnerable, but would be attacked by Japan in the near future.

Following WWI, in accordance with military restrictions imposed by the League of Nations, and the 1922 Washington Agreement on the reduction of navy fleets, Western nations, including Australia, had instigated stringent economic cuts to defence. Contrary to this, Japan made good use of the time between the wars, undertaking a program of military expansion. In 1931, the Imperial Japanese Army occupied Manchuria and less than two years later withdrew from the League of Nations. Under their Nanshin-Ron (southward advancement theory), in blatant defiance of Article 22 of the Covenant of the League of Nations, all former German island colonies over which Japan had been granted mandates were fortified with military and naval bases. This unprecedented activity was a clear indicator of aggressive ambition.

On 14 February 1941, the Japanese Ambassador to Washington DC, Admiral Kichisaburo Monura, on behalf of his government, informed the United States Secretary of State, Cordell Hull, that recognition of Japan as the power in the Pacific was a prerequisite for peace. This prompted a reaction from the United States (US), and pressure was placed on the Australian Government to garrison Rabaul so that, if required, a major United States Naval (USN) fleet base could be established. Rabaul offered not only a wonderful deep-sea port, but opportunity for an adversary to interdict sea lanes, and Allied lines of communications between Australia and the United States. The US promised additional fortifications for the protection and expansion of the anchorage at

Rabaul, for British and American fleets. Also promised, armaments: mines, six 7-inch coastal guns, eight 3-inch anti-aircraft guns, and 12 heavy machine guns.[13] As the United States was not at war, however, there could be no commitment of troops on the ground.

By 1941, there was a large Japanese naval and military presence 700 miles (1,127km) due north of Rabaul, on the islands of Truk and Ponape in the Carolines, and even closer, on Kapingamarangi, a mere 320 miles (515km) from Rabaul. The north-east area of Australia was covered with a virtual offensive umbrella.[14] Japanese intelligence gathering had also been overt. Passenger-cargo ships frequented Rabaul and other Pacific ports, carrying little cargo, but passengers exhibiting a great 'propensity for photography'.[15] Rabaul residents were well acquainted with Komini, the Japanese Consul who owned the 'largest shipbuilding operation and slips in Rabaul'.[16] He soon assumed the rank of Captain in the Imperial Japanese Navy.[17]

Yet successive Australian governments dithered and the attention of military strategists remained firmly on the war to save Britain. They held secure in the belief that United States forces in the Philippines, British forces in Hong Kong and the fortress of Singapore, which British Prime Minister Winston Churchill boasted was 'impregnable', would defy any thoughts of aggression from Japan. They were also imbued with a total disbelief that any Eastern nation had the capability, or audacity, to attack the West. Racist philosophies were heavily entrenched in white Australia.

Lieutenant Lorna Margaret Whyte (NFX180288) was one of the six Australian Army nurses stationed in Rabaul. Lorna believed:

The popular belief held at the time that Japan was a poor nation full of myopic little men who could not fire a rifle [18]

Lorna was soon forced to reassess this view. Contrary to 'popular belief', by early November the Japanese South Seas Force had been issued with the operational order that, after securing Guam, it was to assemble in Truk and occupy Rabaul.[19]

For residents and *Lark Force* troops, there was no honest

information from men in authority and consequentially no real sense of impending danger – their thoughts remained on enjoying the remainder of their time in the tropics and going home.

Just before 8 a.m. on 7 December 1941, hundreds of Japanese fighter planes attacked the United States Navy (USN) base at Pearl Harbor near Honolulu, Hawaii. The surprise attack found the Americans ill-prepared and the two-hour barrage was devastating. A total of 12 ships were sunk or beached, and 9 others were damaged, including the American battleships USS Arizona and USS Oklahoma; 160 aircraft were destroyed and 150 damaged. More than 2,300 Americans were killed and another 1,000 wounded. The day after the assault, US President Franklin D. Roosevelt declared 7 December 1941 'a date which will live in infamy.'

In early December, a coastwatcher recruited by Lt Cdr Feldt notified Rabaul of major Japanese activity. Lt McKenzie sent the report immediately to the Commander-in-Chief (C-in-C), Hong Kong. The C-in-C, Hong Kong, signalled the Rabaul Naval Intelligence Office: 'Your signal. I am not concerned.'[20] At 8 a.m. on 8 December 1941, Japanese troops engaged British and Commonwealth troops close to Hong Kong. The few British aircraft available were quickly destroyed. The defending forces were hopelessly outnumbered, and retreated from Kowloon Peninsula to Hong Kong Island on 11 December. When calls to surrender were rejected, Japanese artillery and aircraft conducted an intense bombardment of Hong Kong on 15 December, and five days later their troops controlled half the island.

The Japanese were committing atrocities against European and Chinese missionaries and civilians.[21] The reservoir, the British garrison's water supply, was captured, and on 24 December Japanese soldiers entered St Stephen's College field hospital, tortured and killed more than 60 wounded soldiers, nurses and doctors. On what was later called 'Black Christmas', Sir Mark Aitchison Young, Governor of Hong Kong, surrendered. While Japan suffered 2,754 casualties, 11,848 British troops died and a further 5,000 were taken prisoner. The civilian population was left at the mercy of the invading army.

Intelligence officers in Rabaul could but wonder why the highest

The unconcerned faces of 12 Platoon B Company, 2/22nd AIF. Few returned to Australia. Back row left to right: Alf Fry, Jack Moyle, Jack Sutherland, unknown, unknown, R. Long, Norm Webster, Williams, Jim Parker, Edward Austin Fisher, John Andrew Wilson, Eric Douglas Firmstone, Robert Buchanan Hannah. Middle row: Don Searle, Percy Kerr, Sgt Russ Kelly, Lt G. Braden, Charles Robins, unknown, John Cameron, Ronald Long Stanley Allan Cameron, Sydney James Arthur Parker, Gordon Henri Braden. Front row: unknown, Neville Edward Hercules Curtis, Wallace Ross Melville, David Render, John Mervyn Render, William Francis Ladner, unknown, Syd McGregor. Johnson

military authority in Hong Kong had signalled how unconcerned he was about Rabaul. Vivid reports of the rapid and effective invasion, of the treatment of soldiers and civilians alike, were sent south to Australia. The lack of concern for the much smaller garrison force in Rabaul was breathtaking and disturbing. On 23 December an intercepted Japanese radio broadcast announced that Rabaul had been attacked. It was premature, but made it blatantly clear to the Rabaul intelligence staff that 'we were evidently included in the Japanese scheme of conquest.'[22]

Australian authorities were in a state of shock, and as they argued as to who was responsible for not taking the Japanese threat more seriously, enemy forces grouped closer to Australia. The seriousness of the situation was slow to be appreciated on the ground in New Britain;

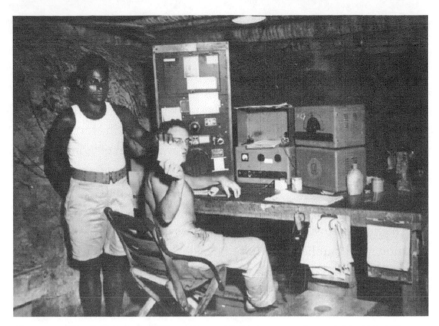

Coastwatchers and their indigenous assistants proved crucial to the Allies
Pacific campaign. AWM

in a letter home, Pte John George 'Jack' Groat (VX23647), with either
false bravado or lack of comprehension, wrote:

> *What do you think of the greasy little Japs? They have ruined*
> *our chances of ever getting any leave home, so we will make*
> *them pay dearly for it if they ever come this way.*[23]

On 12 December 1941, Australian authorities finally admitted to the
seriousness of the situation. An official cable sent to Richard Gavin
Gardiner Casey, the Australian Ambassador in Washington DC,
acknowledged that the promised United States fortification of Rabaul
was extremely unlikely. 'It would appear under present circumstances
that the proposed plan would be greatly delayed or even impossible
to fulfil '[24] The same day, the War Cabinet in Melbourne announced:
'women and children, other than missionaries, who may wish to remain,
and nurses', were to be 'compulsorily evacuated from the Mandated
Territory of New Guinea and Papua.'[25]

As early as 1940 it had been suggested that the approximately 3,000 Australian women and children living in Papua and New Guinea should be encouraged to leave for Australia. However, the Administrator in Port Moresby, the Honourable Leonard Murray, was loath to force families to leave their homes unnecessarily and to incur the costs of their evacuation and resettlement in Australia. Again, in March 1941, the Australian War Cabinet had discussed the evacuation of 'non-essential' civil personnel from Rabaul.[26] Again, the logistics and expense of an evacuation of residents from the TNG was too daunting; evacuation might also leave the Government open to expenses involved with their resettlement in Australia. The decision was deferred.

Individual families were left to decide for themselves without clear guidance, and the decision was difficult for many. For those who had lived in Rabaul most of their lives, there was no network of emotional or financial support in Australia. Where would they go? Where would they live? How could they afford to live? The General Secretary of Methodist Overseas Missions, the Rev. Dr John Burton, wrote to TNG missionaries about the 'conflict of opinion regarding the seriousness of the situation'[27] and attempted to reassure them that the consensus was that there was, 'no evidence of any specific danger in New Guinea.'[28] As late as the middle of November 1941, he admitted that 'decision-making was still ambivalent'. The best the Australian War Cabinet offered in November 1941 was a warning that 'in the event of war' it may not be possible to make 'special arrangements to transfer women and children to Australia.'[29]

There were very mixed messages. By September 1941, Burns Philp, the territory shipping agent, was advising that women and children should not travel to the territories, and in November, passengers were obliged to sign an indemnity notice warning of the dangers. Soon only 'essential travel' permits were issued. Yet women on leave in Australia were being allowed by the Australian Government to return to Rabaul. The only official exchange was that evacuation should be undertaken 'purely voluntarily' and 'as unobtrusively as possible to avoid panic.'[30] From July 1941, more than 100 women had left or were preparing to leave New Britain.[31]

It took until Japan entered the war before the Australian War Cabinet, under the codename 'Z day',[32] issued the order for the compulsory evacuation of all European women and children from Rabaul by 20 December. Evacuation orders were broadcast over Rabaul radio on 16, 18 and 20 December. Women were limited to a baggage allowance of 30 pounds (13kg) with an extra 15 pounds (7kg) for each child.[33] Males over the age of 16 were to remain in Rabaul with their fathers. But even then 'compulsory evacuation' was open to interpretation. Individual women asked and were given permission to remain. Six government nurses were offered evacuation but elected to remain, as did the four Methodist nurses. The Australian Army nurses were not offered that opportunity, 'as it was deemed their duty to stay with the men.'[34]

Women missionaries were allowed to choose. Many, including the Catholic Sacred Heart Mission nuns, stayed.

Gladys Baker was used to taking charge and simply getting done what was needed. Her day commenced before dawn and her duties were rigorous. 'Life here may be quiet, but it is never dull.'[35] Few would agree that Gladys Baker's life was 'quiet' or routine. Life on Langu, a copra plantation of 800 acres (324ha) on Witu Island, New Guinea, 40 miles (64km) north of New Britain, never could be. Her husband, Bill, was another WWI ex-serviceman who took up the Australian Government soldier resettlements call to settle in the mandated territories. Bill unfortunately died of blood poisoning in 1934 and, whereas the more fainthearted would have returned to a less strenuous and perhaps more 'civilized' lifestyle, Gladys stayed. She was proud that her plantation produced an average yield of between 45 and 50 tons of copra a month.

By 6 a.m. on any given day, Gladys had detailed the day's work to her employees. After a hasty breakfast, she supervised 70–80 indigenous workers out on the plantation. The heat and humidity meant that after lunch she indulged in an hour's 'rest' until 1 p.m., when she returned to the fields until her workers ceased, at around 3.30 p.m. Among her projects were the building of a huge hot-air kiln copra-dryer, infrastructure such as bridges, and two concrete loading structures to expedite the loading of copra onto ships. She found it necessary to be 'involved' as much as possible, to demonstrate what needed to be done. She had assumed responsibility, not only for the workers but for the sustenance and health of their families. One of her priorities had been to build a small hospital for the local people and it was there she routinely finished her day, as she was one of the very few with any medical knowledge.

On 4 December 1939, *The Sydney Morning Herald* featured Gladys Baker in a three-paragraph article, within the 'Women's Supplement'. The article was sandwiched between a small feature citing the difficulties facing a housewife unable to procure sufficient fruit and butter for her Christmas cake, and a large advertisement depicting a coiffured lady and 'Mischief – the refreshing perfume that remains fresh.'[36] The reporter felt it best to soften the report by emphasizing that Mrs Baker maintained civility by 'dressing for dinner every night.' 'Life here may be quiet but it is never dull',[37] was already an understatement and 'Life' was about to become even more exciting.

Frilly tablecloths and ornate Christmas snow decorations may have been foremost in the Christmas Day celebrations for women in Australia, but not for Gladys Baker.

I arranged the usual sing sing for the natives but I doubted if we would ever have another Christmas on Langu for a long time. Almost a week before Christmas the first of many Jap reconnaissance planes came over ... In case of bombing I made the natives take shelter in the reinforced concrete culverts I had helped them build. Some Zeroes came too with the Rising Sun glinting on their wings and I hated the scream as they dived to look at Langu and at the plantation anchorages.[38]

Gladys Baker was allowed to remain in TNG because of her medical experience, a decision that soon impacted on *Lark Force* troops.

A constant stream of women and children arrived in Rabaul from all over the territories; the township was in a state of confusion, 'accommodation was stretched beyond its capacity.'[39] Many had to be shipped or airlifted into the main centres from the outlying areas. They were leaving their men and their homes and, for many of them, the only life they had known. Nellie Simpson, arriving from remote New Hanover with her missionary husband Tom and baby Margaret, discovered that 'nobody was worried about us in Rabaul because they were all worrying about themselves.'[40] The Dunbar family were at the Korandindi Plantation on the Mavulu River in the North Bainings. Life was cut off in this part of the world, and the first the family knew of the precarious situation was on Boxing Day, when a government official disembarked from a trawler anchored in the river. It was a shock to hear him imply that 'the invasion of Rabaul by Japanese was imminent.' The family were told to pack essential items into four suitcases, as they would leave in four hours. 'What a shock.'[41]

Women and children were bundled onto ships. Nellie Simpson remembered:

We were all crying, leaving everybody. It was a sad affair ...
all the men ran up, rushed up the big pier and we went past it,
and that was the last ... [we ever saw of them].[42]

The *Neptuna* and *Macdhui* sailed from Rabaul on 22 December and a Douglas DC-3 left a week later. Other families, delayed by weather and transport, had to wait for later ships and flights. It was 15 January before almost all Australian women and children had been evacuated.

Questions as to why there was to be no evacuation for non-European women and children were met with stony silence. China was supposedly an Australian ally. Terrible crimes had been committed against Chinese women as the Japanese conquered China – some of which were depicted in Australian recruiting propaganda. The swell of bitterness felt within the non-European population of Rabaul escalated, and was further exacerbated by a leaflet describing arrangements for Refuge Valley, on Namanula Ridge. The orders were that the upper portion was reserved for Europeans, the lower was for the Asiatic population, along with a 'smaller area convenient to the Europeans, for their native servants with "car parking available".'[43] Questions as to when civilian men were to be evacuated went unanswered. Questions as to when *Lark Force* was to be returned to Australia dared not be asked.

Nursing Sister Alice Bowman sketched Neptuna *departing Rabaul with the title 'Forlorn men in pensive mood'.* Bowman[44]

Endnotes

1. Selby, p.9.
2. Ibid., p.13.
3. Gamble, B. *Darkest Hour*, p.51.
4. A.J. 'Scanlan, John Joseph (1890–1962)', *Australian Dictionary of Biography*, National Centre of Biography, Australian National University, adb.anu.edu.au/biography/scanlan-john-joseph-8349/text14653, published first in hardcopy 1988, accessed online 31 uly 2016.
5. Ibid.
6. Aplin, D.A. Rabaul 1942, 2/22nd Battalion AIF *Lark Force* Association, McCarron Bird, 1980, p.37.
7. primeministers.naa.gov.au/primeministers/menzies/in-office.aspx accessed 1 August 2016.
8. Ibid.
9. Ibid.
10. Ibid.
11. Gill, J.C.H. 'Feldt, Eric Augustas (1899–1968)', *Australian Dictionary of Biography,* National Centre of Biography, Australian National University, adb.anu.edu.au/biography/feldt-eric-augustas-10163/text17953, published first in hardcopy 1996, accessed online 31 uly 2016.
12. Gill, J.C.H. 'The last days of Rabaul. (December 13, 1941 to January 23, 1942)', *Journal of the Royal Historical Society of Queensland*, vol 6, 1961, Royal Historical Society of Queensland, 23 March 23, 1961, p.639. espace.library.uq.edu.au/view/UQ:212613/s00855804_1960_1961_6_3_635.pdf, accessed 11 May 2016.
13. Gamble, p.53.
14. Ibid., p.641.
15. *Montevideo Maru*, Submission, p.10.
16. www.jje.info/lostlives/exhib/odean/index.html Derek Westoby O'Dean.
17. Ibid.
18. Nikakis, G. *He's Not Coming Home*, p.65.
19. *Montevideo Maru*, Submission, p.15.
20. Gill, J.C.H. 'The last days of Rabaul', p.641.
21. At the Salesian Mission on the Chai Wan Road, the Japanese massacred nuns and members of the medical staff there after they had surrendered.
22. Gill, 'The last days of Rabaul', p.646.
23. Johnson, C. *Little Hell*, p.52.
24. A2671/1, 333/41, War Cabinet Agendum, National Archives, Canberra.
25. Ibid.
26. A518, BJ16/2/1, Part 1, and Part 2, National Archives, Canberra.
27. Reeson, M. *Whereabouts Unknown*, Albatross, 1993, p.60.
28. Henderson, M. *Yours sincerely Tom*, p.117.
29. A518, BJ16/2/1, Part 1, National Archives, Canberra.
30. Henderson, p.117.
31. Reeson, *A Very Long War*, p.4.
32. A518, BJ16/2/1, Part 2, National Archives, Canberra.
33. *Montevideo Maru*, Submission, p.13.
34. Ibid.
35. *The Sydney Morning Herald*, 4 December 1939.
36. Ibid.
37. Ibid.
38. Papua New Guinea Association of Australia, *Una Voce,* June 2002, p.14.
39. Henderson, p.118.
40. Reeson, *A Very Long War*, p.10.
41. www.pngaa.net/Library/Evacuate.htm Dick & Robyn Dunbar-Reid.
42. Reeson, *A Very Long War*, p.10.
43. Reeson, M. *Whereabouts Unknown*, pp.59–60.
44. Bowman, A.M. *Not Now Tomorrow: ima nai ashita*, Daisy Press, 1996, p.18.

CHAPTER SIX

THE BEGINNING OF THE END

'There shall be no faint hearts, no thought of surrender, every man shall die in his pit.'

Colonel Joseph Scanlan, Commanding Officer, *Lark Force*

Gnr David Bloomfield scanned the horizon. It was a spectacular view up here on Observatory Hill. When the AA battery was moved here on 7 December the gunners renamed the vantage point Frisbee Ridge, after the blond moustache sported by their Battery CO, Lt David Selby. The colours were simply amazing – deeper, stronger than any in his native Sydney. He was grateful that it was cooler here than down in Malaguna Road camp, the breeze easing the stifling heat and humidity, as well as

Composite of Rabaul Harbour from Observatory Hill taken in 1945, hence area severely damaged from Allied bombing. AWM

dispersing the sulphurous dust continually emitting from the Tavurvur and Vulcan volcanoes. The tremors were unnerving and he couldn't get used to them.

The AA battery had missed out on the Christmas Day lunch enjoyed by rest of the 2/22nd. Heavy, hot Christmas lunches were traditionally celebrated in Australian homes, more in keeping with European climes than with the hot summers of the southern hemisphere. Even stranger was that traditional fare was presented in tropical Rabaul, but it was a pleasing reminder of home. Gnr Tom Cogan wrote home:

We had a very pleasant time. The army turned on turkey and ham, which was most enjoyable and plum pudding and cream. We also had a bottle of Fosters.[1]

To his wife Anne in Melbourne, Pte Joseph William 'Joe' Jeffrey (VX29427) wrote:

Everything was layed [sic] out nice, and we had Roast Turkey, Plum Pudding and of course tomato soup to begin with. We had plenty of beer and wine ... some of the boys sang, and some recited.[2]

The best the AA cook could manage was to toss some curry into the tinned bully beef. It didn't seem quite fair, why couldn't some Christmas food have been sent up to the militia boys?

It was, however, good to be away from the 2/22nd, in with other members of 'The Rabble Force'. At first, the name was a little insulting but then it was embraced. There had been a couple of scuffles down below when militiamen were taunted with the name 'choco'. This may have resulted in the organisation of a boxing tournament the previous October. They may have been young and militia, but they weren't soft and acquitted themselves well, surprising the AIF blokes with wins in four divisions, including heavyweight.[3] Gnr Des MacMullen (NX191482), a big sturdy former miner, had achieved that – not bad for a 'choco' who was only 19. It was good to have a militia mate who had won the heavyweight boxing. Yes, it was nice being high and separate from the regulars.

David Bloomfield had had a privileged upbringing – living in a grand home with a maid, able to indulge in many sports, and afforded a secondary education at the prestigious Scots College in Sydney, where he was an enthusiastic member of the school cadet corps. He grew into a physically capable youth, in part for reasons of self-preservation.

Because I was Jewish … my father had been wise in having me taught to box so I could acquit myself reasonably well. I'd say that I won more than I lost. I got the respect of people by the fact that I could acquit myself quite well with my fists.[4]

Enlisting just seemed the natural thing to do, even if you were only 17 and studying accountancy. He told the Martin Place recruiter he was 18. 'You come back and see me in about two years' time and I'll enlist you,' he was told. Bloomfield was 'annoyed', so he took a bus 'out to Moore Park recruiting department. They didn't refuse me there.'[5]

When he returned home he simply told his mother he 'wouldn't be home for tea tomorrow night, Mum.' The 'why?' caused consternation but the son met the threats to have him withdrawn with: 'I'll re-join under a different name and you won't know where I am.'[6] It just seemed like an 'adventure' that he didn't want to miss.[7] His firs preference was the Black Watch, the 2/30th Battalion, because they wore the same kilt he had worn at Scots College, but Lt David Selby attended the same Sydney synagogue, and decided that Bloomfield, with his education level, should join him in artillery.

Gnr David Bloomfield looked out over an innocuous, peaceful harbour, to the two steep-sided rocks that rose abruptly from the middle of Simpson Harbour. These

David Bloomfield, 17, on enlistment. Bloomfield

uninhabited rocks were named 'The Beehives', but the Tolais called them Davapia, 'the ground of the fishing line', because there was once a fishing village at the foot of the rock face, testimony to how hard life was in this region. Bloomfield had joined up for the adventure but there had been little adventure so far, unless you counted volcanic eruptions. He wished he was where the war action was, asking himself more than once 'there must have been a reason for us going to Rabaul?'[8]

Every day there was gun drill but no live ammunition was ever fired. Not only was there a shortage of ammunition, but that slight crack in the breechblock of no.2 gun was a concern. Only one of the officers and two sergeants had ever witnessed a live firing; the rest of the 54-man AA battery 'had never heard a three-inch gun fired.'[9] Gun drill meant merely going through the motions. One of the gunners walked or ran, holding a long piece of timber with a model aeroplane on the end, on which the gun layers focussed. This duty was detailed to the unit gunner guilty of the most disciplinary infringements, and dubbed by his peers mockingly as 'duty pilot officer'. On Saturdays there was a little more excitement, when the Royal Australian Air Force (RAAF) 24 Squadron (Sqn) Lockheed Hudson flew in with mail and then flew out again. Gun crews pretended to shoot it down. 'That was the only actual live aircraft that we had to practice on.'[10]

Nonetheless, since 8 December 1941, there was a sense of anticipation in camp – something was going to happen. *Lark Force* members had been as stunned as the rest of the world when Japanese forces attacked the US fleet in Hawaii's Pearl Harbor on 7 December. The sense of unease increased with the evacuation – first the bulk of the TNG administration, and then European women and children. Pte Thomas Edward Hartley (VX44999), a member of the 2/22 machine gun platoon, felt that without the melee of people, interspersed with the happy voices of children, 'It did not seem much like Christmas to me.'[11] Pte John George 'Jack' Groat (VX23647) wrote to his aunt of his regrets that this was his first Christmas away from home, and how he really hoped 'this darned war is all over and that we are home for next Xmas.'[12] Pte Hartley harboured a few more doubts: 'serious things are around these parts', and he was concerned how 'just about all the battalion [is] unfit for action, but of course we have to fight on.'[13] It took little expertise to realize that *Lark Force* was hopelessly undermanned and under-equipped to withstand an invasion.

On Christmas Day, a Japanese reconnaissance aircraft had buzzed Rabaul. A light flashing Morse code was seen and mistrust of German missionaries and New Guinea German residents increased – with Germany and Japan now being allies. Gnr David Bloomfield was a member of a squad that tried to track down where the signalling was coming from one evening, but the guilty party realized and ceased. Captain Selby ordered guards on the guns.

The second-in-command of the AA unit, Lt Peter Wallace Fisher, was born in Sydney on 4 October 1916, the eldest of the three children of Wallace George Fisher and Annie Gladys (nee Madsen). Like the junior Gunner Bloomfield, Fisher grew up in comfortable circumstances and also attended one of Sydney's best schools, Sydney Church of England Grammar School (Shore). He, too, had a passion for tennis and cricket, and like the unit CO, Lt Selby, studied law. Following graduation with honours from Sydney University, Fisher chose to study accountancy, while training with the Army Reserve. Bloomfield was in Fisher's gun crew; but he would have preferred to be in Selby's. Fisher was fair enough but had 'a very narrow corridor of thinking, he was a textbook lieutenant.'[14] Selby was more of a 'father image, he was a very nice man', not 'just because he was Jewish, but he was just a nice man.'[15]

The order had come from Scanlan's HQ that, should there be an invasion, the AA battery was to fire down on landing craft approaching the beaches. The expectation was ludicrous, Bloomfield thought: 'even at seventeen and half I said to myself, "That's crazy."'[16] If the guns could be depressed that far they would probably roll down the mountain and also leave the crew defenceless from air attack. This did nothing to improve confidence in the Commander and his staff.

It was a bright Sunday morning on 4 January 1942, coming up to that welcome morning cup of tea – 10.30 a.m. The view was so completely benign. They saw it before they heard it, a single Kawasaki four-engine flying boat bomber. An hour later, an arrowhead formation of 22 bombers passed swiftly over their position, and released bombloads on

Lukanai aerodrome and the adjacent Rapindik Native Hospital.

There was hardly time to think before Lt Fisher, in the command post below the level of the guns, gave the order to fire. All their training was finally put to use. The gun layers, who physically operated the direction of the guns, turned the guns towards the enemy, the fuses were set, the loaders punched the shells into the breech, the breech snapped forward and the firing lever was pulled. Bloomfield operated one of two deflection dials and needed to wait for the order from Lt Fisher on the settings. With no UB-7 rangefinder, only a ringside telescope, the duty officer had to guess the height. The initial angle was 13,000 feet (3962m), well below the formation. Fisher immediately corrected the height to 15,000 feet (4572m) and reported, 'managed to rock one plane before they disappeared.'[17] Loader of no.1 gun was Gnr Lionel Hawes (NX191453), 20, from Woodville, South Australia (SA), and loader of no.2 gun was Gnr Jeffrey Charles Seamark (NX191481), 19, from Macksville, NSW. Seamark had meticulously polished the first shell and proudly told Fisher he would keep the shell casing and return it to Australia, because this was 'the first shot from an Australian Mandated Territory'[18] and it had been shot by militia!

CO Anti-Aircraft Battery and Military Landing Craft Defence unit, Lt David Selby (right); second-in-command Lt Peter Wallace Fisher (left). AWM

AA battery, New Guinea, 1942. AWM

CO 24 Squadron, John Margrave Lerew. AWM

Unfortunately, neither Seamark nor the shell casing returned to Australia.

The gun crews were shocked by the noise, heat and physical impact of their first live shoot. When the ringing in their ears subsided, there was elation that at least they had finally fired in anger, and lived to tell the tale. Concerns remained as to their ineffectiveness. 'We were using WW1 antiquated obsolete equipment.'[19] Word came that though none of *Lark Force* was killed, 12 indigenous New Guineans were dead and another 30 had been injured. Coastwatcher Cornelius 'Con' Page on Tabar Island had warned of the approaching aircraft but the information never made it to the artillery.

There had been a small rise in *Lark Force* optimism when the RAAF arrived during the first and second weeks of December. RAAF 24 Squadron had formed at Amberley Airbase in Queensland on 17 June 1940, before moving to Townsville to conduct reconnaissance and maritime duties, and further training. The squadron then left for Rabaul to provide aerial defence for New Britain. First the Hudson bombers arrived, and then the Wirraways. From the beginning of 1942, the strength of 24 Squadron in Rabaul was four Hudsons, six Wirraways and 130 staff, commanded by Wing Commander John Margrave Lerew.

Lerew was born in Hamilton, Victoria, in August 1912 and was educated at Scotch College, Melbourne. While studying part-time for a civil engineering degree at the University of Melbourne, he served with various militia units and developed a love of fast cars, culminating in a third place in the 1930 Australian Grand Prix. The promise of greater speed saw him enlist in the RAAF in 1932. Lerew quickly became known not only as a very good pilot, but as someone willing to offer candid comment or 'impish irreverence'.[20] Vunakanau airfield, Rabaul, afforded very little shelter for staff or aircraft.

RAAF HQ, Melbourne, demanded rapid results against the enemy, be they reconnaissance or direct contact. On 15 December,

Flight Lieutenant (Flt Lt) Kenneth James Erwin (261863), 23, from Sydney, made a photographic reconnaissance Hudson flight over Kapingamarangi Island, Micronesia. He came under anti-aircraft fire but he and his crew recorded 19 barges, two lighters and a launch, lying off shore. Two slipways had also been built on the beach.[21] The next operation was a flight of three Hudsons; one piloted by Erwin, and the others by Squadron Leader (Sqn Ldr) John Francis Murphy (262), 24, and Flt Lt Paul Pryde Paterson (260515), 26, from Perth, who spotted a ship north of Kapingamarangi that they unsuccessfully bombed.[22]

RAAF superiors in Australia, lacking an understanding of the conditions in New Britain, advised Lerew that the results had been 'lamentable', and they were 'perturbed' enough to threaten him with being relieved of his command. In his inimitable style Lerew signalled: 'disappointment in the lack of assistance rendered by the Almighty.'[23] His next signal was equally to the point, declaring his staff 'totally inadequate to cope' with the demands ordered of them and that:

> *It is regretted that all these misunderstandings and annoying*
> *delays have occurred creating a position in which more worry*
> *is being caused from the south, than from the enemy situated*
> *in the north.*[24]

The Hudson bombing and reconnaissance operations continued, and on 30 December three much-needed replacement Hudsons reached Lakunai Airfield.

Hudson light bomber. AWM

There were difficulties also in directing Wirraway operations. The Wirraway flight operating from Lakunai consisted of five pilots, five observers and six ground staff. Around 50 indigenous workers gradually built, and camoufla ed, dispersal bays and squadron quarters. But progress was 'distressingly slow', due to poor roads and a lack of transport, and was hampered further by a lack of cooperation between civilians and the military.[25] It was some time before Vunakanau and Lakunai airfields were linked by even one, unreliable, telephone line. Wirraway crews mounted morning reconnaissance patrols. The unrealistic expectations of the Australian Air Board were highlighted in a signal concerning the need for an attack similar to the 'opening phase of the attack on HMS *Repulse* by Japanese pilots' and concluded with the rather dramatic sentence: 'The Empire expects much of a few.'[26]

The signal and comparison were equally absurd. The Japanese were armed with a large number of modern and very capable fighters that were already proven in battle.

Contrary to Australian military beliefs, Japanese pilots were expert and committed. Lerew had a handful of Wirraways, and a tiny unit of exhausted pilots. 'Wirraway' was the Aboriginal word for 'challenge', and challenging was a most apt word for the position where RAAF 24

Wirraways. AWM

Squadron found themselves. The Commonwealth Aircraft Corporation (CAC) Wirraway was a training and general-purpose military aircraft, with a top speed of around 191 knots (220mph, 354km/h), armed with two .303 inch (7.7mm) Vickers Mk V machine guns, synchronized to fire through the propeller arc, and one .303 inch (7.7mm) Vickers GO machine gun on a flexible mount in the rear cockpit. It could carry two bombs if the navigator vacated. The Japanese Mitsubishi A6M Zero was a long range, pilot-only fighter aircraft, with a top speed of around 287 knots (330mph, 532km/h), armed with two 20mm cannons, two .303 inch (7.7mm) machine guns and two 66 pound (30kg) or 130 pound (59kg) bombs.

On New Year's Day, Lerew led the Hudsons on another raid against Kapingamarangi Island, igniting a fuel dump that was still burning when the squadron returned to follow up the attack two days later. Between 4 and 7 January, Vunakanau airfield suffered four Japanese bomber raids. Gnr Tom Cogan wrote home to his sister in Perth, about how excited the gunners were to at last see 'action', and in a bright vein wrote:

During the first air raid here, I was having my morning
shave and after consideration eventually moved quick smart
at a rate hitherto unknown to myself and others ... Owing to
censorship I can not elaborate on proceedings here as much as
I'd like to, except to assure you all I am safe and sound.[27]

Somewhat bizarrely he went on to advise: 'in answer to your query of Air Raid shelter, put it near the Jack [Jacaranda] tree and you'll be safe sis.'[28]

On 6 January, the 4,000-ton *Malaita II* and the inter-island 300-ton *Mako* entered the harbour. Onboard *Malaita II* were six signallers. They must have wondered what they were disembarking into and why they had been sent to an island under siege. That night, Vunakanau airfield was bombed again by Kawanishi flying boats in a 'V' formation. The AA boys blazed away but rounds burst short. The RAAF had no time to take off before half the airfield was destroyed. Orders came

Coastwatcher photograph of Japanese bombers flying towards Rabaul. AWM

from Australia that Malaita was not to unload its cargo of boom defence gear, and was to return to Australia. On 8 January, Malaita cast off its mooring lines and sailed out of Simpson Harbour. Onboard were the last evacuating European women and children, as well as Japanese internees. There were berths available for many more passengers. Sub Lt Gill believed: 'We got the clear indication that we had been given away by the Commonwealth.'[29]

On 7 January, coastwatchers spotted 18 Japanese twin-engine bombers flying south. Nothing could be done. Minutes later 78 bombs were dropped on Vunakanau. Sub Lt Gill wrote: 'This time they really hurt us.'[30] The Hudsons were being serviced and refuelled; one was entirely destroyed and two were damaged. A Wirraway was also damaged, as well as airfield buildings. Although the remaining Wirraway crews scrambled to intercept the attackers, their rate of climb was so poor that only one engaged the enemy. Lerew signalled RAAF HQ that he desperately needed at least six 'modern fighters' – none came.

On 9 January, Flt Lt Robert Alfred Yeowart (270647) nursed his Hudson back to New Britain. His life had changed remarkably since he had worked as a Brisbane accountant – on the previous day it had been two years since he had enlisted in the RAAF. Yeowart wasn't aware that he was completing the longest sea reconnaissance operation ever undertaken by a RAAF land-based aircraft – 1,405 miles (2261km). He was just hoping that the fuel held out. His crew were holding their breath until they heard the crunching noise of the landing gear of their Hudson, nicknamed 'Tit Willow', touch down. It had been a tiring and unsettling operation. Pilot and crew, Flying Officer McDonnell and Sgts Marriner and Ellis, RAAF, had just observed and photographed a massive concentration of aircraft and shipping gathered at the Truk islands.[31] In Toll Harbour alone, they counted an aircraft carrier, 11 other warships plus other ships. There were around a dozen float planes, and the airfield was wingtip to wingtip bombers, around 27. They made a photographic run and the anti-aircraft fire opened up; the tip of the Hudson's tail plane was shot away.[32] It took little imagination to realize this was an invasion force, which could only be headed south. Yeowart just hoped someone, other than Lerew, listened to his report.

Pte Tom Hartley, in a letter to his sister Betty on 12 January, admitted 'they' had been bombed 'four times so far', and that 'most of the Chinese have evacuated their shops in Chinatown, they must have got the wind-up.'[33] He still considered the situation not to be particularly concerning: 'The British forces seem to be slowing up the Japs. I think they will only last about a year, but one can never tell.'[34] The bombing of Rabaul intensified [35] Bloomfield and his fellow volunteers re-evaluated the 'adventure' they had wished for. 'We were young I don't think any of us realised what getting killed was all about.'[36] On 20 January, that became a reality for the Australians.

On 20 January, the Zeros came in very fast. The sky was soon full of Japanese carrier-based aircraft – 40 fighters and 80 bombers. Sub Lt Cornelius Lyons 'Con' Page, RANVR, a former planter, now Coastwatcher on Tabar Island, east of New Ireland, sent a radio warning to Scanlan's HQ. The message never reached the artillerymen, or the RAAF. Within months, Page was captured and executed in May 1942.[37]

Lt Peter Fisher was duty officer on Frisbee Ridge when he noticed 'Wirraways' patrolling at 14,000 feet, which was unusual. The sudden realization that the aircraft were 'Zero fighters' was chilling. The Wirraway crews scrambled to get their aircraft into the air quickly, but the battle in the skies was a one-sided affair, and the RAAF planes and their crews disintegrated in flames in the skies over Rabaul. For the artillerymen witnessing the scene from Frisbee Ridge, it was horrific. Lt Peter Fisher described the:

Fierce dogfight ... the horror of the scene, made the more real when two minutes later the first Wirraway went spiralling into the sea, smoke and flame pouring from its engine and breaking up as it fell. Five Wirraways were lost in a matter of minutes.[38]

Another watching horrified as 2/22nd Sgt Frank Septimus Smith:

For sheer, cold-blooded heroism, I have never seen anything to compare with the bravery of the pilots of those Wirraways. They knew they were doomed but they had all the guts in the world.[39]

Two Wirraway crews were already in the air on patrol. They were Flying Officer (FO) John Cameron Lowe (402662) and observer Sgt Albert Clive Ashford (3210), both 26 and from NSW, and Queenslanders Sgt George Robert Herring (405410), 21, and observer Pilot Officer (PO) Albert George Claire (273495), 27. Lowe and Ashford were attacked by six Zeros, a hopeless engagement given that the Wirraway was totally outclassed in manoeuvrability, firepower and speed. Their lives came to a fiery end at 5,000 feet (1524m). Herring and Claire were similarly engaged in a one-sided battle and spun out of control. Herring regained enough control to crash-land, with both aircrew wounded in the legs by enemy gunfire. These two crews had already been in the air; the Wirraways climbing to assist were simply too vulnerable. PO Robert Alfred Blackman (402844), 20, a bookkeeper born in Binnaway, NSW; Sgt Stanley Ernest Woodcroft (22630), 23, a Brisbane insurance clerk; Sgt Charles Frederick Bromley (405391), 19, a jackeroo from Richmond, Queensland; and Sgt Richard Walsh (5803), 25, from Toowoomba, Queensland, a researcher in cotton production in his pre-war life, died quickly.

The Wirraway flown by Sgt William Otho Kemp Hewett (04405), 20, from Bordertown, SA, with observer FO John Vincent Tyrrell (3491), 24, from Melbourne, had commenced an attack on a flying boat when a Zero dived on them. Hewett, 'stalled the Wirraway out of a turn but the Zero pilot was waiting for him.'[40] The Wirraway was raked with cannon fire. 'Pieces flew off the wings and fuselage and a bullet smashed Hewett's knee. He temporarily lost consciousness.'[41] The plane went into a spin and Tyrrell, who had been standing up at the gun, was thrown from the cockpit. He clutched desperately for the ripcord of his parachute. The cord snagged on the cockpit and the parachute opened. Tyrrell came down in a tree. AIF soldiers arrived suddenly to apprehend the 'Japanese parachutist.'[42] They were surprised when the RAAF observer addressed them in colourful Australian. Despite his wounds, Hewett successfully pulled his aircraft out of the spin and crash-landed at Vunakanau.

Two remaining Wirraway crews were battling to stay alive. Flight Sergeant (Flt Sgt) Malcolm Graeme Milne (407586), 26, a salesman from Glenelg, SA, and observer, Sgt Raymond Stanley Harber (32803), a Sydney accountant who had celebrated his 23rd birthday two days prior, were playing tag team with a much greater force. Cloud cover provided the means of escape. In the other Wirraway were Flt Lt Ronald Charles Gordon Little (403059), 27, a public servant who had lived in the Sydney suburb of Coogee, and observer Don Ross Sheppard (031436), a former Adelaide-based salesman who was wondering if he would celebrate his 23rd birthday in a fortnight. Zeroes were everywhere and the speed and the skill with which their pilots pushed them through the air was as mesmerizing as it was scary. Milne managed to finally land their training aircraft with part of its tail missing – at least they were down. As the sixth Wirraway had climbed, its engine shut down at 500 feet (152m) and the aircraft crashed into trees.

The crew, Flt Lt Bruce Anderson and FO Col Butterworth, both survived.

They survived because their engine had failed.

The attack had lasted less than 10 minutes and, of the eight crews that had taken off, six aircrew had been killed and five injured. Three of the eight Wirraways were lost in combat, one was wrecked and two seriously damaged. Official RAAF historian, Alan Stephens, has written that the posting to Rabaul of RAAF 24 Squadron and their obsolete aircraft by the Australian War Cabinet was 'an act of delinquency',[43] and all that could be achieved was 'futile'.[44] In their removed, closeted world, Air Board ordered Lerew to attack the approaching Japanese convoy with 'all available aircraft'.[45] In Rabaul, this amounted to one Hudson. The lone medium bomber did take to the air and Lerew wired his superiors: 'Nos Morituri te saluitamus.' It is unknown if this message was understood, but the Roman gladiator exclamation as they entered mortal combat – 'We who are about to die salute you' – went unanswered.[46]

The AA battery fired as quickly as they could, firing through open sights because there was no time for commands and the Zeros were so close. Above was the drone of bombers, many bombers. The ridge shuddered as bombs fell. A bomber spiralled downwards and crashed – the battery had shot down an aircraft – but if anything registered, it was a brief 'that's one down, ninety plus others' to go, recalled Gnr Bloomfield [47] The bombers opened systematically on both airfields. Attention turned to the harbour and dive-bombers attacked shipping. Westralia was an unseaworthy hulk, but was still targeted. The Norwegian 5,100 gross ton freighter, MV *Herstein*, which had just finished loading copra at the BP wharf, was a larger prize. Three bombs hit amidships, one exploding in the engine room. The resulting fire spread quickly. The freighter's anti-aircraft guns continued firing until a bomb exploded in the bridge area, when the crew jumped overboard and swam ashore. The wharf and ship were both blazing fiercely Swedish Steward, Karl Thorsell, was killed.

MV *Herstein* was a new ship, launched in 1939 and chartered by the Australian Government to assist in the transportation of 4,250 troops and 10,000 tons of equipment to reinforce Port Moresby, New Guinea. *Herstein* departed Sydney on 27 December 1941, in convoy with the Blue Funnel Line SS *Sarpedon*, the Cunard Line *Aquitania*, and four navy cruiser escorts. The convoy reached Port Moresby on 4 January. The convoy of ships all returned to Australia, except for

MV Herstein. www.warsailors.com/singleships/herstein

Herstein. The Norwegian ship was ordered to Rabaul. The Captain, Gottfred M. Gundersen, was instructed to collect, not soldiers or civilians and remaining residents from a besieged town, but 2,000 tons of copra. *Herstein* arrived on 14 January. A week later the ship was a burning wreck.

Japanese authorities admitted to the loss of seven aircraft on 20 January, a small consolation for the exhausted AA artillerymen: 'we were all too shattered.'[48] They had sat fascinated in Australian film theatres as aircraft were shot down, and had even cheered when the bad guys met their match in a hero in a flying helmet and white scarf. The reality was entirely different. 'Having seen the Wirraways shot down it was a very depressing group of young fellas' who retired to the mess hall and would have preferred a 'good stiff Scotch [whiskey]'.[49] Their efforts did not go unnoticed. The CO of the 2/22nd, Lt Col Carr, sent Selby a congratulatory note. Capt David Chadwick Hutchinson-Smith (NX70289) was CO of the anti-tank battery and had watched how '81 bombers and 45 fighters attacked', in a very professional manner, and 'the AA effectively blazed away by guess and by God, without adequate instruments, at every plane in sight.'[50]

Staff Sgt (S/Sgt) Victor Harold Turner (VX15628), R Coy., company 2/22, and his men watched horrified from below at the carnage in the sky and wrote 'we saw them die ... their deaths marked the end of our ten months of hampered and useless effort.'[51] The garrison had been severely disadvantaged by a 'lack of supplies, reinforcements and red tape.'[52] Turner had been flabbergasted when he had been refused permission to cut down the palm trees where his unit was dug-in, which interfered with their field of fire. Duncan described how 'our position is vulnerable both from the sea and the rear.'[53]

Capt Hutchinson-Smith was similarly concerned by the unpreparedness, lack of men and poorly equipped disposition. How could the force possibly defend against what appeared to be overwhelming odds? How could this tiny garrison defend '50 odd miles of perfect landing beaches' from any invasion? He knew what was to follow; they all knew, deep down in their guts, even if few spoke of it. *Lark Force* CO, Col Joseph Scanlan, had been unapproachable, distant. The only statement he had made to his troops was on Christmas Day. Amid the Christmas crackers, turkey and plum pudding, Scanlan declared: 'There shall be no faint hearts, no thought of surrender, every man shall die in his pit.'[54]

The next words Capt Hutchinson-Smith wrote in his diary were '22/23 January ... wild and tempestuous'.[55]

Endnotes

1. www.jje.info/lostlives/people/cogantej. html
2. Johnson, p.51.
3. Fisher, P. PR89/0716, AWM, Canberra.
4. australiansatwarfilmar hive.unsw.edu. au/archive/1778-david-bloomfield
5. Ibid.
6. Ibid.
7. Ibid.
8. Ibid.
9. Ibid.
10. Ibid.
11. Johnson, p.46.
12. www.jje.info/lostlives/people/groatjg. html
13. Johnson, p.55.
14. australiansatwarfilmar hive.unsw.edu. au/archive/1778-david-bloomfield
15. Ibid.
16. Ibid.
17. Fisher, P.W. Papers, PR89/0716, AWM, Canberra.
18. australiansatwarfilmar hive.unsw.edu. au/archive/1778-david-bloomfield
19. Ibid.
20. Gillison, D. *Royal Australian Air Force, 1939–1942*, Australia in the War of 1939–1945, Series 3, Vol.1, Australian War Memorial, Canberra, 1962, p.270.
21. Ibid., p.269.
22. Ibid.
23. Ibid., p.270.
24. Ibid.
25. Ibid., p.271.
26. Ibid., p.269.
27. www.jje.info/lostlives/people/cogantej. html
28. Ibid.
29. Gill, J.C.H. 'The last days of Rabaul: (December 13, 1941 to January 23, 1942)', p.652.
30. Ibid.
31. Yeowart, R.A. PR9/73, AWM, Canberra.
32. Gillison, D. *Royal Australian Air Force, 1939–1942*, p.317.
33. Johnson, p.55.
34. Ibid.
35. Members of the RAAF killed on 19 January 1942 were: Sgt Oliver George Frederick Claxton (400552) 32, NSW; Flying Officer ames Sinclair McIntyre, (402995) 23, NSW; Flt Lt Paul Pryde Paterson (260515) 26, Vic; Cpl James Arthur Wilson (9164) 24, NSW.
36. australiansatwarfilmar hive.unsw.edu. au/archive/1778-david-bloomfield
37. Gill, 'The last days of Rabaul', p.398.
38. Fisher, P. PR89/0716, AWM, Canberra.
39. Johnson, p.60.
40. Gillison, p.355.
41. Ibid.
42. Ibid.
43. Stephens, A. *The Royal Australian Air Force*, Australian Centenary History of Defence, Vol II, Oxford, 2001, p.135.
44. Ibid.
45. Ibid.
46. Lerew, J.M. EXDOC168, AWM.
47. australiansatwarfilmar hive.unsw.edu. au/archive/1778-david-bloomfield
48. Ibid.
49. Ibid.
50. Hutchinson-Smith, D.II. MSS 1534, AWM, Canberra.
51. Turner, V.H. PR01469, Diary, AWM, Canberra.
52. Ibid.
53. Ibid.
54. *Montevideo Maru* Association, Submission, p.15.
55. Hutchinson-Smith.

CHAPTER SEVEN

SACRIFICED AND ABANDONED

*'A sorry muddle, with the 1,500 troops about to be
sacrificed on the altar of political ineptitude.'*

Sub Lieutenant J.C.H. Gill

Lark Force Commanding Officer, Colonel Joseph Scanlan, proved to be
inflexible and unwilling to accept advice from subordinates – to waiver
from the traditional 'command and control' military tenet. Scanlan
did not question his superiors in Australia and sought no variation
to his orders, despite the changing conditions in the Pacific. He did
not alter the fi•ed beach and airfield defence dispositions Lt Col Carr
had implemented, yet faith in Carr's leadership had long evaporated.[1]
Scanlan made no plans for withdrawal. In January 1942, *Lark Force* felt
the full impact of this obduracy.

Intelligence officer Sub Lt Con Gill (RANVR) thought that if the
situation wasn't so serious it was laughable.

*We had no steel helmets and when some pieces of shrapnel
… thudded down nearby we hurriedly got hold of some
lead covered code books and held those on our heads for
protection.*[2]

Simpson Harbour, the calm before the storm. Hasluck

Six months earlier, Gill had prepared a plan for the denial of port facilities in the Mandated Territories. The plan was 'scoffed at' by the 8th military district commandant, who derided him for his 'scorched earth policy'.[3] Gill was given a 'ticking off ' and his superior remarked confidently that, even if 'the Japanese did take Rabaul we might take it back in a matter of weeks' and 'we' would need the port installations that Gill 'was proposing to destroy'.[4] Gill and Lt Hugh McKenzie were frustrated with the trivializing of their intelligence reports and recommendations, as 'the policymakers vacillated from holding Rabaul to the last man, to evacuation, and back again.'[5] No plans were implemented to destroy Rabaul's infrastructure prior to invasion.

Lt David Selby, AA commander, was also frustrated. He visited Col Scanlan in Headquarters (HQ), and reiterated how the Japanese raids were avoiding damage to wharves, road junctions, the wireless station and camp buildings – clearly they were going to invade. Selby asked: 'what the plans were should a withdrawal become necessary?'[6] 'The reply I received was disconcerting: "That is a defeatist attitude, Selby!"'[7]

Rumours were rife and affecting morale, so Selby suggested a daily garrison news bulletin. HQ advised him that his suggestion was 'impracticable'. Selby did not agree, jotted down some notes from a radio news broadcast, and issued a sheet entitled 'AA News Bulletin' to his gunners. It proved to be so popular that he issued one a day. Selby

Lt A.L. Robinson (left) and Maj J.K. McCarthy (right) in 1944. Downs

sent a copy to HQ, and received a request that HQ be added to the distribution list.

'As the officer responsible for these young lives, I had a heavy load on my mind.'[8] Selby contacted HQ again for further orders in the advent of an invasion. The answer came: 'You're going a bit fast for us. We haven't got up to that yet.'[9] Considering that the AA unit was in an elevated position, Selby asked for star shells so his artillerymen could light up the harbour in the advent of a night invasion; his request was refused.

On New Year's Day came the order, each word in capital letters and underlined: 'THERE SHALL BE NO WITHDRAWAL.'[10] *Lark Force* officers realized that Scanlan was probably relaying the order from Australia, but they believed certain plans needed to be made urgently. The Army Service Corps officer requested that his men be permitted to hide portions of the battalion's two-year supply of tinned food in the mountains and along the coast – food dumps for future force resistance and survival. Scanlan refused.

Second-in-command of 2/22nd, Major John Claud Mollard (VX43446) and Captain Ernest Smyth Appel (VX8370), in charge of troops at Vunakanau Airfield, decided to act without the knowledge of their superiors and moved three truckloads of tinned food to Malabunga Mission, which proved to be a lifesaving initiative.

John Keith McCarthy was a restless man, always had been, since his birth in Melbourne in 1905. After completing his leaving certificate at Christian Brothers' College, McCarthy became a jackeroo in NSW. He tried various occupations, from working in a department store to cutting cane in northern Queensland. In 1927, McCarthy sailed for New Guinea. Here the tall, strongly built man, with classic Celtic colouring and a 'natural curiosity, energy and humanity', found his vocation, first with the Department of Native Affairs at Kokopo, then alone at a new station at Malutu, among the Nakanai people of central New Britain.[11] In 1929, he undertook a course in native affairs at the University of Sydney, before serving throughout New Guinea in a number of positions.

McCarthy's 37th birthday was 20 January 1942. Rabaul had been left devastated, and without air or sea defence. A motley group of troops, trained in desert warfare, were left to defend a place and people he felt strongly protective of. His concern had resulted in the evacuation of his wife, Jean. It wasn't the first time, but McCarthy offered his services to Col Scanlan. His knowledge of the local terrain and culture was beyond reproach. In however much time they had, he could instruct officers and soldiers in the lay of the land and jungle warfare; his offer was refused.[12]

Wing Commander Lerew was still reeling from the death of so many of his men. He received orders from the Air Board that he should take the remaining Hudson to Port Moresby and assume command, and that the remaining RAAF aircrew and ground crew join *Lark Force* infantry. Lerew ignored those orders. He had devised an evacuation plan not long after his arrival in Rabaul – trained RAAF personnel were more important elsewhere. Lerew ordered the Hudson loaded with the wounded and any other personnel it could carry and, before dawn on 22 January, the Hudson struggled into the air. The aircraft barely made it to Port Moresby. After refuelling, the aircraft flew on to Townsville with its precious cargo of injured servicemen. At one stage it began to lose altitude so everything but people was jettisoned, and the Hudson finall landed in mainland Australia.[13] Lerew informed Scanlan that he and his remaining men intended to implement his devised escape plan in the advent of an invasion. They began to evacuate on 22 January, with as many as possible rescued from pre-determined positions by Catalina aircraft, others to make their way independently. Only three RAAF personnel failed to escape Rabaul.

In October 1941, John Curtin had become Prime Minister. Unlike Menzies, he was determined to return Australian forces to protect the Australian mainland. Unlike Menzies, he forcefully pursued a United States alliance and protection policy, and in 1942 placed Australian defence forces at the disposal of US General Douglas MacArthur, the Allied Commander in the south-west Pacific.

But 1941 had been a year of procrastination, poor decisions and lost opportunity, and Curtin was struggling to catch-up with implemented strategic decisions. The Australian War Cabinet, acting on military advice and diplomatic pressure, had agreed to garrison forces on outlying islands. On 15 December, the Chiefs of Staff had argued that the evacuation of troops from Rabaul was impossible because of the effect it 'would have on the minds of the Dutch', in Dutch East Indies.[14]

Having deployed undermanned and underarmed island units with little or no air cover or naval support throughout islands north of Australia, those in the highest authority decided that these garrisons could offer 'only token resistance'.[15] The Chiefs of Staff, bunkered down in conference rooms in Melbourne, had actually decided by mid-1941 that *Lark Force* could not be effective against the naval and military forces Japan had already assembled in the Caroline Islands. A secret

William Mahony: 'Long distance thinking', the failure of British PM Winston Churchill to acknowledge the Japanese threat and to return Australian troops, speaking with PM John Curtin, Daily Telegraph, 1942.

john.curtin.edu.au/shapingthenation/essay/leader

army minute, dated 2 August 1941, admitted that 'to secure Rabaul against attack would require a scale of defence beyond the resources at its disposal.'[16]

The decision had been made that thousands of troops were to be sacrificed. The Rabaul garrison, like the other 'bird' forces, were expected 'to do their duty and inflict heavy casualties on the Japanese before becoming casualties themselves.'[17] Inertia on the part of officialdom meant that Rabaul's civilians were doomed to the same fate. The Acting Administrator, Harold Hillis Page, lacked the ability to make independent decisions. Page cabled his superiors for permission to evacuate the remaining European civilians. His plea should have been received with serious credibility, given his family ties to the Government – but it wasn't. His brother, the former Australian PM Sir Earle Page, had been appointed Australian envoy in London and sat on the British War Cabinet. In December 1941, Earle Page had declared to the same war cabinet that 'Australia would never stand our men being deserted.'[18] Yet on 12 December 1941, the Chief of Naval Staff

General MacArthur and PM Curtin meet in Australia in March 1942.

National Archives

had sent a cablegram to the Rt Hon R.G. Casey, Australian Minister in Washington DC, stating: 'it is considered better to maintain Rabaul only as an advanced air operational base, its present small garrison being regarded as hostages to fortune.'[19] Earle Page left London for a six-day Christmas holiday with relatives in Belfast,[20] another example of the lack of awareness and failure in communication of those in power. Earle Page returned to Australia in June 1942, having had severe pneumonia, caused by 'since January the worst period of acute mental distress of my whole life.'[21]

The civilian population in Rabaul was 'already confused and frustrated by a policy of secrecy.'[22] They received no official instructions on how to evacuate. There remained an obsession with the civilian supervision of the native population, indicated in a cable sent to Harold Page that read: 'the situation is in hand, carry on as usual.'[23] Page appointed the architect and civil engineer Robert Leeuwin 'Nobby' Clark, a member of the Legislative Council, and President of the Returned and Services League, as Chief Civil Warden. Clark, an ex-WWII Australian Flying Corps and long-time Rabaul resident, was unable to obtain advice on evacuation or civil defence from either civilian or military authority.[24] 'The truth was there that was no plan and no organization.'[25] The Administrator, in Lae, was ill and unable to assist. Major General Basil Moorhouse Morris DSO, GOC, Commandant of the 8th Military District, Port Moresby, had – according to historian Ian Downs – 'troubles of his own', and 'was obsessed' with being 'rid of the civilian Administrator of Papua, Leonard Murray', so he could achieve 'total control of all activities by military government.'[26] 'Nobby' Clark did his best by introducing a civilian air-raid precautions plan, issuing instructions to dig slit trenches near homes and work places, and to proceed to a refuge area in the valley at Namanula Ridge should the alarm be sounded.

Harold Page sent another telegram, more urgent than his last; in his opinion nothing further could be achieved by his government employees remaining, when Japanese internment was likely.[27] The Chiefs of Staff again emphasized the importance of government officials remaining at their posts until ordered to leave.[28] Another message announced that civilian European men could evacuate for Lae from 21 January. By 21 January, most civilians had already left Rabaul, seeking refuge near Namanula.

Having made no plans for the general evacuation of civilians, using small boats or other transport, Page and Treasurer H.O. Townsend departed by car for an outlying plantation.

The Asian and mixed-race population were alarmed and resentful that their women and children had not been evacuated, unlike from other parts of New Guinea, such as Lae and Salamaua. In Rabaul, Chinese telephonists ceased work on Christmas Eve and Chinese tradesmen 'could no longer be relied upon for defence works.'[29] Page had then contacted Australia, requesting that an army engineer unit be sent to Rabaul. The Chinese Ambulance Auxiliary organized by NGVR Warrant Officer Robert Leslie Kennedy (NGX496) – because non-Europeans were not allowed guns – struggled to muster. Ben Cheong, Siu Ban Cheong, Leo Kam On and Leo Chee Chai were the only four who reported for full-time duty. After four days assisting the wounded,

Left to right: Lorna Whyte, Pte Hennessy, Mavis Cullen, Cpl Blake, Kay Parker.

they were advised to destroy their uniforms and return to the Chinese community.

Three hundred native police staged a demonstration because their rifles and ammunition were buried, after being told they were not allowed to fight.[30] Sub Lt Gill could only shake his head and think: 'it was a sorry muddle, with the 1,500 troops about to be sacrificed on the altar of political ineptitude.'[31]

Army nurse Lt Lorna Whyte could scarcely believe that she had shared the popular belief that 'Japan was a poor nation full of myopic little men who could not fire a rifle.'[32] Nor that she had felt so completely confident that British forces would quickly defeat any Japanese recalcitrant. Apart from surviving the heat in their heavy uniforms, the nurses had found their duties reasonably easy. So too

Lt Lorna Whyte.
www.angellpro.com.au/rabaul

members of the 2/10 Field Ambulance. For Pte Billy Cook (NX56978) and his unit mates, particularly the other 'Cs': Ptes Roger Attwater (NX47047), 23, from North Sydney, Ron Cantwell (NX46687), 25, Des Collins (NX57343), 22, Stewart Caston (NX60008), 23 and Tom Clissold (NX57642), 28, life had been stress free. With the exit of the Administrator, the military hospital had been moved to Government House on Namanula Ridge, a real improvement after tents.

Also on duty at Namanula Hospital was civilian nursing sister Alice Bowman. Sister Bowman was born in 1912 in Longreach, Queensland. Growing up in the harsh conditions of the Channel country she believed that she could manage the harsh conditions of New Britain and, with both general nursing and midwifery qualifications, she was well received in 1939 at the European Hospital, Rabaul. She enjoyed spending her off-duty hours writing and sketching, and unlike some, Sister Bowman considered it 'of prime importance to understand and speak the language of Pidgin', regardless of the 'many efforts made by Australian authorities to discourage the use of Pidgin English', because

Namanula Hospital. Bowman

'it was considered, among other things, demeaning.'[33] There were hundreds of dialects in New Britain, and Pidgin was the only way she could communicate with the indigenous peoples. When *Lark Force* arrived, she was kept busy assisting with young troops ill prepared for the unforgiving tropical conditions, who quickly suffered malaria and dysentery. Like army nurse Lt Lorna Whyte, Bowman wondered how:

> *The Japanese were viewed as being somewhat primitive ... it seems strange that there could have been so much ignorance and complacency surrounding the Japanese.*[34]

Their world of medical staff was turned upside down when the bombs rained down. Mutilated bodies arrived. Many died and amputations were common; women and children were not immune, and medical staff worked around the clock to save lives. Maj Palmer worked feverishly:

> *The operating theatre was like a slaughterhouse, bloodied swabs and dressings were thrown into a corner none of them being cleaned up until the last of the patients were treated.*[35]

The President of the Rabaul branch of the Australian Labor Party sent a personal cable to Prime Minister Curtin. 'Despite any information to the contrary after today's attack on Rabaul you may anticipate total loss here.'[36]

The many reports and cables created by intelligence officers MacKenzie and Gill had, it appeared to them, been largely ignored by the highest powers in New Guinea and Australia. They were now instructed to continue to broadcast. With no issued wireless equipment of their own, they were forced to resort to a borrowed teleradio, and the Amalgamated Wireless Australasia (AWA) station in Rabaul. AWA ceased operations on 21 January. A signal from the British Admiralty had ordered them to destroy their ship's confidential books (CBs), cyphers, and signal books. Commonly, a small station like New Britain held few CBs, but because pre-Pearl Harbour military strategy considered Rabaul to be a desirable Allied fleet base, the Rabaul office held an unusually large quantity of CBs. CBs were constructed with lead-weighted covers, 'to hasten their descent to the ocean bed in the event of risk of capture afloat '[37] There were no instructions as to how to destroy these on land. The officers dug a large trench and over seven hours they tore, ripped, attacked with tomahawks and fed the CBs into a 'roaring fire' [38] Looking at the empty safes, MacKenzie and Gill decided: 'things ought to be made interesting for the Japanese.'[39] They placed reams of unused stationery, lead bars, rocks, anything they could find, before locking the safes and throwing the keys into the harbour.

Hopefully the enemy would find that 'irritating' at least.[40]

For NGVR volunteers, officialdom had shown a frustrating lack of urgency and a 'fatuous incompetence'.[41] Rabaul and the surrounding region was their home, their livelihood, and these were facing total destruction. For members of the NGVR, this could not be more personal, yet their experience and resources were not being utilized. Loosely under the control of Col Scanlan and his staff, they had not been fully mobilized.

Admittedly, they were unpaid volunteers, armed with obsolete weapons, but their intelligence, skills and local knowledge were high.

On 20 January, schoolteacher and NGVR Sgt Francis William Ryan (NGX501), 42, initiated a muster of NGVR volunteers. They met on the parade ground in the Botanical Gardens – a cross-section of men

Gwen and Lionel Dix. AWM   *Charles Houghton.* AWM

and backgrounds, intent on the defence of their town. Sgt Charles Ian MacLean (NGX475), 36, was a dentist; Rifleman Bernard Alphonsus O'Connor (NGX408), 35, was an entomologist; Rifleman William Robert Reynolds (NGX480), 21, was a Commonwealth Bank employee; Cpl Robert Allan Bird (NGX500), 34, was a Customs Department official; Sgt Victor Aikenan Florance (NGX508), 53, was a solicitor. They carried small arms and 100 rounds of .303 rifle ammunition. They loaded themselves into a truck with a mortar and two Vickers machine guns and drove to the Lakunai Airfield. Soon others joined NGVR ranks. Plantation manager Charles William Booth Houghton, 35, changed his civilian clothes for uniform, and became Rifle an (Rfn) (NGX510). Recently married Lionel Stephen Dix, 27, became Rfn (NGX504).

Lark Force troops were uneasy. Col Scanlan and his staff were rarely seen and rumour had it that Scanlan remained in denial, believing that a brigade would arrive from Australia.[42] Their officers seemed uninformed; what was going on? What had started as a thought rarely voiced – would ships and aircraft arrive soon to evacuate those who remained? – was now being asked forcibly. The troop's feelings of being beleaguered and doomed were exacerbated by the lack of communication from their superiors. Between mid-December 1941

Happier days in Rabaul. AWM

and mid-January 1942, five ships had berthed in Rabaul, yet there were no contingency plans for their use. The 330-ton inter-island ferry, Matafele, was at the wharf – it just needed a crew. A flotilla of smaller vessels just needed to be commandeered – but Acting Administrator Page had already left Rabaul.

Even the most junior member of *Lark Force* understood the gravity of the situation. Eighteen-year-old Gnr David Bloomfield decided: 'The Japs probably knew more about our equipment than we did. Or as much.'[43] They all realized that they were armed with obsolete weapons; suddenly the happy, laid-back times in a tropical paradise seemed long distant.

Up with the Praed Point battery, Sgt Frederick Stanley Vasey (SX11435) remembered how he had written home to his family in Adelaide on 2 December: 'Please don't send any more parcels up here, as in all probability I'll be home for Christmas.'[44] It was well past Christmas and they were still waiting. He wondered what the family at home were thinking and if he should ask them to begin sending the very welcome comfort packages again. He had no answers for the younger blokes, and no one more senior in rank, including the Praed Point CO, Major James Rowland Purcell (TX6041), seemed to know what was going on; or at least, weren't telling the troops. Two days ago, the bombs had come close to his 6-inch battery – a terrifying day, particularly for all the youngsters he served with. Everyone was nervous and, although 21 January had been quiet, it was a only supreme optimist who believed the attacks were over. Vasey spoke calmly to his no.1 crew as 22 January dawned: Bombadier (Bdr) Ken Carmichael (SX11443), 22, from Nagambie, Victoria; Gnr Tasman Gallagher (TX4395), 21, from Hobart; Gnr Robert Hannaford (SX11447), 21, from Cudlee Creek, South Australia; Gnr Clarence Harrison (VX129361), 21, from Melbourne; Gnr Harold Thomas (VX129384), 27, also from Melbourne, as was Percy Gray (VX129342), 21. As the sun rose, the normally calm horizon was full of aircraft.

The air-raid alarm sounded and the AA crews on Frisbee Ridge ran to their guns. 'We saw them coming in from the northeast.'[45] But the dive bombers kept well out of range, instead flying straight at Praed Point battery and 'bombed the hell out of it.'[46] The heavy battery crews stood no chance. From Frisbee Ridge, Lt Peter Fisher watched with a feeling of total helplessness as the Praed Point emplacement was destroyed with 'devastating efficiency'[47] by 1100-pound (500kg) bombs. They took their time, waiting for the dust to clear before the next wave of bombers delivered more devastation. The top gun was blown from its platform and tumbled down onto the bottom gun emplacement, just as the engineers had warned. Men were buried alive. The AA crews were helpless, 'we couldn't do a thing, we just stood by and watched it', said Gnr David Bloomfield [48]

The no. 1 Sgt Vasey gun crew were blown up or buried. Gnr Arthur Enever (TX4401), 21, was dug out, but he died of his wounds shortly after. The Fortress Engineers Sapper (Spr) John McLeod Bennett (QX64918), 21, from Brisbane, Spr Frederick Clissold (VX129401), 20, of Broken Hill, NSW, and Cpl Douglas McHenry Sandison (SX38281), 20, from Adelaide, were killed as they sheltered in a dugout, buried alive.

Gnr Gordon Abel AWM

The 18-year-old Gnr Gordon Abel survived, but only just. He had lain as flat as he could in a shallow stormwater drain. The bombs were 'daisy cutter bombs', anti-personnel, with graze fuses, which meant they exploded on touch and flung shrapnel – 'old door knobs, door latches, and bits of all kinds

Sgt Bert Smith. Johnson

of scrap metal' – indiscriminately through the air with the power of rifle bullets.[49] Abel felt a searing pain in the middle of his back, as if a hole was burning through his body. Someone flicked red hot shrapnel off his shirt. The noise made by the bombs, and the screams of fellow gunners were terrifying – a memory that remained etched in survivors' minds forever.

Climbing out of the dirt and debris, the sight was even more 'shocking' for the youthful Abel; survivors found 'a few of our mates with no heads at all.'[50] The camp was destroyed, their guns were completely ruined and there were no contingency plans. The adventure had lost all lustre for the Tasmanians who had left their state young and naive. Concussed and disoriented, Praed Point survivors gathered their rifles, unfired since arriving in Rabaul, some ammunition and received one water bottle each. There was no food because, as they learned later, due to their youth and militia status 'some officers thought we might run away.'[51]

Scanlan's HQ intercepted a message from a Catalina flying boat that enemy cruisers were steaming towards Rabaul; Kavieng had already been heavily attacked. He instructed Lt Col Carr that to avoid the troops being massacred by naval gunfire, they should be moved from the Malaguna camp, which lay exposed on the Simpson Harbour foreshore, to an improvised army headquarters at Raluana. Scanlan had little confidence in his soldiers as plainly demonstrated when, believing the truth would cause panic, he ordered that troops be told this was 'an exercise only'. This directive resulted in soldiers going to battle stations without hard rations, quinine or other essential items. The order made little sense to Sgt Ashley Vance Dore (VX42841) or other members of his 30-strong platoon. Following orders, Dore:

Pte Percy Pearson. Johnson   *S/Sgt Vic Turner.* Johnson

Moved out with only the minimum gear, shirt, shorts and tin
hat, plus also in my case a Thompson sub machine gun and
haversack full of spare magazines and ammunition. I had fired
a sub machine gun once.[52]

Sgt Herbert William 'Bert' Smith (VX46514), A Company 2/22, was
worried; 'without air supremacy, infantry and ground troops' had little
chance.[53] Staff Sgt (S/Sgt) Victor Harold Turner (VX15628), R Company
2/22, was a veteran of service with the British Army in India; it seemed
to him that things were falling apart. Col Scanlan 'has not been seen',
and his last order had been not particularly confidence building: 'Every
man will fight to the last. He will not surrender to anyone.'[54] A feeling
of depending disaster lay heavy in the air.

After months of preparing fixed defences, like at Lakunai Airfield,
troops were being withdrawn to beach positions on the other side of
Simpson Harbour. Turner's Company were trying to recover from
the bombing of Lukunai, so blatantly done that Japanese aircrew had
'leaned over the side of their planes to see more clearly', and performed
acrobatics as they returned to their carriers. His men were covered

in dust and dirt, and the sun was blazing down – they already looked defeated. Drenched in sweat, as they climbed up the face of Matupi Pass the volcanic dust raining down on them, 'was hell'.[55] His company marched down the slope to the bay, 'only to be told we have to turn and march all the way back.'[56] Turner was struggling to sustain the morale of his unit, but 'I'm tired tonight, so tired it all seems as though nothing matters any more.'[57]

The return trip was 'like a bad dream ... I realised the ridiculous futility of it all and wanted to laugh ... nobody has much hope.'[58]

Others were faced with the same confusion of orders. Private Percy Pearson, D Company 2/22, couldn't believe that 'our months of work on the coast round Talili Bay was useless.'[59] So much time had been spent rolling out barbed wire in the north of New Britain and, even with his limited military experience, he could see the Japanese were about to sail comfortably into Simpson Harbour. Pearson was detailed to build roadblocks and to mine roads – tricky when civilians were still escaping Rabaul.

Confusion continued. NGVR Sgt Ryan was ordered to move his machine guns and mortar to a new position at Vulcan Island. This gave his small band of NGVR about one mile (1600m) to defend. The plan was to prevent the Japanese from moving up to Vunakanau from Vulcan Beach. However, not only was it already dark but 'we had no tools and found it difficult to make a new position for our guns and mortar.'[60] NGVR Cpl Basil George Challis (NG13) used his hands and kept digging, until at waist level, he hit water. They had no further contact with other units and, feeling very alone, waited.

The morale of the AA unit had taken a big slump after watching their fellow artillerymen at Praed Point die. Then their truck arrived back without the day's rations. Malaguna camp was deserted and the Army Service Corps stores were locked up. With his rising anxiety clear in comments such as: 'The infantry have dumped us. We've been forgotten. What happens now?', Lt David Selby instructed his battery quartermaster, Sgt Gilchrist, to go to Malaguna camp with an axe, break open the store, and take the rations.[61]

By mid-afternoon the ocean was full of enemy ships. Selby counted 25, including an aircraft carrier, five other warships and 19 transports. 'Faced with the grim reality of their approach, I was obsessed by a feeling of finality, of complete impotence.'[62] Thoughts of his wife and daughter loomed large – 'war is no game for married men and fathers.'[63] But war was war and it did not discriminate: sons, husbands, fathers, brothers were all about to be subjected to it. As if his thoughts had a greater power, there was an 'incredible, earth-shattering explosion'.[64] An army team had destroyed a dump of RAAF bombs opposite Malaguna camp, but they had severely underestimated the effect. The explosion was so violent that it wrecked town buildings but, even more importantly, it broke the valves in all wireless sets in the Rabaul district. *Lark Force* now lost all communication with the outside world.

Selby had been ordered to destroy his guns. The order didn't sit well with the AA CO, or his battery. 'It was with a heavy heart' that he and his men moved.[65] Crews placed a shell down each gun barrel and one down the breech; then, after taking cover, pulled the firing. Metal flew and all that as left was twisted metal. Selby had been told that there was no additional transport for his unit – they had indeed been deserted. Assembling his men, he issued each with a clip of ammunition for their .303 rifles. Few had fired a rifle. There were boxes of grenades, but no one knew:

whether the boxes marked with green was four or seven second fuses, or vice versa. So here we had hand grenades ready to pull the pin and throw, but we didn't know whether to throw them high or to throw them low.[66]

The battery had one three-ton truck and a utility. Officially, the three-ton truck had a maximum prescribed load of 18 men, but 40 crowded into it and the remainder overloaded the utility.

Selby had been instructed to go to the forward headquarters (HQ), but the locality of the forward HQ had not been sent to the AA unit. Selby decided to drive to Three Ways and then ask directions from Captain McGinnis of B Company. Upon arrival at Three Ways, the AA unit was ordered to unload and dig in. After following this order, another was given – to proceed to Raluana Beach. No one knew where Raluana was, but they reloaded their trucks and proceeded south-east.

The rain was falling heavily and, as headlights could not be used because of blackout restrictions, troops took it in turns to walk on the near side of the trucks, at the edge of the track. When they finally arrived at Raluana, Captain Frank Eric Shier (VX44908) was struggling to coordinate the retreating troops. Lt Alexander Richard Tolmer (VX35754) and his soldiers were at the mission, Lt Lennox Douglas Henry (VX38976) and his platoon were right of the mission and Lt George Alfred Charles Milne (VX44781) had taken a platoon to the small water reservoir with five NGVR manning a medium machine gun.

Shier was left with the remainder of Y Company, which contained no infantry soldiers but comprised 'the odds and ends, postal unit, mess waiters, clerks',[67] and now AA gunners. 'We all had bayonets so we were soldiers', joked Gnr David Bloomfield. He volunteered to be a member of the Vickers machine-gun detachment and, with six other volunteers, stayed on the beach, while the others moved further inland. S/Sgt Vic Turner was an experienced soldier and now he regarded the AA gunners with new admiration. 'Kids, only boys. These boys.'[68] He shook his head: 'Fourteen hundred of us! Fourteen hundred to face what?'[69] Then they waited, this ill-assortment of militia and support *Lark Force* troops, lying on a mound of earth with bayoneted rifles – rifles no one had fired in action. The wait was agonizing. 'Visibility was practically nil', described Capt Hutchinson-Smith, making 'the tense atmosphere ... eerie and unnatural.'[70]

Endnotes

1. Gamble, B. *Darkest Hour*, p.51.
2. Gill, *The Last Days of Rabaul*, p.656.
3. Ibid., p.657.
4. Ibid.
5. Ibid.
6. Selby, D. *Hell and High Fever*, p.24.
7. Ibid.
8. Ibid., p.23.
9. Ibid.
10. Ibid., p.24.
11. H.N. Nelson, 'McCarthy, John Keith (1905–1976)', *Australian Dictionary of Biography*, National Centre of Biography, Australian National University, adb.anu.edu.au/ biography/ mccarthy-john-keith-10910/text19375, accessed online 20 August 2016; first published in hardcopy in *Australian Dictionary of Biography*, Volume 15, (MUP), 2000.
12. McCarthy, J.K. *Patrol into Yesterday: My New Guinea Years*, Cheshire, 1963, p.189.
13. Gillison, pp.356–358.
14. Horner, D.M. *Crisis of Command: Australian Generalship and the Japanese Threat, 1941–1943*, ANU, 1978, p.35.
15. *Montevideo Maru Association*, Submission, p.12.
16. Ibid.
17. Ibid.
18. Horner, D.M. *High Command*, Allen & Unwin, 1982, p.150. See also, Warren, A. *Britain's Greatest Defeat: Singapore 1942*, A&C Black, 2006, p.180.
19. A2671/1,333/41, War Cabinet Agenda files, National Archives, Canberra.
20. McCosker, A. *Masked Eden, A History of the Australians in New Guinea*, Matala, 1998, p.184
21. Bridge, C. 'Page, Sir Earle Christmas (1880–1961)', *Australian Dictionary of Biography*, National Centre of Biography, Australian National University, adb.anu.edu.au/ biography/ page-sir-earle-christmas-7941/

text13821, published first in hardcopy 1988, accessed online 21 August 2016.
22. Downs, p.47.
23. McCosker, p.179.
24. Hall. T. *New Guinea, 1942–1944*, Methuen, London, 1981, p.14.
25. Downs, p.50.
26. Ibid., p.56.
27. Sweeting, p.673.
28. A5954 532/1, National Archives, Canberra.
29. Downs, p.49.
30. Ibid., p.55.
31. Gill, p.656.
32. Nikakis, p.65.
33. Bowman, *Not now tomorrow*, p.4.
34. Ibid., p.xiv.
35. Palmer, J.P. MSS2155, AWM.
36. Hall, p.17.
37. Gill, p.664.
38. Ibid., p.665.
39. Ibid.
40. Ibid.
41. Downs, p.46.
42. *Montevideo Maru Association*, Submission, p.15.
43. australiansatwarfilmar hive unsw edu au/archive/1778-david-bloomfield
44. Vasey, F.S. Letters, PR04644, AWM.
45. australiansatwarfilmar hive.unsw.edu. au/archive/1778-david-bloomfield
46. Ibid.
47. Fisher, P. PR89/0716, papers, Australian War Memorial, Canberra.
48. australiansatwarfilmar hive.unsw.edu. au/archive/1778-david-bloomfield
49. Abel, R.G. MSS1623, 'Gnr Gordon Abel Rueben Gordon's war', Australian War Memorial, Canberra.
50. Ibid.
51. Ibid.
52. Dore, A.V. PR01835, 'Escape from Rabaul', Australian War Memorial, Canberra.
53. Johnson, p.60.

54. Turner, V.H. PR01469, Diary, Australian War Memorial, Canberra.
55. Ibid.
56. Ibid.
57. Ibid.
58. Ibid.
59. Johnson, p.74.
60. Downs, p.59
61. Selby, p.33.
62. Ibid., p.34.
63. Ibid., p.35.
64. Ibid., p.37.
65. Ibid.
66. australiansatwarfilmar hive.unsw.edu. au/archive/1778-david-bloomfield
67. Selby, p.38.
68. Turner, VH,. PR01469
69. Ibid.
70. Hutchinson-Smith, MSS1534.

CHAPTER EIGHT

SITUATION HOPELESS

*'There is no longer satisfaction to be
had from this slaughter.'*

Sgt Victor Turner

On 22 January, between 3,000 and 4,000 Japanese troops stormed ashore at neighbouring New Ireland and the 1st Independent Company retreated. Formed in May 1941, and trained at Victoria's Wilsons Promontory, the 1st Independent was another force raised to serve in the Middle East.[1] However, there was dissention within the Australian Army as to the need for a specialist commando unit, and it was not until Japan entered the war that that question was answered.[2] Under the command of Major James Edmonds-Wilson (SX9608) from July 1941, around 158 officers and men were dispersed throughout New Ireland – at Buka on Bougainville, Lorengau on Manus Island, Port Vila in the New Hebrides, and Tulagi and Guadalcanal in the Solomon Islands – to protect Kavieng airfield, and act as island observers.[3] Having received comprehensive military training, the commandos, if faced with a superior force, were to destroy military installations and other key infrastructure before resorting to guerrilla warfare.

They prided themselves in being more qualified, even elitist, than the regular Australian Army. This also came with increased expectation.

Pte Petersen.   *Pte George.*

The Independent Company favoured country men as they were robust, multi-skilled and capable of using initiative. Private (Pte) Harvey James Petersen (QX7985), a cheerful 23-year-old, was named after his family farm on Harvey Creek, south of Cairns – the New Ireland tropics really didn't feel like the lush tropics of North Queensland. Pte Ronald Angus Fraser (NX68894), 21, was from Boggabri, a small town in north-western NSW – there was no jungle in Narrabri Shire unless you counted the palm tree planted next to the railway station. The winter climate of Glenn Innes was one of the coldest in NSW, which had not

exactly prepared Pte Arthur John George (NX41372), 22, for New Guinea. Tenterfield, NSW, about 57 miles (92km) north of Glenn Innes, is another town with misty picturesque landscapes. For later generations, Tenterfield was famous for the song written and performed by Peter Allen, 'Tenterfield Saddler', a tribute to his grandfather who ran the saddlery from 1908 to 1960. For

Pte Fraser at home in Boggabri. AWM

earlier generations, the town was renowned for being where eloquent NSW Premier Sir Henry Parkes delivered his famous 'birth of our nation' speech in 1889. This rousing speech was decisive in the federation of the colonies into the nation of Australia in 1901.

Lance Corporal Kevin Geyer. Geyer

Lance Corporal Kevin Victor Geyer (NX47935) was born in Tenterfield on 13 March 1918. His paternal ancestry was German, his maternal side less spoken of because of 'generational denial/embarrassment, caused by the social pressures of those times.'[4] Kevin's maternal grandmother was Annie Taylor, of the Dunghutti Aboriginal people of the Kempsey area, who married Luke Whitton, a stockman of the Ngarabal people.

William Godfrey Geyer and Harriett Geyer (nee Whitton) were a couple tied to the land by ancestry and choice, as were their 10 children, and the road on which their farm was located would be renamed Geyer Road. Kevin was the second youngest and 'a deft shot, potting rabbits for their pelts and meat', who spent 'countless hours keeping birds off the ripening stone fruit crops.'[5]

The Great Depression was cruel and Kevin Geyer took employment wherever he could, including at a local timber mill and a grocery store. He matured into a strong resourceful man with a strong Christian faith.

There was a family tradition of volunteer war service and Kevin enlisted at Newcastle, NSW, on 5 September 1940, aged 22 – one of the many resourceful country men selected for service with 1 Independent.

The Turner brothers were inseparable. Mark Sylvester Turner and Jessie Turner of Willoughby, NSW, could not have been prouder because, despite the seven-year age difference, their boys developed into men with different temperaments and skills but remained close. Sidney 'Sid' Stewart was the eldest, born in 1915; Dudley James was born in 1919; and Daryl George in 1922. Sid was a NSW travelling salesman, a man's man with an eye for the ladies.[6] Dudley was a Sydney-based clerk, except for when he worked as a shearer on his grandparents'

Dudley, Daryl and Sidney Turner. Dale

farm. Dudley 'Dud' was the 'runt of the litter', and his broken nose was testimony to his love of 'a drink, a laugh and a fight '[7] With three boys and two girls, Ona and Alexis, at home there was never a dull moment in the Turner household.

In 1940, Sid and Dud were keen to enlist in the army, but Daryl was barely 17 and had just left school. There was no way the Turner brothers were going to leave him behind yet 'no one would take on Mum.'[8] So they approached their father. With his words that they must stay together ringing in their ears, they reported to the recruiting office in June 1940 with a plan – both Dud and Dal would alter their dates of birth. They stood closely in line with Daryl in the middle, protected as always. The subterfuge worked and they were soon VX57050, VX57051 and VX57052. They then convinced the authorities that it was in the army's best interest that, following regular AIF training, the three enter 1 Independent and be shipped together to New Ireland.

The island lifestyle did nothing to enhance the military preparedness of 1 Independent. New Ireland was a tiny island and, whereas the commandos were trained for combat, there was none. Lt Alexander Fraser (QX6470) realized 'one severe penalty for the static use of such highly trained troops was boredom.'[9] There was guard training but

Tsang Tsang's pub, Kavieng, a favourite watering hole of 1 Independent soldiers. McNab

mainly life revolved around sports and 'visits to the local club, pubs and the canteen.'[10]

Life was too easy, and photographs home showed that the soldiers were embraced by local families, but this was not what they had been trained for.

On 21 January 1942, Rabaul received a reprieve from bombing because 60 Japanese aircraft bombed Kavieng, New Ireland, 125 miles (201km) to the north-west. The dive-bombing pinpointed the

1 Independent soldiers relaxing at Doyle's plantation near Kavieng. Page/McNab

Independent airfield's machine-gun emplacements. The crew of the commandos' 81-ton schooner *Induna Star* quickly cast off from the Kavieng wharf to reach the shelter of the Albatross channel but the escaping craft made an easy target. The boat's Bren gun team, led by Cpl Gordon Bradley Reed (VX20657), fired until six of the team were wounded and the schooner became wedged on a reef.

The defenders of Kavieng had shot down four planes but clearly this had been a pre-invasion attack. Decisions needed to be made quickly. Maj Edmunds-Wilson visited the hospital where the unit's medical officer, Capt Vincent George Bristow (VX39436), and civilian nurse, Dorothy Maye, were struggling with the influx of civilian and military casualties. The more serious were moved to the Lamacott Mission. Though the *Induna Star* was barely seaworthy, it was taken to Kaut Harbour and emergency repairs were undertaken – it was the only means of escape off New Ireland. A small number of soldiers were left at the airfield to ensure the demolition of the wharves the next morning, and the remainder of 1 Independent moved to Sook River camp. Very early on the morning of 22 January, the Japanese made nine simultaneous landings, between 3,000 and 4,000 troops. Commandos scrambled to blow up the airfield and supply dumps, and destroy wireless equipment – 1 Independent was vastly outnumbered and had little alternative but to retreat.

By 28 January, Maj Edmunds-Wilson realized that his men, who had been through 'jungle and swamp for nine days ... were now suffering from fatigue, malaria and dysentery, and skin diseases.'[11] The *Induna Star* lay on a mud bank. With all possible repairs completed by 30 January, 1 Independent Commandos re-floated and boarded the schooner. At nightfall the escape to Port Moresby was launched. By the next day they had reached Kalili Harbour when an enemy destroyer was sighted. The *Induna Star* quickly hove to in an inlet and hid. With an overcast evening, 'a favourable wind and a heavy following sea'[12] the schooner sailed south. Hopes were high until an enemy aircraft suddenly circled and machine-gunned the boat. A bomb struck amidships, killing three and wounding more. To continue was senseless – the flight of the *Induna Star* was over. An enemy destroyer arrived and sent a boat

Japanese landing at Kavieng and Buka Island. McNab

to take officers and wounded onboard, a line was attached, and the schooner and remnants of 1 Independent were towed to Rabaul and captivity.

There had been an evacuation of New Ireland women and children during December to Australia, but some missionaries, plantation managers and government employees had remained. As in Rabaul, non-European and indigenous residents were not evacuated.

Just days before, District Officer MacDonald had advised the remaining civilians to leave Kavieng.[13] From [21] January, the days were harrowing. Civilians killed during the bombing and invasion included Tung Sing,[14] and [77]-year-old Archibald Corbett Forsyth on his Lemacott Plantation.[15] With [1] Independent Doctor Bristow retreating with his unit, civilian nurse Sister Maye chose to remain with her patients. For military personnel and civilians unable to escape New Ireland, the future was bleak.

Lt Hugh MacKenzie had been ordered that, in the advent of an invasion, he and Sub Lt Gill were to use their New Guinea familiarity and move into the hinterland. From there they were to report Japanese

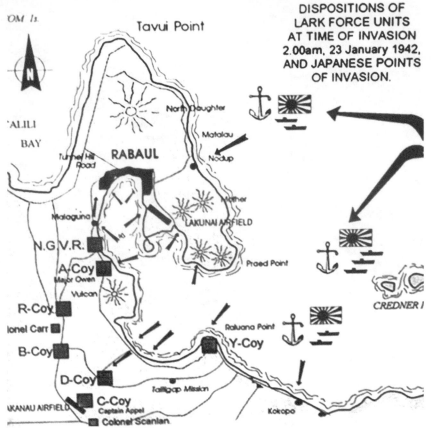

Lark Force *emplacements, 23 January 1942.* NGVR Museum

movements to Port Moresby by the teleradio at Toma. On 22 January, Gill left with NGVR Rifleman Kenneth C.J. Stone to retrieve the teleradio.

When they returned, MacKenzie was clearly perplexed that orders had now been issued that the teleradio was to be destroyed. It made little sense to MacKenzie, Gill and Stone, who retreated to the hills and 'waited for the confused situation to clarify.'[16]

On the island of New Britain, a tiny, ill-prepared, badly equipped, uncoordinated and poorly led garrison, forsaken by their government, faced an overwhelming invasion force estimated to be around 18,000. The coastline was huge and there was no air or sea defence. They were on their own with no hopes for reinforcement and the day Capt Hutchinson-

Neil and Jack Olney in peaceful times. Johnson

Smith described as 'wild and tempestuous' began early.[17] Individual bravery among *Lark Force* and NGVR troops, who lay in the pre-dawn hours of 23 January, would soon be evident, but their situation was hopeless.

A Company 2/22nd Battalion AIF took the brunt of a perfectly orchestrated and executed invasion. On the previous morning after the destruction of Praed Point battery, Maj William Taylor 'Bill' Owen (VX45223) had ordered A Company to move to Vulcan Island. The platoon was made up of around 110 men, excluding machine gunners, mortar detachments and carrier crews. They had been joined by about 50 NGVR, led by Lt Claude Geoffrey 'Geoff' Kilner (NGX457), who manned machine guns and mortars on the northern flank of the harbour defensive line. In No.2 section, 2/22nd twin brothers Ptes Clarence and William Bellingham were watching each

Lt Bill Owen. AWM

other's back, determined to survive. They did but 28 of their company did not. Pte Jock Olney (VX30074), a member of D Company, was remembering what he had written to his sister Marion the previous month about how life in New Britain 'was like the tropics you read about, with the beautiful blue waters and lovely cool nights',[18] and how he and three mates had been sent by the owner of the Rabaul Hotel to spend time at a plantation at Put Put. Olney had been 'staggered by its beauty', and the pure luxury of having a bedroom overlooking the open ocean.[19] Now he had another position overlooking the ocean, but it was not luxurious and the ocean was full of enemy ships.

His company was under the command of Maj Owen; their weapons consisted of one 3-inch mortar, two Vickers machine guns, tommy guns, rifles and a couple of Lewis guns. The soldiers had been reminiscing about Australia and how they intended to enjoy life on their return. Olney had been moved by how each soldier crammed a lifetime into a couple of minutes. R Company, in reserve, was commanded by Capt Colin Lachlan McInnes (VX46497), who had worked in a bank; so too had Maj Owen, less than 18 months before. They heard aircraft noise and for a brief moment experienced elation: 'it's the boys coming to our aid from Moresby.'[20] The optimism quickly evaporated as the aircraft sent down parachute flares and Owens ordered his company to open fire. After that, a blur.

More aircraft and flares cast brilliant light over the harbour. A Company hadn't heard the barges coming ashore or realized that the enemy was so close. At 2.25 a.m., an enemy green flare signalled the commencement of the invasion and the shapes of boats and soldiers appeared. Sgt Kenneth Gregory Hale (VX25895) was staggered not only by their numbers but by the confidence of the invading troops, which was remarkable; one shone a torch, others 'were laughing, talking and striking matches.'[21] Only a few hundred yards away, an enemy officer shouted orders at his soldiers approaching their position. They were subjected to 'a murderous rain of fire' from the barges. An enemy bugle sounded and there was movement in every direction. Olney made one brave trip to replenish ammunition but the string of transports disgorged more and more landing parties.

The NGVR mortars, commanded by Lt James Clarence Archer (NGX458), provided accurate fire as did the machine-gun crew of Pte Edward Peter Saligari (VX24181), but 'even the most dull minded of us could see that our position was hopeless' concluded Olney.[22] Maj Owen was waiting for orders from HQ, but none came. Tragically, Pte George Alexander Rohead (VX41616), the batman (personal servant) to Owen, was killed while carrying a message. Owen's company was outflanked and he ordered a withdrawal. Aircraft from Japanese carriers flew so low the 'grinning faces' of the pilots could be 'clearly seen'.[23] Olney was pleased to be retreating into the jungle; 'little did we know what was ahead of us.'[24]

Pte Harold Maloney (NX27918) had been surprisingly calm. He was asleep when the first shot was fired. Startled fully awake, he found the 'air was alive with darting bullets [at] about 0400' and heard the blood-curdling screams of enemy soldiers. His war began dramatically as two of his mates were hit. His A Company was already being flanked and two platoons pulled out by 5.40 a.m. At 6.45 a.m., 'with the Japs very close', his platoon retreated, faced with a 'terrible climb up a ridge to get out'[25] under withering machine-gun fire. More of his mates fell. Having been told the day before that this was an exercise, they had minimum equipment and had used their tin hats to collect water from a village tank. Down into a gully, another steep climb, they grabbed coconuts as they moved. A native hut offered respite. Tramping boots startled them and they reached for their weapons. Smiles creased faces as they heard cursing, wonderful Aussie swearing, and they could relax again.[26]

Sgt Vic Turner could see the fires over Rabaul; he thought A Company was somewhere nearby at Vulcan – he had heard the chink of entrenching tools as men dug in. His mind was playing tricks: 'God, but it was a nervous business waiting!'[27] Was that a boat? Or just water lapping the beach? Turner believed that he was an experienced soldier, but nothing had prepared him for this: 'swarms of landing craft bringing troops to different points ... our task is impossible.'[28] The world was suddenly full of gunfire as his squad of militia and support soldiers opened fire with mortar and machine guns. Mortar shells burst into the landing barges, bodies exploded and fell into the ocean. Enemy soldiers waded ashore and NGVR Sgt Frank Ryan's Bren gun blazed away. Enemy escort craft returned fire – anti-personnel shells burst around the Australians. An armoured motorboat shepherded two landing barges towards the shore, a mere 200 yards (183m) from his position. Turner was as impressed with the efficiency of the invasion as he was terrified by it – motors so quiet, each landing craft carrying 60 men, the ominous black shapes of giant ships further out; dozens of

Gnr David Bloomfield.

Bloomfield

them disgorging more barges, more invaders.

Nineteen-year-old Gnr David Bloomfield was with Turner. He had lied about his age to enlist and was now attempting to repel thousands, with just 'ten clips of five .303 ammunition and two hand grenades',[29] and the landing barges were right in front of him, overflowing with helmets glistening under the light of flares. This was not supposed to happen; 'they' were not supposed to be capable of this sort of attack. 'It doesn't take long to expend fifty rounds of .303 ammunition.'[30]

He was stunned to see enemy soldiers heaping the bodies of their own dead over the barbed wire and clambering over them onto the beach.

The shrill screams of 'Banzai' as the enemy left the barges, mixed with the cries of their wounded, was chilling. Dawn revealed the shores and shallows littered with bodies – a terrible sight. The brief satisfaction that Sgt Vic Turner felt at repelling the invaders dissipated quickly because 'there is no longer satisfaction to be had from this slaughter.'[31] It was overwhelming, they just kept coming, and any satisfaction of taking the enemy by surprise evaporated. Now clearly in sight were the ugly silhouettes of dozens of transports and destroyers, at least six cruisers, two aircraft carriers and what looked like a battleship. Turner saw them, the enemy, almost lazily pouring ashore, confident, even smoking. His group was in a pincer movement; the enemy was coming from the front and the right.

Capt Allan Gordon Cameron (VX30679) described this terrible day, 23 January 1942, as 'Black Friday'. How could he save his soldiers? They fired their weapons until the barrels burnt hot and their ammunition supplies were spent. There was seemingly no end of targets, 'hordes coming down on the drone area through Vunakanau plantation.'[32] A Company had been overrun on the beach, as had C Company on the upper drome – a strong wedge driven between B and D Companies on the Talliligap Ridge. At 8 a.m., NGVR Lt Archer, who just two days before was carrying out the duties of Custodian of the Rabaul Expropriation Board, ordered Sgt Frank Ryan, a schoolteacher, to destroy the machine guns and withdraw to Vunakanau Airfield and reinforce 2/22nd B and C Companies. Transport was promised but didn't arrive.

Cpl Jack Moyle (VX19428) was feeling neither confident nor brave. He was a bushie, a country lad, who worked the family property at Spring Creek near Tallangatta. Tallangatta is a small town in north-eastern Victoria pleasantly resting on the banks of the Mitta Arm of Lake Hume – a pretty place where family was everything and you made your own fun. Jack had joined the 8th Light Horse Regiment, did a bit of training and joined the monthly camps.[33] At the beginning of June 1940, Jack Moyle and two mates, Pte Alexander George Cardwell (VX20534) and Pte Peter Joseph 'Joe' Kelleher (VX19573) travelled to Melbourne and enlisted in the 2/22nd.

On the morning of 23 January, Joe had left with a patrol to mine the road and hadn't returned. Jack Moyle was lying on a remote tropical island, the rain pelting down, hungry, being eaten alive by thousands of mosquitos, listening to gunfire and wondering what the hell was

Sgt Victor Turner believed that there was no 'satisfaction to be had from this slaughter.' Turner

Invading enemy forces, January 1942. NGVR Museum

going on. Would he still be alive to celebrate his birthday in three days time? He had yet to shoot at anyone.

At about 9 a.m. they were ordered to retreat again; just as well, because the enemy mortar fire as getting too close for comfort, and enemy fighters were 'skimming the coconut palms, machine-gunning and bombing everything they see.'[34] The news wasn't good, possibly '20,000 troops' had invaded, 'so we have no hope of stopping them.'[35] On the terrible and muddy roads, the trucks were making painfully slow progress and the trip was punctuated by stops and mad dashes to the jungle to avoid strafing aircraft fire. Jack Moyle could not help wondering what had happened to his mate Joe Kelleher.

By midday they reached the crossroads behind the airfield. Two hours later, orders were altered yet again and they were told to retrace their steps – only two-thirds of 12 Platoon were left, and very few of B Company. A patrol from B Company left and hadn't returned. Lance Cpl (L/ Cpl) Herbert 'Graeme'

Parsons (VX29259) struggled up the road, bleeding profusely from a wound in the chest. He had been in a truck with Pte James Andrew Ascott (VX25843), Pte Merton George Carmichael (VX23805) and two others. They had been ambushed. Ascott was killed instantly as were two others. Carmichael had jumped out but had been shot dead. Parsons had crawled away from the wreckage. He thought Kelleher's patrol had also been ambushed.[36]

It was pandemonium; troops were being ordered here, there and elsewhere: 'Why we are being split up we don't know.'[37] Moyle and what was left of his company kept moving, stopping only briefly to pick paw-paws – finally some nourishment. A truck arrived and they were taken past the Keravat River. Moyle was told to take a patrol to guard a bridge. His mate, Pte George Cardwell, was with him; they sure were not in Tallangatta anymore.

Capt Cameron, Sgt Russell Kelly (VX33979) and some native police arrived carrying very welcome supplies. Sgt Kelly had the distinctive middle name of Livingstone, which was probably why he preferred to be called 'Kell'. The 2/22nd Sgt set off again to see what else he could salvage for the men and never returned.[38]

George Cardwell, left, and Jack Moyle, right. Moyle

It was another miserable night in the open with rain tumbling down, expecting any minute to be attacked. The attack didn't come so they moved further down the coast. In the daylight the true extent of the chaos became obvious – trucks abandoned, troops carrying any supplies they could, machine guns, ammunition, gas masks and other discarded equipment.

Moyle described how they waded through 'dirty, stinking swamps up to our waist, some chaps fall in the slime under the weight they are carrying.'[39] They were bone weary but had to keep moving.

Their numbers grew and there was news of 'chaps killed that we knew well':[40] Pte Leslie William Smith (VX37810), better known to his mates as 'Curly', was dead; L/Cpl Gordon Douglas Crawford (VX50048), 22. John Skelton Russell (VX26521), 23, died on 22 January, caught up in the machine-gunning of the lower drome, Lakunai. His brother Bob, 21, was unaware his brother was dead, or that their mate, L/Cpl Ormond Copas (VX27001) 23, had just been killed. It was all too much

Sgt John Russell Cpl Bob Russell, left, and L/Cpl Ormond Copas, right.
Bob Russell, aged 21, died on 1 July 1942. Lost Lives

to take in so they just kept moving, except 'no one seems to know where we are going.'[41]

The term 'evacuation of Rabaul' carried a hollow ring, because it was anything but an 'evacuation' – more an uncoordinated escape and attempt to survive. As late as 17 January, Acting Administrator Page had received a message that the Chiefs of Staff in Melbourne 'are considering proposals ... and the matter will be considered by War Cabinet on Monday, 19 January.'[42] Furthermore, the message added that it was not possible to 'anticipate decision' and that the War Cabinet believed 'all Government officials should remain at their posts.'[43] The lack of touch with reality within the Melbourne and Canberra offices as staggering.

On 20 January, the War Cabinet approved the removable of 'unnecessary civilian personnel';[44] there was no one left to receive the signal. With Scanlan and Page long gone, units and individuals remaining in Rabaul needed to look after themselves. By 21 January, most of the civilians had departed for Refuge Gully or distant plantations.

Around 30 Europeans, about a dozen of their native servants and 200 Asian residents remained.[45] Chief Warden 'Nobby' Clark made the bold decision to remain in town to urge residents to get as far away as possible by whatever means they could. Gordon Thomas, editor of the *Rabaul Times*, decided to keep him company.

Maj Palmer's detachment of 2/10 Field Ambulance and the six Australian Army nurses needed to move their patients quickly. Pte Billy

Cook had initially seen the humour in that, when the wail of the air raid sirens was heard, 'the patients beat me to the slit trench even though I was closest.'[46] A day later, 22 January 1942, Sister Lorna Whyte vividly remembered how they were the last to leave Rabaul. 'We had 80 patients and took them in two or three ambulances and some private cars.'[47] As the transport moved slowly through Rabaul, it was impossible not to be saddened by the destruction caused to what had been a gracious and attractive town. The sight of bodies lying in roads was sobering. Some of the roads had been blown up by *Lark Force* troops so the ambulances needed to find back roads.

The rough drive to the Sacred Heart Mission at Vunapope caused further misery to the wounded. 'We finally arrived at Kokopo about 2 o'clock in the morning and straight away we set to work digging slit trenches' wrote Whyte.[48] The mission was soon crowded to capacity. Troops with hollow defeated looks passed through the mission with stories of the frontline action. Radio Tokyo had earlier broadcast that the Rabaul garrison was 'a drunken and immoral crowd.'[49] Pte Billy Cook thought it interesting that the last Radio Tokyo broadcast he had heard admitted that, while around 300 Australians had been killed, 8,000 Japanese had been killed. 'Just as well that we were a drunken and immoral crowd or the ratio of 25 to 1 in casualties could have been greater.'[50] He listened to the stories and thought it sad 'that there were heroic deeds ... that unfortunately will never be recognized, like the soldier 'who died with his finger still bent round the trigger of his Vickers.'[51]

With daylight came a frightening reality, the harbour was full of enemy ships. Whyte remembered: 'We couldn't believe our eyes ... we were all just young Australian girls. We hadn't seen anything much of the outside world.'[52] Further shocks followed for the six Australian army nurses. After two days relentless duty, their energy levels were severely depleted. Nuns relieved them and the nurses went off for a hasty breakfast.

Sister Lorna Wyte.
www.angellpro.com.au/rabaul

When we returned to the hospital, we found that our two
Medical Officers and the Orderlies had gone. They just left us,
all excepting two Orderlies who volunteered to stay behind
and help.[53]

The nurses had no warning that the doctors had decided to leave: 'we thought it was a very cruel thing not to tell us.'[54] A 'cruel thing' was an understatement. Maj Palmer had decided to accompany retreating *Lark Force* troops to the south and Maj Akeroyd accompanied troops to the north. Palmer did not inform the nurses, choosing instead to disappear without facing them with his decision. In his diary he simply mentioned:

'I decided to leave our patients.'[55] His advice to members of the 2/10 Field Ambulance and 2/22nd band was that they should attempt their own escape. Only Cpl Laurence Ashleigh Hudson (NX25197) and Pte Reginald Maxwell Langdon (NX35227) elected to remain. Palmer may have believed that the nurses were not up to what promised to be an arduous retreat but he decided instead to leave them at the mercy of the advancing enemy. At 11 a.m. on 23 January, Sister Kay Parker and Chaplain John May surrendered the sisters, the hospital and around 100 patients to the Japanese.

With the beach lost and the ammunition expended, Gnr David Bloomfield and his group had retreated to where Lt Selby was waiting with the remainder of the unit and the AA utility. It was broken; the clutch was stripped. They piled into the three-tonner and began a treacherous ascent up the hilly, wet road. It was slow progress as the wheels failed to find traction in the mud; shells were exploding around them. Bloomfield was suddenly thrown up in the air. He and two others became pinned under the truck. Selby shouted to the others to right the truck but they couldn't. Bloomfield felt pain in his back as they scraped out the dirt beneath him and pulled him free.

Lt David Selby had always felt like a father figure to his young gunners and now some were dead. The names, numbers, ages and faces of the gunners went through his mind like a bleak roll call: Frederick Brown (NX191483), 20, Gnr Wilfred Emery (NX191484), 19, Lionel

Unlike Lark Force, *the Japanese soldiers were battle-seasoned from their conquests in Hong Kong and Guam.* NGVR Museum

Hawkes (NX191453), 20, John Moran (VX191457), 20, John Sheedy (NX191477), 21, and Des McMullen (NX191482). How could he forget McMullen, the 19-year-old who had won the garrison heavyweight boxing title? A militia youngster beating regular AIF, how that had raised the morale of the AA unit. Selby was going to have a great number of next-of-kin letters to write. How many more?

McMullen's mate, another 19-year-old, David Bloomfield, was beside him, grimacing in pain after being dug out from under a truck. Selby had persuaded Bloomfield into joining the artillery when they met at a Sydney synagogue. Bloomfield had been on the beach and had already witnessed things no teenager should. Selby needed to keep

Bloomfield close, and alive. They come to another hill and the truck refused to go further. The driver told them they must get out and push. The injured Bloomfield and others got off and heaved the back of the truck forward. It started to move, but the driver didn't stop. With difficulty Bloomfield chased, grabbed hold and was heaved onboard – he swore he wouldn't do that again. They finally arrived at Three Ways and Lt Col Carr ordered them to attach themselves to B Company and dig in.

After a short reprieve Selby saw:

Over the ridge about 800 yards away, the enemy appeared like a swarm of black ants, threw themselves down and opened fire with rifle and machine gun [56]

Strangely what he felt next was humour; he wondered what a good commander does in this situation: 'run, crawl or walk. Running seemed both pointless and provocative', but 'crawling was too slow.'[57] Bloomfield, in a lot of pain, may have lost consciousness because when he became aware of gunfire, there was no one around. Another explosion and he started to run as mortars landed around him. 'I did look behind me and I could see this line of figures coming towards us. Not ours.'[58] The pain forgotten, he ran straight into Lt Selby, who was planning to hold up the next truck, at gunpoint if necessary, and take it to Toma. They stopped near several NGVR soldiers, setting up a mortar. The soldiers refused to join them and shouted: 'Get the hell out of here!' As the Selby group turned the next corner they heard machine-gun fire, and 'then no more sounds come from the mortar crew.'[59]

At Toma they finally came across Rear Operational HQ. Selby informed the Sgt Major there that he wished to report to Col Scanlan. The soldier went into a tent and returned saying: 'The colonel's orders are that each man is to fend for himself.'[60] It was an unsatisfactory command at the end of a very unsatisfactory campaign. 'The Battle of Rabaul was over.'[61] Gathering his remaining troops, Selby set out on foot southwards. Abandoned vehicles, 'filled with rations, munitions and stores of all descriptions',[62] littered the track. He ordered the men to salvage what they could carry, to leave the remaining food close-by for other stragglers, and to demolish the vehicles. After a quick meal they set off into the jungle. Selby, 'in my ignorance', assumed 'that we would live in the mountains and carry on guerrilla warfare against the Japanese.'[63] It was an extremely optimistic thought and Selby had no way of knowing the hardships ahead.

Endnotes

1. McCarthy, D. *South-West Pacific Area – First Year: Kokoda to Wau. Australia in the War of 1949– 1945* Official War History Series. Series 1—Army, AWM, 1959, p.85.
2. Horner, D. *SAS: Phantoms of the Jungle—A History of the Australian Special Air Service*, Allen & Unwin, 1989, p.22.
3. Downs, p.19. See also McCarthy, p.39.
4. Geyer, I. Conversation 3 October 2016; email 6 and 9 October 2016.
5. Ibid.
6. Dale, M. Email, 6 and 9 September 2016.
7. Ibid.
8. Ibid.
9. McNab, A. *We Were the First: the Unit History of No. 1 Independent Company*, Australian Military History Publications, 1998, p.17.
10. Ibid., p.16.
11. Wigmore, p.415.
12. Ibid., p.416.
13. www.jje.info/lostlives/exhib/potp/japaneseinvasion.html, accessed 28 August 2016.
14. Ibid.
15. McCosker, A. *Masked Eden: a History of the Australians in New Guinea*, Matala, 1998.
16. Downs, p.66.
17. Wigmore, p.403.
18. Johnson, p.36.
19. Ibid.
20. Olney, W.J. 3DRL 957.
21. Wigmore, p.403.
22. Olney, W.J. 3DRL 957.
23. Ibid.
24. Ibid.
25. Johnson, p.61.
26. Ibid.
27. Turner, PR01469.
28. Ibid.
29. Bloomfield, D. *Rabaul Diary*.
30. Ibid.
31. Turner, PR01469.
32. Cameron, A.G. 3DRL/1088, Diary, AWM.
33. Moyle, J.T. *Escape from Rabaul and the Moyles of Spring Creek*, self-published, p.4.
34. Moyle, p.18.
35. Ibid.
36. Kelleher died on 19 February 1942.
37. Moyle, p.19.
38. Killed on 1 July 1942.
39. Moyle, p.20.
40. Ibid.
41. Ibid.
42. Sweeting, A.J. 'Civilian Wartime Experience in the Territories of Papua and New Guinea', in Hasluck, P. *The Government and the People 1942–1945*, p.673.
43. Ibid.
44. Ibid.
45. Ibid., p.676.
46. Cook, PR90/053.
47. www.angellpro.com.au/rabaul.htm accessed 18 September 2016.
48. Ibid.
49. Cook, PR90/053.
50. Ibid.
51. Ibid.
52. Ibid.
53. Ibid.
54. Ibid.
55. Palmer, E.C. and Cook, W. PR90/053, AWM, Canberra.
56. Selby, *Hell and High Fever*, p.41.
57. Ibid., p.42.
58. australiansatwarfilmar hive.unsw.edu.au/archive/1778-david-bloomfield
59. Ibid.
60. Selby, *Hell and High Fever*, p.41.
61. Ibid., p.43.
62. Ibid.
63. Ibid.

CHAPTER NINE

ESCAPE OR PERISH

'It is the 26th, my birthday, and George gives me a piece of coconut as a birthday present.'

Pte Jack Moyle

The route taken by the invading force had been expertly planned.

Wigmore

Pte John Thomas 'Jack' Moyle appreciated the gesture of his mate Pte George Cardwell, on this birthday, 26 January 1942. A piece of coconut wasn't a bad gift considering he and George were 'hungry and wet and dirty', and had eaten little in the last four days.[1] It was also Australia Day and they were being chased through the alien and challenging terrain of New Britain by well-led, determined Japanese soldiers. It was a day he would never forget; in the evening Moyle suffered a bad attack of malaria, the first of many. The Japanese invasion of New Britain was achieved with clinical efficiency. As many had warned, the Japanese militarization of Pacific islands enabled a rapid advance. As predicted, invasion and occupation had always been the intent. The Nankai Shitai, or South Seas Force, commanded by Major General Tomitaro Horii, had achieved what military experts in Canberra and Melbourne had judged impossible just months previously. Formed in November 1941, the invasion group and its main combat units included the 144th infantry regiment (three battalions), an artillery company, as well as platoons from the 55th cavalry regiment, support regiments and three special naval landing forces – enabling simultaneous landings at beaches around Rabaul.[2] It took just a few hours for the Japanese to stream ashore at Put Put, Kokopo, Raluana, Talili Bay, Mission Point, Kerevat, Pondie, near the junction of the New Road and Maluguna Road and elsewhere, from a massive fleet which had sailed uncontested into Simpson Harbour.

Lack of preparation had left the surviving *Lark Force* troops feeling grim. No escape plan had been made. Orders were confused; rendezvous points were reached only to find they were somewhere else. Stores of food, medical supplies and ammunition had not been established. *Lark Force* was a melee fleeing south by whatever mechanical transport they could find, taking any roads, until the roads disappeared. Men moved in many directions, with no consensus as to where and how. The Rabaul Garrison was in total disarray. They had been told they were on another exercise before they took up positions to face an invasion; this meant minimal equipment and supplies. The *Lark Force* Commander believed this would prevent panic. The same Commanding Officer had refused to allow food and ammunition dumps because that was 'defeatist'. The same authority had rejected the offers of men who familiar with New Britain to instruct his troops in jungle warfare and survival. Now the *Lark Force* troops were totally disorganized, panicked, unprepared and defeated. Much worse was to come.

The main route of withdrawal was to the south coast by Malabunga and Toma roads, across the Warangoi and Kavavas Rivers either to Put Put Harbour on the Gazelle Peninsula or Lemingi at the foot of the Baining Mountains – a mountain range that stretched skywards to a height of 7,999 feet (2,438m). Poorly defined, rugged tracks branched out to the coast, commonly to Adler Bay and Wide Bay. Unfortunately for the retreating *Lark Force* troops these were also accessible for enemy barges.

Mates were looking for mates. Who was dead? Who would lead? Sections and groups of men were trying to re-group as best they could under the command of junior officers. Lt David Ormond 'Mick' Smith (VX23843) had received the dubious honour of a promotion in the field – just 23 days before the invasion. He was now responsible for the lives of 30 men. Smith faced huge decisions.

Did he and his men attempt an inland escape to the north coast or stay on the coast? Both escape routes contained rugged mountains, covered with dense growth and intersected by deep ravines through which ran fast-flowing streams and rivers. Troops had been trained for static desert warfare, not mobile jungle hostilities. Few had any

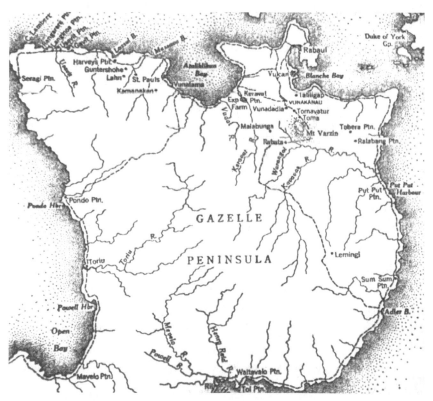

Escape routes from Rabaul, dangerous and demanding. Wigmore

knowledge of the terrain beyond Rabaul or how to live off the land – food was there but they were clueless. Then what? How could they get off the island? Who among the indigenous and European population could be trusted? Who were enemy collaborators?

Arch Taylor had joined the 36th Battalion militia at the age of 17. He impatiently waited until June 1940, when he was allowed to transfer to the AIF at 18. He recalled how he was told by Australian authorities that Japanese soldiers were:

> *About four foot high, they were all myopic, they all had to wear glasses because they couldn't see … they were bad shots and their rifles weren't any good. And they were quite easy to defeat, then not to worry about them.*[3]

By the third week of January, the 19-year-old Taylor had realized that was rubbish. The Japanese were most definitely here and he was running for his life as their aircraft strafed from above, their boats menaced from the ocean and he was being pursued by well-armed soldiers who drove with startling speed. He heard the aircraft, saw the bullets hit the ground, dove into a ditch by the side of the road before feeling the effects of a bomb dropped way too close. His ears were ringing and he was covered in dirt. A truck full of fellow anti-tank artillery soldiers drove past at speed because they thought he was dead. Digging himself out from under the dirt, he spoke to the Australian soldier beside him about the pilot: '"God that bloke was determined."[4] The soldier 'just fell forward and he was dead.' Taylor was shaken, 'that was the first of the Australians that I'd seen killed.'[5]

The smallest and the largest things caused further anxiety and their predicament was too bad to believe. George Cardwell and the rest of his section had left Pte Jack Moyle as he was too weak to accompany them. The next morning Moyle recovered enough to accompany Capt Hutchinson-Smith's group inland. 'We walk and climb until dark. It has been a terrible day, the worst day yet.'[6] Moyle wondered what would happen to the *Lark Force* wounded left behind.

His group arrived at Kamanakan, where Capt John Thornbury

Gnr Gordon Abel. UNSW

Gnr Arch Taylor. Taylor

McCallum (VX45855) and 250 men had gathered. McCallum was not optimistic; there was very little food and the men were already debilitated from lack of rations and sleep. Some were wounded and many were suffering from malaria. McCallum told them that they must break into small groups and 'live off the land' – but no one knew how. They dispersed, hoping to find assistance at plantations and missions. Groups followed tracks that they hoped took them in the right direction. Paranoia set in. Moyle woke the next morning to find his party reduced to four; the rest had moved on without them, 'perhaps they missed us in the dark, or didn't like our company.'[7]

Gnr Gordon Abel was disoriented and still concussed from the bombing of Praed Point. On 24 January 1942, he and 17 other 'young Australian men sat down on a muddy and rain swept track to discuss their future.'[8] His group was made up mainly of 18-year-olds who carried some ammunition, one water bottle and no food because 'some officers thought we might run away.'[9] They scrounged a tin of pea soup that they shared – a teaspoonful each. 'We knew about nothing' – nothing about where to find plantations and missions.[10] There was anger and frustration; they were militia, they were 18 and they felt that they had been deserted by their *Lark Force* Commander.

Imagine what you'd feel like if your boss said 'everyman for himself, you can do what you like. I've got nothing to do with you.' We felt so bloody terrible, by Christ if we'd have found him we'd have shot him dead ourselves. Terrible bloody order.[11]

The youngsters began to walk and stumble up mountains and through rivers, hoping they were going in the right direction. Sustenance was a teaspoonful of McCallum's Scotch whisky each evening for the first 10 days. They had made a pact that if someone could not continue, he would be made comfortable and left. It proved to be a difficult pact to keep. A soldier was in great pain from a tropical rash, which spread so rapidly he struggled to walk and his discomfort was unforgiving. The soldier said he was not going on. They told him that they would all continue the following morning and carry him if they had to. The group woke to find he had slashed his wrists and died. The shock was terrible. They buried him, marked his grave and trudged on. Gnr Gordon Abel decided:

'It's very difficult to know what a hero is. Somebody committing suicide. To us he was a hero.'[12]

The word 'hero' was mentioned a great deal during January through to April 1942, as members of *Lark Force* tried to escape New Britain. It was a title very much open to interpretation and invariably applied unexpectedly. Under great adversity, some men emerged as leaders and others succumbed to being less. In the ensuing years, the established authority awarded medals and tributes that reflected the official status quo. Many were warranted but other acts of selflessness and bravery went unacknowledged.

In his pre-war life, Ernest Smyth Appel was a pharmacist living a fairly predictable routine life in the pleasant beachside Melbourne suburb of St Kilda. In late January 1942, life was

Sgt Bert Smith. AWM

anything but predictable or routine and he was surrounded by confused troops. He was a 2/22nd Captain (VX8370) in retreat in tropical New Britain. His superiors had long since stopped resolving problems, his subordinates looked to him for life-saving decisions. The last order Appel had received from Col Scanlan was to cover the withdrawal. It was left to his own judgement when it was timely to withdraw his own soldiers and where then to retreat. He gathered more and more men along the route and by 26 January they reached the Kamanakan Mission. He had organized the soldiers into advance and rear guards, and carrying parties. Appel held a muster parade and gave a rousing talk to the 285 troops, promising to retrain them so they could once more fight he invaders. 'The men responded well to his appeal.'[13]

Appel divided the soldiers into groups and then despatched several soldiers on horseback to contact and organize other escapees. By 29 January Appel took his company, now numbering around 120, beyond Lahn into the mountains where he moved them into a village, which let them shelter in huts from the unceasing rain. The men were exhausted. Appel believed it imperative that they be allowed to spend the night. He left for Lassul Bay with a small party, leaving instructions for the men to follow the next morning. His group took a wrong route, pushing them 5 miles (8km) off their intended path. Concerned that the main party would arrive before he had reconnoitred Lassul Bay, Appel 'ran every part of the way which was flat or downhill', a distance of 7 miles (11km).[14] Appel was greatly relieved to find the main party had already arrived but that the enemy had departed previously. Appel organized food searches, reconnaissance and standing patrols, and established a headquarters at nearby Harvey's Plantation. More troops had been located by the riders until around 413 were dispersed in groups along the 30 miles (48km) of coastline between Cape Lambert and Ataliklikun Bay.

Pte James Olney referred to Sgt Herbert William 'Bert' Smith (VX46514) as someone 'who proved himself a very fine and capable leader.'[15] In late January Bert Smith was another who felt very separated from his pre-war life. Being an apprentice plumber had ill-prepared him for the responsibility of leading a group when he had no idea where he or they were. They caught up with a group that included NGVR Warrant Officer Robert Leslie Kennedy (NGX496). Kennedy advised them to give themselves up or wait for Col Scanlan. Smith didn't have faith in either option. He asked District Officer (DO) Gregory for some information on the route to the south coast and was surprised that the DO 'was loathe' to offer any assistance.[16]

Smith left the main group with a dozen others and pushed on into the Baining Mountains. Their food consisted of a small portion of bully beef and two army-issue hard biscuits twice a day for each man. They realized they were lost so decided to follow an alternative track. This took them back to the spot they had been days before. A decision was then made to continue down a river, which meant steep muddy climbs. Indigenous New Guineans helped where they could, sharing their own scarce food, but they were bewildered about why soldiers should need to beg for food.

As Gnr Arch Taylor climbed, he looked out over the harbour, so different now.

A beautiful harbour that on previous days was alive with harmless natives … I thought of the beautiful moonlit nights when we used to go for walks along the coconut studded shores. I was now looking at that same panorama, not with a view of admiration but a heart full of hate for below me lay nothing but death and desolation – I had left behind me some mates. I swore to God that I would avenge their deaths. Disillusioned and bewildered I plodded on.[17]

Not long before, he had sent home a photo of him and his mates fishing. He now felt very alone, and thought how good it would be to have company.

Ahead was a small clearing with six men around a fire. Taylor was stricken with fear and dived into the undergrowth. 'God I'm trapped.' He knew he had made too much noise and then: 'I heard a voice "Come out, you yellow bastards" – I knew I was safe.'[18]

Taylor's group emptied their packs to see what was useful and what

Arch Taylor and mates enjoying the water. UNSW

was not. Taylor came to his wallet and paused. 'I looked at my Mother's photo and a photo of my intended wife – and this bucked me up a bit.'[19] Between seven men they had seven tins of bully beef, two tins of soup, seven packets of hard biscuits and enough tea for about two billies. One bloke remarked that that would get them through to the next day. Frank, a heavy-set man who had spent a lot of years humping his swag around Victoria in search of work, shook his head: 'Like bloody hell it will, that will last us six days with a tight belt.'[20] Frank was elected leader. The next days they forged rivers, climbed and climbed, pushed through thick foliage, and the rain never ceased. Along the track they collected more and more stragglers.

The mountain range just kept getting steeper and some of the men were struggling. Frank told them to throw away their guns and bayonets. They reached the peak only to find the descent was just as steep and into a rushing river. Taylor's group had tried to limit their group to 10 strong, a greater number was more likely to be seen and food needed to be shared sparingly. They took shelter in a native hut and their 10 feasted on a tin of bully beef in seven pints of water and 'it was delicious.'[21] One of their group was ill and collapsed. Taylor thought how this soldier had been a Rabaul bank clerk and 'a bank clerk was never meant to go through this.'[22]

Keith Brian Paul was an NGVR rifleman (NGX512) but more in name than in training because the 21-year-old from Moree, NSW, had been working in the Bank of New South Wales in Rabaul less than a month ago. Taylor offered to carry his pack and Paul limped on. Breakfast was a cigarette and a mouthful of water. It was always a difficult decision to leave a sick man. Soldiers moved past or dropped back, all with the same exhausted expression. If they were fortunate, the sick recovered in time to link up with the next stragglers. Taylor's group arrived at a German mission station called Lemingi, with Father Meierhofer in charge. They spent the night in what had been a leper hut.

The following morning Paul felt unable to cross the very steep gorge they faced, a drop of 2,000ft (610m) and the swollen river. Paul told Taylor he would remain. It took them two days to traverse the ravine, by which time another group of Australians had caught up with them. Taylor asked: 'Did you see that fellow called Keith Paul? ... They said, "Yes, he died."'[23] Taylor had grown up inspired by stories of Gallipoli. Two uncles had served there. He remembered how 'enthralled with those stories' he had been and 'thinking it'd be a wonderful thing ... I always wanted to be a soldier.'[24] He now wondered why he had not been told about 'the bad bits' and 'the suffering'.[25]

They had never seen mountains like this. Higher and higher they were forced to climb until they could climb no further and dropped to the ground to sleep. They woke cold, about 7,000 feet (2134m) above sea level. The irony did not escape Taylor; 'it seemed strange to be cold after having five months of stifling heat.'[26] They came to another fast-running river and were grateful when a number of Seven Day Adventists mission boys arrived to pull them over the river, one hand on a vine, one around a soldier and the soldiers' equipment on their heads. One mission boy had crossed this river 28 times and still he forged back and forth as more stragglers arrived. They believed he ferried 200 men. Taylor's group were depleted of energy and the sight of the mission settlement, complete with a sawmill, radio operators, even a magistrate and a Chinese store, was simply incredible. There was a congregation

Fording a swift and swollen river. AWM

of civilians and troops at Adler Bay. Taylor mentioned his birthday was a couple of days before and was presented with half a coconut full of uncooked rice. He was so hungry he ate the uncooked rice washed down with water; 'it was food.'[27]

Colonel Scanlan had remained at Tomavatur Plantation for some time to decide if he should attempt an escape or surrender. 'Eventually, accompanied by five others, he set out for Malabunga' where he was seen 'trudging along the track to Lemingi.'[28] At Lemingi, soldiers were given food by Father Meierhofer. By 25 January, the priest had assisted around 400 troops. 'The men, wet, muddy and weary, were strung out along the track.'[29] If they were fortunate, they found taro roots to cook. Each day they grew weaker but needed to find the energy to continue. Their bodies were battered by slips and falls, their hands were cut and torn from grasping rough vines and undergrowth.

On 24 January, aircraft had been heard and the men had scampered into the scrub. But this time instead of bombs, leaflets were dropped.

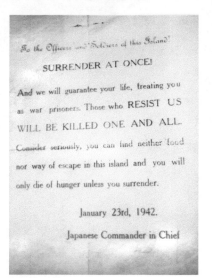

SURRENDER AT ONCE!

And we will guarantee your life, treating you as war prisoners. Those who RESIST US WILL BE KILLED ONE AND ALL. Consider seriously, you can find neither food nor way of escape in this island and you will only die of hunger unless you surrender. January 23rd, 1942. Japanese Commander in Chief

SURRENDER AT ONCE!
And we will guarantee your life, treating you as war prisoners. Those who RESIST US WILL BE KILLED ONE AND ALL. Consider seriously, you can find neither food nor way of escape in this island and you will only die of hunger unless you surrender.[30]

NGVR Museum

One of the first to arrive at Adler Bay, on 27 January, was Lt Edward Wallace Best (VX44505). He found Europeans and Chinese flying a white flag and expressing the desire to surrender. The group included Rabaul Director of Public Works, and NGVR Commanding Officer, Lt Col Charles Ross-Field. A larger group of *Lark Force* troops led by Maj Harold William Nicholls (V83714) arrived and pulled down the white flag. Ross-Field advised them all that they should surrender. Almost to a man they shook their heads and moved on.

Six other groups did the same, including 13 men led by Sgt Bert Smith. He had convinced his men not to give up when they became lost in the mountains, and they followed him on to Wide Bay. The coastal route did nothing to alleviate the men's misery, as they traversed mangrove swamps and coral outcrops by day and were tormented by mosquitos and sandflies by night. Smith gathered seven members of 2/22nd A Company, which brought his group to 20.

Arch Taylor was thinking that it was now 3 February and his 'cobber George's birthday'. Gnr George Henry William Thornton (NX55060) was his lifelong friend. They had been childhood mates and 'as children they

Gnr Arch Taylor. Johnson

An avid collector of photographs, John Cameron, far left, and mates. Lost lives

used to play soldiers.'[31] They enlisted together. Taylor wondered if when they went home they would laugh about the lives they had led as real soldiers. It was Thornton's 19th birthday and Taylor had no idea where his cobber was.[32] Little did Taylor realize that he would never see Thornton again.

Taylor's boots were shredded and his feet torn. He pushed through the mangroves and muddy bank to place his feet painfully into the salt water. He heard machine-gun fire and saw two Japanese soldiers heading straight for him. Two Australians nearby were killed: 'I never knew their names.'[33] Taylor dropped into the mud.

> *They are getting closer – my heart is beating faster – I am*
> *beginning to tremble – I can now hear their footsteps –*
> *they have seen me – they stop, jabber a little and move off.*
> *They must have thought I was dead.*[34]

Taylor lay still for about half an hour. Wide Bay was proving dangerous; another barge full of enemy soldiers was motoring to shore. Taylor scurried off into the high Kunai grass – he was alone again.

Jack Moyle kept falling back due to illness, malaria and diarrhoea –

and it was taking its toll on his spirit. Other B Company blokes arrived and his mood lifted. He was now with L/Cpl Robert Whitton 'Bobby' Langlands (VX44864) and Pte Stanley William Hunter (NGX202) and a member of the NGVR. They arrived at a plantation and killed two ducks. Combined with other foodstuffs they found in the homestead, they enjoyed their best meal for days. They were exhausted, wet through and ill, and Moyle's companions decided to retrace their steps and surrender. He felt torn, 12 of his Platoon B Company mates were bent on surrendering: Pte John Cameron the ardent photographer, the more serious Pte Stan Cameron, Pte Horrie Newman and the likeable clown Pte James Arthur Parker (VX22890). They asked if he was coming. Moyle shook his head, he couldn't agree: 'I'm determined they shall not get me', and with a backwards glance he continued on alone.[35] Stan Hunter was killed on 7 February; Langlands, both Cameron boys, Newman and Parker all died on 1 July.

There was another leaflet drop, this one signed by the 'Japanese Commander in Chief of Landing of Wide Bay.'

Surrender Yourselves. You will die of hunger or be killed by wild savages as there is no means of escape. You will be treated as prisoners of war and when the war is over you will be returned to your motherland. Today we caught many prisoners but killed only those that attacked us.[36]

And then another:

Now that the island is took (sic) and in Japanese hands and tightly surrounded by our navy and air force you have no means of escape. If your religion does not allow you to commit suicide it is up to you to surrender yourself and beg mercy for your troops. You will be responsible for the death of your men.[37]

The romantic tropics had lost all charm. They were really in trouble, weak and hungry, bitten by insects of all kinds, struggling through waist-deep mud, clambering over mangrove roots, very much afraid and didn't even know if their families in Australia were safe. To surrender meant this nightmare could be over. They were soldiers so would be treated with respect. As POWs they were sure to be looked after, their next-of-kin told they were alive, and when the Allies retook Rabaul they could go home.

Groups shook hands and turned back. Others watched them go, torn between staying with their mates and their own personal drive to stay free at all costs. Pte Angus Burnett had tried to watch over brother Edward, even though this had proved difficult when the 2/22nd first hit Rabaul and Edward had partied a little too much. Now the brothers needed to make a decision. Angus was 11 years senior to the 22-year-old Edward and he had found the physical exertion of the last days testing to the extreme. They were brothers, they would stay together, they would surrender. Gordon Abel and his group of young gunners were considering the same.

They had arrived at 'a place called Tol, Tol Plantation.' It was beautiful, a house right on the headland, rivers close by and 'coconut trees, thousands of coconuts', and their weary legs moved just that much faster. There were a lot of 22nd Battalion soldiers already there. It was a beautiful place but:

> We thought to ourselves we wouldn't like to stay with that many people because it would be tempting to the Japs to catch that many people together. It'd be bingo. So we went and slept, they gave us a couple of coconuts each and we went and laid in the bush just on the edge of the plantation and we had a sleep.[38]

The noise woke them, barges full of enemy soldiers coming ashore. Abel's group had no guns. They were bare-footed and unarmed teenagers, 'but you still feel bad because you done (sic) nothing' recalled Abel.[39] They moved back into the undergrowth. The shooting made them look. Three Australian soldiers had been lined up and shot. The gunners fell into the river and hid under leaves until night. Abel repeated to himself 'you still feel bad because you done nothing.'[40]

Members of the 2/10 Field Ambulance and 2/22nd band had

Pte Billy Cook. NGVR
Museum

been told by their Commanding Officer, Maj Palmer, to leave the hospital and attempt an escape into the mountains. They decided to drive the ambulances as far as they could but had travelled only a short distance before they found Pte Thomas Richard Connop (VX22066) with a broken leg. Capt Sandy Edwin John Robertson (NX35101), Pte Maxwell Henry Pearsall (VX24376), Pte Albert Fernandez (NX19620), Pte Billy Cook and Pte Frank Harold Hennessy (NX27487) stayed and set the leg, before attempting to continue on with the injured soldier.

They found Malabunga Mission deserted. Fernandez volunteered to return to the hospital with Connop. Both were captured and died on 1 July 1942.

The remainder of the 2/10 Field Ambulance finally caught up with Maj Palmer at Lemingi and set up a first aid station with the medical supplies they had carried across the mountains. They needed to stay to care for the sick and wounded but Palmer insisted on moving off with the bulk of the troops and the medical men went with him, clawing their way up and over the mountain range. Their first sight of the ocean was wonderful; they had arrived at Tol Plantation.

A group of troops led by Maj Owen had pushed through on the route to Put Put. Near Taliligap, they found Japanese soldiers but managed to skirt around them and continued unhindered. On 25 January, they met Acting Administrator Harold Page and three other administration officials. Page warned them that he had sent a message of surrender to the Japanese. The *Lark Force* officers and soldiers left quickly. They arrived at Ralabang Plantation at dusk and asked the three civilians at the homestead for food. The initial reply was that was there was none available.

By 1945, Benjamin George Dawson (VX47614) had attained the rank of Lt Col and was CO of B Company, 1st New Guinea Infantry Battalion. But in January 1942 he was a 21-year-old, hungry, weary Lieutenant with a group of equally exhausted and hungry soldiers – he was in no mood for pleasantries.

'I lifted a plate of scones off the table and said: "This will do for the time being."'[41] Eventually they were given food for one day. Plantation staff argued that there were '300 natives to feed.' Dawson appreciated that but he was amazed when they told him the reserves needed to be kept because they didn't know how long it would be 'before

Lt Col Dawson. AWM

they could get rice from the Japanese. The unreality of their outlook shocked us.'[42]

On foot and by raft, the Owen and Dawson groups reached Adler Bay by the last day in January. There they found a large number of *Lark Force* troops ready to surrender. The troops looked defeated and had lost the will to continue. Owen, accompanied by Sgt John Alfred Morgan (VX21651) and Pte Valentine Patrick Glynn (VX24088), set out from Adler Bay on a fast trip to Tol. Owen feared that the retreating soldiers would waste food so was desperate to get ahead of them to take charge. Arriving at Tol, he found a large gathering of troops and food already scarce. Owen decided to push on the following morning, having been joined by Majors Mollard and Palmer, Captain Goodman, and a small number of troops. They were well clear when five landing craft full of troops neared the beach. The Japanese systematically combed the area around Tol and Waitavalo plantations – there was no escape for those who had not left so swiftly.

Members of the 2/10 Field Ambulance and 2/22nd band had spent a couple of restful days at Tol and were preparing to move inland when the Japanese came ashore. They moved away but stopped to rest. They lay in the open air and discussed what they were going to do when they arrived back in Australia. Pte Billy Cook remembered how:

Ron Cantwell promised us he would stand the best feed we could buy and Dick Buck said that he would be responsible for the liquor arrangements.[43]

It was a pleasant fantasy, broken when a soldier came running towards them shouting 'The bastards are here.'[44] Japanese soldiers surrounded them. Cook ran and hid but, upon seeing his mates with their hands raised, he emerged and stood with them. They were herded back to Tol Plantation. For Cook, it was the first time he had come face to face with the enemy. Strangely, he did not feel threatened. 'Their impassive faces struck me as dull, rather than the faces of supermen.'[45] Cook was helping a wounded soldier and was ordered to leave him. 'I looked back at the man ... with a Jap standing over him.'[46] The soldier raised himself on one elbow and waved. 'He was a brave man. The Jap caught up with us about ten minutes later.'[47] They had no doubt what had taken place. In the beginning the troops were buoyed, as they were fed at midday and at night before being placed in a large hut to sleep. Early the following morning, the prisoners were assembled outside the hut and marched to Tol Plantation house. Two Australian officers were taken away. Members of the 2/10 Field Ambulance and the 2/22 ex-Salvation Army band wore Red Cross armbands; they were non-combatants. They were confident that this assured them of favourable treatment and they wanted to stay together. They made up the largest section of the estimated 160 captured. Cook was unimpressed that the enemy soldiers had ransacked their packs, concerned that the only items of interest were 'photographs (particularly female) and tobacco.[48] Medical supplies were trodden on and spoilt, including thousands of quinine tablets.'[49] *Lark Force* troops were now searched, which was unsettling for Cook: It took 'all our self-control to stand it and allow those yellow monkeys to dive their hands into our pockets.'[50] Watches were yanked from wrists and rings pulled from fingers. Their captors were acting more and more fiercely, waving their rifles with long bayonets attached. 'They were jabbering excitedly and there seemed to be a spirited exchange as to what to do next', observed Cook.[51]

The Australians were pushed towards the jungle. The medical personnel pointed to their Red Cross armbands and were surprised when these were torn from their uniforms and they were stripped of other identification. This did not feel right and, when their thumbs were tied behind them with fishing line, the nerves increased. Groups of two and three were then tied together. This was not the treatment they had imagined. They were prodded towards a coconut grove, stopped and pushed to the ground. The Japanese officer in charge unsheathed his sword and cut the bindings of the first Australian in line. He was motioned to his feet and a Japanese soldier took him into the jungle. The remaining Australians looked quizzically at each other. Then came a terrible scream and the Japanese soldier re-emerged, wiping blood from his bayonet.

Endnotes

1. Moyle, p.20
2. Wigmore, p.410
3. australiansatwarfilmarchive.unsw. edu.au/archive/113-archibald-taylor accessed 19 June 2016.
4. Ibid.
5. Ibid.
6. Moyle, p.22.
7. Ibid., p.23.
8. Abel, MSS1623.
9. Ibid.
10. Ibid.
11. Ibid.
12. Ibid.
13. Wigmore, p.655.
14. Ibid., p.656.
15. Olney 3DRL 957 VX35583, AWM, Canberra.
16. Smith statement
17. Taylor, A. MSS1533, AWM, Canberra.
18. Ibid.
19. Ibid.
20. Ibid.
21. Ibid.
22. Ibid.
23. Ibid. Paul had struggled on with another group but was killed by the Japanese on 4 February 1942.
24. Ibid.
25. Ibid.
26. Ibid.
27. Ibid.
28. Wigmore, p.661.
29. Ibid., p.662.
30. NGVR Museum, Brisbane.
31. Wigmore, p.662.
32. Thornton died on 1 July 1942.
33. Taylor.
34. Ibid.
35. Moyle, p.23.
36. Fisher, P. PR89/0716.
37. Ibid.
38. Abel, G. MSS1623.
39. Ibid.
40. Ibid.
41. Wigmore, p.663.
42. Ibid.
43. Cook, W. AWM54 607/9/1.
44. Cook, W. 'Action Rabaul', Chapter Three in Connolly, R. and Wilson, B. (eds.) *Medical Soldiers 2/10 Australian Field Ambulance 8 Division 1940–45*, 2/10 Australian Field Ambulance Association, 1985, p.94.
45. Cook, W. AWM54 607/9/1 and Palmer, E.C. and Cook, W. PR90/053, AWM, Canberra.
46. Ibid.
47. Ibid.
48. Cook, W. *Medical Soldiers*, p.95.
49. Ibid.
50. Ibid., p.96.
51. Palmer, E.C. and Cook, W. PR90/053.

CHAPTER TEN

GRUESOME DEATH

'I lay there past caring – I wanted to die.'

Pte Billy Cook

The minds of the prisoners struggled to make sense of the circumstances and process that there was no escape and that death was imminent. Never could the *Lark Force* troops, tied together with fishing line and rope, have imagined that they would die on 4 February 1942 so gruesomely at the hands of Japanese soldiers. Pte Billy Cook had come out with his hands up the previous day to stay with his mates, particularly the other 'C's he enlisted with: Ron Cantwell, Bill Collins, Stewie Caston and Tom Clissohold. Roger Attwater, the Buck brothers – Richard and Cecil – Harry Galloway, Frank Hennessy, Gordon Hudson, Bill Ramage and Tom Webb were there – all members of the 2/10 Field Ambulance, all non-combatants. It had just seemed right to remain together.

Random thoughts raced. There were brothers; apart from the Buck boys, there were the Burnetts, Angus and Edward; Fred and Bill McNickle; and another set of twins, Colin and Charles Roy. Didn't that mean something? The McNickles were not even frontline soldiers but attached to army supply. There were young militia, including AA Gnr Albert Thomas Curtis (N109935), 19, AA Bombardier Bruce Gordon

2/10 Field Ambulance, Rabaul – only seven survived. AWM

Davies (N107781), 21 and Spr Raymond Baumgartner (Q90858), AA Gnr Lawrence Robinson (NX191466) was only 18; how was he even sent to New Britain? There were members of the Salvation Army 2/22nd band – medical orderlies who had also been wearing Red Cross brassards before these were torn off by the enemy, who now threatened them with swords, bayonets and rifles. Pte Trevor William George 'Bill' Haines (VX37510), 28, a fine tenor horn player and Pte Ronald Harry Cook (VX37490), 21, an accomplished trombonist, both had been members of the Salvation Army's premier band, Melbourne's Territorial Staff Band. There was no logic to what was happening and to whom. This wasn't right!

Twenty-two men had sat on the beach at Wide Bay with a white flag. They had been separated from the other unarmed troops and taken to Rabaul. After being compelled to write their names, ranks and serial numbers in a book, the remaining troops, their thumbs cruelly tied behind them and roped together in groups, had been pushed towards a coconut grove. Faces were haunted but stoic, as the men knew they were about to die. Billy Cook recalled his conversation with Stewart Caston just days before. Caston had said: 'I wish that I could put the calendar on two weeks so that I would know what happens.'[1] Cook had replied 'you might be sorry.'[2] The soldier on his right was praying quietly and the soldier on his left was saying over and over to himself: 'God, what a way to die!'[3] The future was bleak but Cook decided he was 'pretty proud of being an Australian that day.'[4]

Cook caught a glimpse of mate Ron Cantwell 'trying to work his thumbs free' before a guard 'jerked at his bonds, nearly pulling Ron down.'[5] A member of *Lark Force* attempted to run, only to be slashed by an officer's sword and then shot. Another said loudly 'well, fellows this looks like it.'[6] Cook felt numb:

I didn't feel scared. I was just full of wonder that this was happening to me, not sure that it wasn't just a horrible dream.[7]

Another of Cook's 'C' medical mates, Clissold, commented: 'Well Cookie we'll know what the other world is like.'[8] Clissold was shot dead in front of Cook.

Several Australians were bayonetted close-by, one cursing: 'You yellow bastards, you will pay for this when our chaps get you.'[9] Then it was Collins's turn.

Collins was ordered by the officer to walk on alone and the officer fired. Hit in the left shoulder, Collins fell forward. 'He fired two more shots at me ... [one] hit me in the left wrist, the other in the right hand.'[10] Collins fainted. When he stirred, all was quiet and he realized the second shot had severed the fishing line and his hands were free.

Unfortunately that gunshot had also caught him in the back and paralysed his legs. 'I could not move for quite a considerable time.'[11] As movement returned, Collins lurched to his feet; the sight of all the bodies was horrifying. For five days he wandered, surviving only on water until he found himself at Waitavelo Plantation. Finding two seriously wounded soldiers there, Collins helped them to a house, gave them water and left to find assistance. By the time he was found by a party, which included Maj Palmer, Collins was in a terrible state. When the group returned to the house, they found that an enemy destroyer had shelled the house, setting it alight with the wounded Australians inside – one believed to be Pte Stanley Albert French (VX20598), former corps Sgt Maj of the Salvation Army Camberwell Corps and, at

37, the oldest member of the 2/22nd band, a baritone player and the husband of Evelyn.

On the way back to Rabaul, Pte Arthur William Robinson (VX24099) had become aware of a guard's inattentiveness. He was thinking to himself that he didn't wish to be 'done in' in cold blood.[12] Robinson was fortunate insofar as he was not tethered to others. As the track came to an S-bend, he fell into high Kunai grass. The next soldier in line bravely muttered 'lower sport' and Robinson crouched down further.[13] For three days Robinson wandered. When New Britain planter Vic Pennefather found Robinson, he was delirious and his still-bound hands were in a 'shocking state'.[14]

Pte Clifford Marshall (VX24254) had seen the Japanese landing craft approach Tol and had 'gone bush' with about 30 others, mostly soldiers of D Company 2/2nd. They watched as their fellows were taken prisoner, given food and appeared 'reasonably well treated.'[15] Hunger was acute so it seemed reasonable to surrender – a decision he regretted as he was herded along a narrow path to his death. Marshall watched as the Japanese officer drew his sword and slashed the rope linking the leading group of Australians before an enemy soldier pushed the first Australian further up the track. His blood-curdling scream left his fate in no doubt. The officer smiled and gestured to the bayonet and the rifle; 'did they want to be shot or stabbed to death.'[16] The troops were certain a bullet was the better option but it made no difference; the officer simply grinned and his soldiers proceeded to murder the Australians as the enemy soldiers preferred.

The diminutive 41-year-old Scot, Pte John Robert Copland (VX28345) from Kirkcubright and Melbourne, was taken away. So, too, was the very tall Pte Bruce Evans (VX23858) 22, from Melbourne's South Yarra. He was followed by the baby-faced, not yet 21, 2/22nd Pte Douglas Arthur Gallahar (VX24932) from Mornington, Victoria.

It was now Marshall's turn. He was stabbed from behind, in the back, on the arm and side and again lower down on the side. One bayonet thrust speared through the back of his left shoulder, passing right through his body to the top of his chest beneath the left collarbone. Marshall crumpled and, whether due to survival instinct or shock,

LEFT: *Pte Copland.* CENTRE: *Pte Evans.* RIGHT: *Gnr Gallahar.* National Archives

he lay still, listening to the screams of other *Lark Force* troops being massacred. Japanese soldiers then returned and shot men lying on the ground to ensure they were dead. Marshall was bleeding freely and he probably fainted. It was dusk when he pulled himself to his feet and stumbled away. Lieutenants Frederic Lomas[17] and Benjamin Dawson found Marshall, who attempted to evade the Australians.

> *He was delirious, walking along with an empty tin in one hand,*
> *the other tucked in his shirt front, which was full of blood ...*
> *We caught him, and learned the story of the massacre of Tol.*[18]

Billy Cook was in the second-last group of three. What he had witnessed defied comprehension. Japanese soldiers fell in behind them. The first blow knocked the three *Lark Force* captives to the ground. Their captors stood above them and stabbed. Cook was bayoneted five times, 'each stab being accompanied by a snarling grunt.'[19] He felt the pushing and pulling of the weapon before the pain hit. His head was pressed into the dirt by the weight of the man on top of him. The Japanese moved away until the soldier next to Cook let out a groan. They returned and bayoneted the soldier again. Cook willed himself not to make a sound but he had simply run out of oxygen and had to breathe. Cook was stabbed six more times. The final bayonet thrust went through his ear into his mouth, severing the temporal artery and the blood gushed.

Assuming Cook was finally dead, the Japanese left.

Cook was still alive. His body was severely traumatized and he couldn't focus. It would be easy just to succumb to the fog. Cook 'lay there past caring – I wanted to die.'[20] The pain was now just numbness with a feeling that his head had become a balloon, a bit like 'it does at the dentist when they inject the anaesthetic.'[21]

> *That was the end, I went out of the pain and the sunlight into a darkness that I knew was death and that I welcomed. Out of the darkness I could hear a voice, my wife's voice, calling to me clearly and softly. I'll swear to that.*[22]

Flies and other insects had been attracted to the blood and he struggled to see.

> *I gave up the idea of dying.*
> *I didn't know where the hell I was going, and perhaps in the end I'd die anyway but I just didn't want to die there.*[23]

The voice provided the incentive for him to move. Cook pushed bodies

Collins, left, and Cook, right. Cook

clear as he tried not to look at their faces. The Buck twins were dead, so too the Roy twins, the Burnett brothers and McNickle brothers. The 2/10 Field Ambulance had been wiped out, including the other 'C's.

Cook's slight frame enabled him to work his still-tied arms down and around his feet. Bringing his hands to his face, he chewed through the fishing line. His medical training demanded that he get to the ocean to disinfect his wounds. The pain was horrendous as he fell into the salt water. He spent the ensuing days in a daze of fainting spells and pain, and being tormented by mosquitoes and sandflies.

William McNickle, LEFT, *and Fred McNickle,* RIGHT. Johnson

Peering through his one good eye, Cook detected smoke about three miles (5km) away. 'The three miles took ten hours.'[24] His damaged throat made it difficult to speak and the same bayonet thrust had left him quite deaf. Cook's sudden appearance was completely shocking to the *Lark Force* group led by Col Scanlan. The *Lark Force* CO gave Cook one of his own shirts but then decided that Cook needed medical treatment, so with a native guide sent him back to where it was believed NGVR Warrant Officer Bob Kennedy was camped. Fearful of being caught with an Australian soldier, the guide disappeared and Cook was left to struggle on alone. His condition worsened due to malaria, fatigue and hunger. Cook was close to death when he stumbled into *Lark Force* Fort Engineer, Cpl Melvin Reginald 'Eric' Edwards (SX38278) and 2/22nd Lance Sgt Harry Burgess Sisson (VX39297) and Pte Harry Gibson (VX23917).

They retraced a route Cook had already taken too many times but his fellow soldiers were sharing the only food they had, 'a pound of barley' which was 'counted in grains to ensure an equal share.'[25] They came to a stream and found small water snails, which they boiled and ate. Passing Tol was particularly terrible for Cook.

We had to pass the spot where the massacre had been
committed and it took all my willpower to keep going. I carried

a razor blade in my hand, with the intention of committing
suicide rather than be captured again ... I could see boots and
tin hats lying around.[26]

Again it was Col Scanlan and his party they found. The *Lark Force* Commander was wearing full summer dress, having decided that he would surrender with seven other officers. Cook was unimpressed. If the Colonel was surrendering because he hoped to stop atrocities, 'his surrender would have been in vain' because 'the atrocities had been committed – practically all the troops had either passed Tol or had been captured.'[27] Cook had no intention of surrendering, and he and his small group quietly disappeared into the undergrowth. For days they travelled. Harry Sissons had some money and this allowed them to purchase food at a village. Unfortunately, Cook rolled on a stone during the night and re-broke his ribs. At some stage, Cook and Edwards became separated from Sisson and Gibson. Edwards had eaten some poisonous berries and was suffering abdominal pains and passing blood.

A mission run by 'a German' (Father John Meierhofer) who 'treated us coldly' offered no relief and then they came across some unfriendly natives, who started to hurl stones from slings at them – for Cook this was one continuing nightmare. Capturing and butchering a small pig did nothing to improve relations, until they paid. After that, at each village they were kindly treated and provided with food. Cook's companion Edwards had fallen by the wayside, unable to continue on due to illness. Cook had been told that a group, which included 2/10 Field Ambulance CO Maj Palmer, was not far ahead and he was determined to catch them up for medical treatment. It was several more days before Cook walked into a village to be greeted by Palmer. The relief was immense. With Palmer's words: 'Cook, you're a tough old Bastard' ringing in his ears, Billy Cook could at last sleep, and sleep he did, for 16 hours.[28]

Cook was woken; it was time to move as the Australians tried to keep ahead of the Japanese. Over the ensuing days Cook struggled to keep up with this group, due to the severity of his malaria attacks. Each night came the recurring nightmares, which drove him out of huts into the undergrowth. Cook finally collapsed and Maj Palmer placed a thermometer in his mouth. 'I waited until his attention was elsewhere, then I took it out and shook it down to 101 degrees.'[29] Cook, soaked in perspiration and staggering side to side, was allowed to continue. At the next campsite, he admitted to Palmer that his temperature had been 105 degrees (40.5°C). Palmer 'just shook his head.'[30] There was no way Cook was going to be left behind again and, with quinine, his health began to improve to the point that he could laugh again.

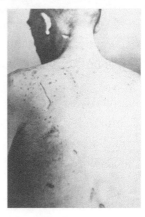

The healed back of Pte Billy Cook. Cook

> *One very humorous incident ... Our progress had been stopped by a deep river, on the other side of which was a native village. Sandflies were thick ... we were trying to attract the attention of the villagers ... It was not possible ... so Tom Law [L/Cpl Thomas Albert Henry Law (VX23621)] started to swim ... As soon as he reached the opposite bank, swarms of sandflies attacked him – Tom started to run right into the village – naked and wearing a fearsome black beard. Every native had one look at him and started running.*[31]

Eventually Law conveyed to the villagers that he was friend not foe, and the dilemma facing the soldiers. The New Guineans lost no time in bringing the Australians across by canoe.

Further relief came when they arrived at Mal Mal Mission, run by Father Ted Harris, and at Drina River plantation. At Drina, groups under the leadership of Lt Owen were well organized and with some food for all. Owen had organized work parties to plant vegetables until sickness made this impossible. By the end of March, Cook was providing medical treatment to others with the help of the NGVR's Cpl Jim Peterson.

To his surprise, Cook met up with two other survivors from the

LEFT: *Hugh 'Nipper' Webster.* T.Webster RIGHT: *Pte Norman Walkley.* Johnson

4 February massacres – 'Nipper' Webster and 'Smacker' Hazelgrove, each with their own harrowing story. 'Nipper' was making a speedy recovery from his gunshot wounds but 'Smacker' was not recovering as well. He had been hit by 'what was thought was an explosive bullet, right through the shoulder blade, and he had a very nasty wound', according to Cook.[32]

There had been little warning before AA Gnr Maxwell 'Smacker' Hazelgrove (N109824) felt the impact of the bullets in his back and fell forwards. It was a blur but the 19-year-old from the pretty and peaceful town of Bega, NSW, knew he needed to move. Body and mind were bewildered and it took all his willpower to push away the bloodied bodies of men who had been friends. It took hours to free his hands. Hazelgrove staggered to the beach but could go no further. Two days later he was found by none other than a fellow AA gunner.

It was the 19-year-old Gnr David Bloomfield who stumbled across the 19-year-old Hazelgrove. He studied the prone body, the shirt caked in blood, and as he rolled Hazelgrove over he saw 'several jagged holes' in his back, including a very large shoulder wound.[33] Hazelgrove was exclaiming: 'Quick you've got to get out of here, the Japs are in the plantation.' As Bloomfield tried to reassure him, the wounded gunner shouted: 'Laurie Robinson and the others are all dead.'[34] It was yet another ordeal for Hazelgrove as Bloomfield supported him back to the party led by their AA CO Lt David Selby.

There was something in a name, and particularly the letter 'W', according to brothers Les and Walter Whittle. They had enlisted the same day as their best mates Pte Hugh 'Nipper' Webster and Pte Norm Walkley. As a symbol of mateship, they each had a 'W' tattooed on their arms and were known in D Company 2/22nd henceforth as 'the four W's'. On 4 February 1942, the four were marched to Waitavolo House not far from Tol. They supported each other as best they could as they were pushed into a line facing the enemy, who had rifles raised. The shots were rapid. Webster was shot in the side and arm, and fainted. When he stirred the Japanese were gone, and Les and Walter Whittle were dead. Walkley was barely alive, having been shot in the chest, arm and buttocks.

After three days, they mustered up the strength to leave but Walkley soon fell behind and Webster was unable to find him. Webster also came across Col Scanlan's party and, like Cook, found Scanlan about to surrender. Webster decided his previous interaction with the Japanese had been anything but pleasant, so he limped off alone. Walkley wandered in a daze, until he was found on 14 February by Lt Peter Ernest Figgis (VX44411). There was little that could be done for the severely wounded Walkley and he died of his wounds on 1 March 1942, at Wain Village near Cape Orford. It is believed that, during the first week of February, there were at least four separate massacres of Australians in New Britain. In May 1942, an Australian Court of Enquiry concluded there had been 144 *Lark Force* victims. Members of the NGVR were not included in the enquiry findings, nor were civilians. NGVR men massacred on 4 February 1942 at Tol included: Bombardier John Barrie (NGX497), 42, husband of Beatrice; Rfn Edwin Fischer Johnson (NGX494), 30, husband of Mary; and Rabaul Solicitor Rfn James Lee Street (NGX495), 43. Street had also served in WWI. Having put up his age to enlist, he survived three years of carnage on

James Street, boy soldier WWI. AWM

the Western Front. His wife Violet had been evacuated to Australia at the end of 1941. Also killed was the recently married Rfn Lionel Stephen Dix (NGX504), 27. The former Rabaul Bank clerk, 21-year-old Rfn Keith Brian Paul (NGX512), who had struggled across the mountains with 2/22nd Pte Jack Moyle until he could go no further, had revived enough to make it to the coast only to be killed at Tol.

Capt David Hutchinson-Smith was disappointed as more and more of his group left to surrender. Consensus was then to go with a young native, who'd offered to take them further south to a place called Gasmata. Hutchinson-Smith was feeling 'far from happy' with this decision – he was struggling with trust, angered by how many New Britain residents were blatantly assisting the enemy to capture Australians. What were their reasons? Were they disenchanted with British/Australian governance? Did they believe the Japanese offered them a better life? There were reports of a man 'who spoke like an Australian' working as an interpreter with the Japanese.[35] Hutchinson-Smith's distrust proved warranted when he and his group were delivered to Gasmata.

Jack Eric Daymond was the Assistant District Officer in charge of the Gasmata District. A patrol officer under his jurisdiction, Eric Mitchell, warned Australia of the presence of the Japanese fleet off Rabaul. Foolishly, the Australian radio service broadcast the message. Hearing the broadcast, the Japanese promptly sent a landing party to Gasmata to silence the radio. On 9 February, Daymond and Medical Assistant Richard Thomas 'Dickie' Squires, and shortly afterwards Mitchell, were taken prisoners-of-war (POWs). Gasmata was well occupied.

Capt Hutchinson-Smith realized that his war, and that of the troops with him, was over.

Suddenly we spied a prone figure behind a light machine
gun at the left of the path in a well-camouflaged position.
He was covering our small group and we realised that now
we must raise our hands in the distasteful token of surrender,
and this we did most reluctantly. Immediately a strange
figure detached itself from the bushes on the right of the track

and raced towards us with a peculiar ape-like gait, moving noiselessly and with great speed. In a moment or two I found myself looking into the ugly, sweating countenance of a Japanese who presented his bayonet uncomfortably close to my fluttering heart. The feeling was indescribably odd.[36]

On 8 March 1942, Gasmata was the scene of yet another massacre when between 16 and 20 troops were bayoneted and shot.

Few who visited South Gippsland, Victoria, would deny the picturesque qualities of the low, rolling granite hills and lush farming communities that descend to the coast at Wilsons Promontory, the southernmost point of mainland Australia. A principal town of the region is Leongatha, around 62 miles (100km) south-east of Melbourne. In 1941, 16 men left the Leongatha district to enlist in the 2/22nd and became part of *Lark Force*.

Only three returned. Six died on 1 July 1942, one died later in the war and six were massacred at Gasmata: Pte James Butterworth (VX42459) of Dumbalk, Pte Francis William James (VX38952) of Leongatha, Pte Albert Ernest Kuhne (VX43383) of Dumbalk, L/Cpl Harry Alfred Millsom (VX51030) of Tarwin and the Bellingham brothers, Bill and Tom, sons of Harry and Annie Bellingham. Pte Clarence Thomas Bellingham (VX28007), 2/22 Battalion, was 33 and Pte William Henry Bellingham (VX28017) was 34. They had lived and worked on the family farm at Nerrena. Life was monotonous and unexciting, so war and the army had promised something else.[37]

Soldiers are trained to fight, not to run away. The Rabaul Garrison force was ill prepared for battle and completely unprepared for capture or escape. A failure to provide contingency plans for withdrawal and Col Scanlon's command 'every man for himself ' created chaos and disintegration. Throughout February and March, troops looked to their officers to lead but their officers were as unprepared for this retreat as the troops were. AA Lt Peter Fisher had led men out of Rabaul but he had no more clue as to where they were going or how they would get off the island. Days and days were spent through mud, rain and jungle. His group came across 2/22nd CO Lt Col Carr drawing a map and discussing native foods and customs with the Inspector of Police, Bruce Ball.

Too little, too late? The irony was inescapable. Fisher and his group 'pushed on scavenging into hilly country, tired, hungry wet.'[38] They came across more and more officers and soldiers, all feeling the strain of mountain climbing. 'The tracks were now very steep and the heavy tropical rain made them slippery.'[39] Each night he would share the food ration: 'a biscuit and half a lemon and a piece of taro occasionally.'[40] He had no answers to the questions etched on faces.

At the mouth of the Merai River, Fisher was relieved to meet up with Maj John Mollard and AA CO Lt David Selby and then Lt Owen. Owen 'shared a magnificent tin of raisins, one handful each – the best meal for days.'[41] They were in the vicinity of Tol Plantation when they heard shots; they reasoned soldiers were shooting pigs and cattle but 'to our unbelievable astonishment it was not pigs and cattle.'[42] They came across the group that included *Lark Force* CO Col Scanlan and were astonished that news of the massacres was greeted by Scanlan 'with the greatest scepticism', even when Lt Selby appeared with the wounded

Maj Mollard and Col Scanlan after they surrendered. Johnson

Gnr Hazelgrove and Pte Marshall.[43] Fisher was further 'astonished to hear [that Scanlan] had decided to return to Rabaul' and even 'more astonished to learn of Maj Mollard's decision to accompany him.'[44]

'Astonished' was not strong enough a word for the normally mild-mannered Lt David Selby. He was feeling the strain of the previous days. He had been encouraged to continue on by photographs of his wife, baby and mother. The images, he now discovered, had been washed away by the river crossings. Selby had led his exhausted group to another mission and, on seeing the livestock, felt confident that Father John Meierhofer would be as generous as his brother, Father Alphons Meierhofer of Lamingi Mission. This Father Meierhofer, however, refused all requests for first aid, shelter and food. The Japanese had been at the mission shortly before and said they would return for the livestock – the repercussions could be grave. Selby was more interested in the here and now, and two chickens were killed and provided a much-appreciated meal for his troops. The following day, it was a relief to arrive at the camp of Lt Owen and Maj Palmer and secure badly needed medical treatment for Tol survivors Marshall and Hazelgrove. But now Col Scanlan and Maj Mollard were surrendering. Selby was totally unimpressed.

> *There was the Commandant in a blaze of glory complete with summer-weight uniform, collar and tie, red gorgets and red cap band. He was wearing new boots and had cut his hair and shaved … a startling contrast to our ragged shorts and shirts, battered boots and stubbly beards.*[45]

Scanlan had asked Mollard to address the troops on his behalf. At first Mollard refused as he had consistently encouraged the troops not to surrender. The Commandant insisted. 'It's your job. You are in charge now.'[46] An 'obviously upset' Mollard gave an address which Selby found profoundly depressing, 'more than anything which had happened on the track', and a 'heavy gloom settled over us.'[47]

With the departure of the senior officers, next in command was Lt Bill Owen, now left with the responsibility of guiding a party of around 150 men to safety. Men were dying and few had the strength to continue. Lt David Selby accepted the responsibility for recording deaths. There was no escaping his feelings of disbelief and despair when writing 'exhaustion and starvation' beside the name of a 20-year-old; or 'dysentery' and 'malaria' beside the names of troops who had laughed and enjoyed life just over a month ago. The camps at Wunung Plantation and Drina River Plantation were the final destination. A message was sent to those on the south coast who were physically incapable of trekking to Drina or Wunung that they should remain at Palmalmal Plantation and keep watch for aircraft or other means of rescue; as unlikely as this might be, there was little alternative. Unless there was a miracle, hundreds of *Lark Force* troops were not going to escape New Britain.

Endnotes

1. Cook, W. AM54 607/9/1, AWM, Canberra.
2. Ibid.
3. Ibid.
4. Ibid.
5. Ibid.
6. Ibid.
7. Ibid.
8. Ibid.
9. Stone, Holland. *El Tigre*, p.39.
10. Ibid.
11. Ibid.
12. Wigmore, p.666.
13. Ibid.
14. A461, AF420/1/1 Part 1, 'Enemy breaches of all the rules of warfare (including Japanese atrocities) Part One', National Archives, Canberra.
15. Ibid.
16. Ibid.
17. Lt (later Maj) Frederic John Lomas (VX2207), later a member of the 2/7 Commando Squadron.
18. Wigmore, p.667.
19. Cook, AWM54 607/9/1.
20. Ibid.
21. Ibid.
22. Ibid.
23. Ibid.
24. Ibid.
25. Cook, W. Chapter Three: 'Action: Rabaul', in Connolly, R. and Wilson, B. *Medical Soldiers 2/10 Australian Field Ambulance 8 Div 1940–45*, 2/10 Australian Field Ambulance Association, 1985, p101.
26. 26. Ibid., p.102.
27. Ibid.
28. Ibid., p.108.
29. Ibid., p.109.
30. Ibid.
31. Ibid.
32. Ibid.
33. Bloomfield, D. *Rabaul Diary: Escaping Captivity in 1942*, Australian Military History Publications, 2001, p.38.
34. Ibid.
35. Hutchinson-Smith, D. MSS1533.
36. Ibid.
37. Killed on 1 July 1942 were Jack Howard, Fred Broadbent, Fred Ketels, Jimmy Kavanagh, Arthur Oliver and Tom Sangster.
38. Fisher, P. PR89/0716, AWM, Canberra.
39. Ibid.
40. Ibid.
41. Ibid.
42. Ibid.
43. Ibid.
44. Ibid.
45. Selby, D.M. *Hell and High Fever*, Currawong, 1956, p.83.
46. Ibid., p.84.
47. Ibid., p.86.

CHAPTER ELEVEN

DESPERATE

*'It was a gross error of judgment –
it was utter stupidity.'*

Maj John McCarthy

The cloth-covered volume was marked 'Top Secret' and the author, Superintendent of Police in New Guinea, Col John Walstab, ensured that all new patrol and police officers read the 'Blue Book' thoroughly. It contained 'the plan I have written for action if New Guinea is overrun by the enemy.'[1] Walstab's experience in both military and New Guinea affairs was beyond reproach. He had enlisted in October 1914 as a Captain with the AIF 5th Battalion. Wounded at Gallipoli in the Battle of Krithia on 8 May 1915, by November 1916 he had been promoted to the rank of Lt Col and was in command of the battalion. In 1917, he was awarded the Distinguished Service Order (DSO). Walstab held the position of Superintendent of Police in New Guinea between 1927 and 1942.[2] In Rabaul prior to the commencement of WWII, he established the New Guinea Volunteer Rifles (NGVR).

The 'Blue Book' axiom was: 'Never fight a pitched battle. Hit, then run!'[3] The text strongly recommended that District and Patrol Officers establish small ammunition and food dumps in isolated jungle areas. In the advent of an invasion:

Pivotal to the rescue of New Britain survivors were Col Walstab, left rpngcnames, *Keith McCarthy, centre* Johnson, *and Bill Harry, right.* Jackson

> *Native police and selected native plantation workers, plus local*
> *Europeans such as planters, who knew the country and could*
> *live off it were to be accepted as volunteer 'troops'.*[4]

Walstab was advised that Australian Army Headquarters had 'approved' the book and the doctrine within[5] but clearly this was not the case. Advice based on long experience in New Guinea, and New Britain in particular, was ignored by those who filled comfortable Australian military and government offices, and who had never put foot in the mandated territory; it was dismissed by the Commandant of *Lark Force*.

Like Walstab, Assistant District Officer (ADO) Keith McCarthy was a tall, strongly built man with purpose. In 1927 McCarthy sailed for the Mandated Territory of New Guinea, having found 'a government position that matched his natural curiosity, energy and humanity.'[6] He had commenced his position with the Department of Native Affairs at Kokopo, near Rabaul. He had a natural affinity with and concern for the indigenous people, and spent most of his days travelling the wilds of New Guinea on foot or by canoe in the company of native New Guinea policemen. In just a two-and-a-half-month period in 1933, he and his men walked 240 miles (386km) through harsh and hostile country, during which one was killed and McCarthy was struck by arrows in

Pondo Plantation. J.Holland

the thigh and stomach.[7] The arrow to the stomach, he remarked, had 'ruined the beautiful symmetry' of his navel.[8]

McCarthy had read the 'Blue Book' from cover to cover and entirely agreed with Walstab. He lamented that Walstab's plan was never implemented by the Australian Army.

> *The Blue Book plan, to my mind, was made even better by the fact that it could work in conjunction with a scheme already being operated by the Royal Australian Navy ... Thanks to efforts of my former District Officer at Madang, Eric Feldt, planters and other non-officials had been appointed ... each with his 3B set [radio transmitting sets] and each responsible for a defined area.[9]*

Lt Cdr Feldt and his Coastwatcher network had implemented part of the Walstab's plan and McCarthy intended to execute the main part of the 'Blue Book' strategy. Feldt believed that 'if ever a man was given a difficult assignment'[10] it was this; and that Keith McCarthy was the man for the job:

> *His affections and emotions governed him, but when his fine, free carelessness had landed him in trouble, he could extricate*

himself, logic guiding his Celtic fervour until the danger was past.[11]

On McCarthy's initiative, improvisation skills and physical stamina depended the lives of hundreds.

Stationed at Talasea on the western end of New Britain, McCarthy had boarded his launch with his 17-year-old native teleradio operator, Trevor Bruce, planter Rod Marsland and several native police, and sailed up the coast to Pondo Plantation 50 miles (80km) south-west of Rabaul. Pondo was a large plantation and factory that manufactured desiccated coconut. On arrival, he discovered that the Japanese had already visited Pondo and blown up the plantation schooner and several buildings. The manager, Albert Evensen, and his European staff – who included Bill Korn, D'Arcy Hallam and Andy Anderson – had been warned not to associate with Australian troops.

McCarthy knew all the men personally. Although they had placed large white flags on poles on the beach, the large stock of rice and meat would be willingly shared and Pondo was the logical rendezvous point to embark for Australia.

McCarthy despatched runners to gather men who had lived in New Guinea for many years. More and more New Britain residents arrived, such as planter Ken Douglas and Frank Holland from the timber camp, whom McCarthy knew as a brave and 'excellent' bushman.[12] The 'Blue Book' plan was fast becoming a reality. McCarthy intended team members to walk or sail by small craft and canoe, and spread throughout New Britain, contacting the retreating men and assembling them at contact points before small plantation vessels could transport them to Pondo.

McCarthy recalled with frustration his numerous futile offers to Col Scanlan to instruct *Lark Force* troops about survival in the hinterland and his suggestions concerning ammunition and food dumps.

Another who answered the call was Pte Bill Harry (VX24800), a rarity within *Lark Force*. 'Bill' was his preferred name as the name he was christened with, Cuthbert Oswald Harry, was a bit of a mouthful. Bill was a country lad, born to a family of Victorian farmers, and this gave him an advantage over the city born. An even bigger advantage came when Bill, serving with the intelligence section of Colonel Scanlan's staff, surveyed the surrounding area. He'd spent valuable weeks moving into the hinterland past Rabaul, befriending missionaries, accompanying them on patrols and familiarizing himself with jungle villages and tracks. Over the ensuing months Harry, sometimes alone and sometimes

New Britain indigenous police proved invaluable in the rescue of Lark Force. Johnson

with others, dodged the enemy and gathered *Lark Force* men wherever he went. On one occasion, Harry was given four days to pass evacuation information to a group on the coast and return through the mountains. He travelled day and night, and returned two days later. For 11 weeks he lived on sweet potatoes, taro and fish, but despaired as he came across starving *Lark Force* soldiers stricken 'with fever and dysentery'. In every second or third village, Harry found 'two or three soldiers dying.'[13]

Information concerning Japanese occupation was patchy, and plans and chosen routes needed to be adjusted rapidly. Unlike his counterparts, McCarthy fully intended to use his armed native police. Among the first refugees were sullen and bitter Rabaul native police.

The Australian Government! Why didn't they let the police fight the Japanese? Why did they take our rifles from us just before the Japanese landed? They buried our rifles and now we are running like frightened women. We would have fought with the soldiers![14]

When McCarthy heard this, 'the more angry I got.'[15] He firmly believed that 'a well-trained constabulary' should have been allowed to fight for their country and there was the further insult of burying their guns. 'It was a gross error of judgment – it was utter stupidity.'[16] He immediately re-armed the native police who quickly proved invaluable.

McCarthy needed those still in authority to listen and this was not always easy. Capt Allan Cameron, 2/22nd, had arrived with 11 troops in the small pinnace Dulcy loaned by Mrs Kjillert. Cameron requested the ADO to send a message to Port Moresby asking for a Catalina aircraft to collect him. McCarthy was troubled, as he wished to evacuate as many men as possible and a Catalina would only have room for a few. Cameron believed that the soldiers were already done for; he doubted McCarthy 'could even get them to move! Their spirit is gone. You'd be wasting your time and energies.'[17] McCarthy refused to send the message. 'Cameron became annoyed. He ordered me to send it.

When I still refused there was nothing he could do.'[18] During their travels, McCarthy's team were also collecting provisions from deserted plantations for a voyage to Australia. Military Headquarters in Port Moresby advised McCarthy not to attempt such a perilous voyage. McCarthy considered the alternative much worse and ignored the order. He set off to coordinate a fleet of local boats.

Returning to Pondo, McCarthy discovered Cameron and Albert Evenson in violent argument. Cameron wrote: 'Big rumpus with Evenson … can't understand that man. He lives under a white flag. Need to watch him.'[19] Cameron wanted to take charge of the entire food supply. Evenson refused, arguing that he would share but needed to consider his staff, native workers and any future arrivals. Evenson was becoming increasingly 'emotional', as was Cameron. McCarthy attempted to adjudicate but he and Cameron were both strong personalities. For McCarthy it was an irritation he could have done without.

Bitter hatred existed between the two men … things were bad enough without personal wars too … Cameron demanded that I no longer listen to Evenson and added for good measure: 'You're an Army Sergeant! You are under my orders … furthermore I instruct you to hand over your WT set to me![20]

This was too much for McCarthy. When Cameron threatened him with 'eleven armed men' McCarthy 'lost his temper.'[21] "'Why you stupid ass," I roared, "I've got twenty armed police!'"[22] McCarthy declared there was no time for a 'private war' and went off to assist Evenson and his staff with the arrival of more troops, 'most of them in the last stages of starvation and suffering from malaria.'[23] He and Rod Marsland spent the night perfecting the evacuation plan. They took stock of the boats at their disposal; more were desperately needed before the voyage to Australia could be accomplished. The following morning, Marsland began repairs on the Pondo schooner *Malabuka* and they were buoyed by the arrival of Leong Chu in the tiny launch *Dufaur*. The elderly Chinese caused rare smiles when he exclaimed: 'Business bugger up!' so he was here to help.[24]

The condition of the arriving troops highlighted that speed was of the essence, but to gather the scattered force meant covering hundreds of miles. News that ADO Jack Daymond was captive and Gasmata was occupied further closed their options. A message from Military Headquarters (HQ) Port Moresby placed McCarthy in charge. On 20 February, he gave the now disgruntled Capt Cameron and his men charge of launch Dulcy to traverse the Talasea stretch of coastline, looking for survivors.

McCarthy started his own trek on foot into the mountains. He was overwhelmed as he came across more and more and more troops suffering from malaria and dysentery, starving and with their clothes in tatters. McCarthy pointed out to one group begging for food that they were lying in a native food garden. He dug up a few roots. 'Nobody had taught them ... soon the men were eating, cursing the Army that had failed to train them.'[25] Occasionally, a plantation manager needed to be persuaded to supply the detachment with food but most, such as plantation men Bill Mason, Frank Conroy and his young son Joe, did so willingly and then assisted the sick and weak to Pondo.

The relief of completing the journey was short-lived for McCarthy. Bert Olander had accompanied Capt Cameron's party onboard Dulcy to set up a staging camp further down the coast. He now rushed up to McCarthy, 'his face almost black with rage. "That bloke Cameron!"'[26] Cameron had put Olander ashore and instead sailed off for the New

Guinea mainland. 'That's the last we'll see of them or the Dulcy,' exploded Olander.[27] McCarthy, too, was very annoyed. He already had more than 100 troops who were 'haggard skeletons' and countless more coming with Frank Holland that he needed to get off the island, and Cameron had cut and run taking with him a precious boat.[28] Cameron arrived at Salamaua on 3 March.

A small over-the-horizon cavalry appeared in the form of Gladys Baker and her launch. On 4 December 1939, *The Sydney Morning Herald* had featured Gladys Baker in the 'Women's Supplement' sandwiched between an article about Christmas cakes and a perfume advertisement. Gladys Baker and husband Bill owned a copra plantation of 800 acres (324ha) on Witu Island, 40 miles (64km) north of New Britain. After Bill died in 1934, Gladys remained to run the plantation, Langu, and manage the indigenous workers and their families. She refused to evacuate to Australia with the other European women and children, arguing that many indigenous families depended on her and that the medical knowledge she had gained over the years might well be of use following an invasion.

Faced with what might be her last Christmas at Langu, Gladys Baker had attempted to make it as normal as others by arranging a 'sing sing for the natives.'[29] Japanese reconnaissance aircraft had flown over her plantation on Christmas Day. News of the bombing of Rabaul came to her 'by drums and smoke signals down the mainland of New Britain and my boys picked it up.'[30] She endeavoured to persuade the crew of Lakatoi to leave for Australia with a party of Witu residents but they believed such a voyage was too treacherous. On 24 January, Gladys Baker loaded her 27-foot (8m) pinnace Langu the Second with food and set off for New Britain's west coast. Her boat's speed was only nine knots, but she and her crew established food dumps along the Aria River. She sent the boat and crew off to seek information on the evacuation of any Australian soldiers while returning on a smaller launch to Langu on 14 February. They were intercepted by a Japanese seaplane and Gladys Baker hid under the after-decking in the bilge.

I heard footsteps on the deck accompanied by a flood of fluent

Pidgin. The Japs had boarded us and were questioning the natives. The native boys told one of the two in answer to the questions that their master had gone to Sydney a long time ago and that they were going back to the plantation on Witu to pick up a load of workers to take them back to their villages.[31]

When the seaplane took off, Gladys Baker re-emerged proud of the bravery of her crew. They returned to Langu and, two days later, Langu the Second and crew arrived. Her native crew were upset. 'The Australians, the head boy told me with tears in his eyes, were "sick fella masters too much."'[32] She immediately loaded the pinnace with food and medical supplies. 'I overloaded dangerously because I had 15 tons by measurement on a 5½ ton boat.'[33] Baker and her crew met up with Keith McCarthy, who put her in charge of the Iboki camp. McCarthy wrote:

'kind-hearted Mrs Gladys Baker ... took charge of the sick and organized the place.'[34] Initially she 'cooked for and nursed the 13 boys who were sick' and when they were well enough they were transferred. Baker decided good use should be made of her 'mud-ticket', which she had gained because 'of my knowledge of New Britain waters' so with no more wounded to treat she took the pinnace and 'sailed up the coast towards Rabaul to see if I could find more troops.'[35]

Baker came across a boat stranded on a reef. She left the pinnace and crew to observe, and returned by canoe to Iboki. To her relief, the stranded boat had been a mission boat and, having cleared the reef, arrived at Iboki with Captain Apel and 34 other troops. Two days later, her own pinnace returned with a further 15 soldiers and another boat brought more. 'Some of them were very sick and others were wounded ... Escapees continued to trickle in until we numbered 191 in all.'[36] The demands on Gladys Baker for care and attention had increased exponentially. Over a 16-day period she managed around 13 hours

Frank Holland. J.Holland

sleep. The troops were ill with dysentery, malaria and tropical ulcers, many suffering from very severe fevers. 'Their systems were craving for salt and sugar.'[37]

I remember being struck by the number of ginger beards. I worked night and day caring for them and feeding them.[38]

Frank Holland was pleased that his wife Mabel and children John and Ann were safely back in Australia. He had volunteered for one of the most dangerous rescue missions, to lead a patrol of six native police across the island to the south coast, emerging at Tol Plantation. This route was rugged and trackless, and was inhabited by the Mokolkol, a fierce treacherous group notorious for slaying intruders with long-handled axes. Pondo's manager Evenson had assisted in recruiting volunteer native carriers. Holland and his group set off on 20 February, moving inland from Pondo.

Left to right: L/Cpl John Henry Johnson (VX23546), Pte Harold George Tomison (VX23365), Maj John Akeroyd and Pte Norman Cole (VX24021). Johnson died 1 July 1942. AWM

Capt Ernest Appel's pre-war occupation was as a pharmacist, so he was well aware of how fragile the health of his retreating troops was and he wished that he had access to the medicines he had back then. His original group of 285 at Kamanakan Mission had grown after he despatched soldiers on horseback to make contact with others. He had also undertaken a trek of 100 miles (161km) on horseback and on foot, visiting gathered parties and urging them on. He estimated that there were now around 413 troops dispersed around the coastline between Cape Lambert and Ataliklikun Bay. On the

Native police and carriers made the journey to Pondo possible for many.

Johnson

night of 21 February, Cpl John Malcolm Headlam (VX20614) rode into Appel's camp with the most heartening news – Keith McCarthy had implemented a rescue plan and help was on its way. Holland had come across Headlam, whom he regarded as an 'energetic and competent' non-commissioned officer.[39] Headlam was suffering from malaria and Holland took him to Langinoa, where they found 30 troops on the verge of starvation. They had eaten all the European food but had 'failed to recognize 50 hectares of bearing tapioca growing with 20 yards of them.'[40] Headlam insisted on riding back to give Appel the news.

During his trek, Holland had located Lincoln Bell, a fellow timber-cutter, planter, trader and excellent bushman. Bell was a great addition to the operation, particularly when they were attacked. The attack came not from the Japanese but the Mokolkol.

> *Myself and the police boys opened fire. The Mokolkol charged*
> *our line swinging their axes as they came, about a dozen of*
> *them. One big fellow close to me was shot at by both my police*
> *boys and myself. We dropped him.*[41]

Frank Holland's rescue trek. Stone/Holland

Another was killed before the remainder disappeared into the jungle. One of Holland's party had a slashed arm but it could have been much worse and they hastily moved on. The jungle was thick with trees so high the sun was rarely seen. Rivers were forded and the group continued to labour up steep, muddy mountains and slide down slopes, grasping at vines to slow their descent.

At Kasalea, Holland found the NGVR's Alfred Lampton Robinson (NGX263) who told him the story of Tol. It was now with even greater urgency that Holland and his party moved on. Holland then found Tol survivor Pte Bill Collins with three others. Collins's story of 'this barbarous affair of cold-blooded killings' was horrific.[42] Frank Holland despatched runners on ahead, conveying his approach and plan to evacuate to the north coast before the enemy returned.

On receiving the evacuation news, Capt Appel moved his 145 men towards Pondo. Eight men too ill for the trek were assisted to the hospital at St Paul's, established by 2/22nd Medical Officer Maj John Finch Akeroyd (VX18194), who bravely decided to remain.

The native police and carriers were proving indispensable for their hunting, shooting, language skills and knowledge of the terrain. Pte Bill Harry arrived and, after advice from Holland, disappeared into the bush again in search of other sick and hungry *Lark Force* troops. At Ril, Holland met up with the 2/22nd CO, Lt Col Carr. Carr was ill and was receptive to Holland's advice, although Holland told him 'that should we get out we owed everything to Mr J.K. McCarthy who started the scheme.'[43]

Holland was on the move again, having left four of the native police with Carr to guide his group back to the main camp. It was a relief to meet

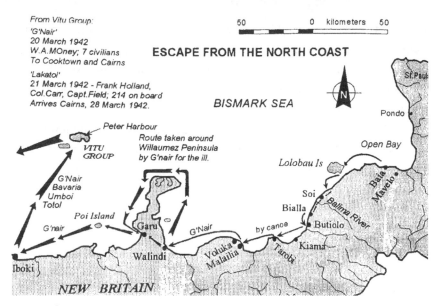

Escape from north coast of New Britain. Stone/Holland

up with Inspector of Police Bruce Ball and his party, which included New Guinea Police Warrant Officers, Ronald William Feetum, Alexander Morrison Sinclair, D. Crawley, H. Thexton and J. Palmer. There was now an assortment of military and civilians: the police contingent, Carr, Sub Lt Con Gill, two RANR sailors, Captains Smith and McLeod, six police constables, three timber merchants, one electrician, agricultural expert Larry Dwyer, seven privates of the AIF, six police boys, 20 native carriers and several other civilians – a total of 52 to be sustained and guided to the north coast – a huge responsibility.[44]

The spirits of the travellers were high. With some food in their bellies and new hope for survival, they laboured on. Holland hoped that this would be sustained as they moved back through hostile Mokolkol country. It was disturbing when Royal Australian Naval Reserve (RANR) Writer Thomas Ian Douglas (PM3146) and RANR Yeoman of Signals George Phillip Thomas Knight (S1782) needed to be left at Karlai Mission. Very ill with dysentery, they could not undertake the arduous climb. Chief Yeoman of Signals Stephen Lamont (PM1325) courageously elected to remain with them. Lamont was a tough Irish-born Chief Yeoman who was soon to turn 50. Holland wrote: 'After saying good bye to our two sick mates and a very brave man we sorrowfully move off.'[45] The exact fate of Douglas and Knight is unknown as both deaths 'from illness' are recorded as 5 March 1942. Lamont died on 1 July 1942, his name inexplicably unrecorded at Bika Paka War Cemetery, New Britain.

As Frank Holland led his bedraggled group through the mountains, he was troubled by thoughts of what to do if the Japanese had returned to Pondo and captured McCarthy and others. What if there were no boats? The responsibility weighed heavily but he chastized himself: 'these thought were no good to anyone.' Trying to purvey a sense of confidence, he pushed on.[46] This motley group of men spread out in a long single line, heads down as they climbed. New Britain resident George 'Pop' Brown, afflicted with a damaged knee, fell back. Two native police fell back with him, declaring him 'man true' because Brown had never complained.

Holland continued to organize food and rest stops, and dispense first aid. The men had begun to ask 'how much further?' Holland estimated a day and a half but the weakened men had slowed. Having drawn a map for Lt Col Carr, Holland went off ahead so as to return with assistance. It was a wise decision; a day later a runner handed him a letter from McCarthy:

*You are NOT under any circumstances to go back to Pondo.
It is dangerous. Get all your party at Watu as soon as possible
... Best of luck ... Cheers and thanks for what I know is an
excellent job on your part. Signed Mac.*[47]

Holland's party finally arrived at the Watu Landing but their ordeal was far from over.

It took another week by foot and canoe to rendezvous down the coast at Iboki with the main party of escapees. At Waloka, he had found McCarthy and Marsland organizing boats. Malahuka had broken down; McCarthy again rued the disappearance of Dulcy. McCarthy was happy to see his friend 'gaunt but still cheerful' and impressed, but not surprised, with what Holland had achieved.[48] The mission priest produced a small bottle of wine. It was probably intended for communion but he had decided that 'Mac, Rod and myself' should have a drink for 'the success of the show.'[49] Moving on to Walinda, Holland found Sgt Bert Smith impressively in charge.[50] Arriving at Iboki on 17 March, Holland found Mrs Gladys Baker 'doing a wonderful job here with the sick men dressing sores and treating fever etc.'[51]

McCarthy continued to struggle with the chasm that remained between the reality of the situation and the unrealistic expectations of officialdom. Having contacted military authorities in Port Moresby for advice concerning the hundreds of escapees, he received instructions that they should be brought to the New Guinea mainland and then marched over the New Guinea Highlands to Chimbu. The march of around 75 miles (121km) over mountains thousands of feet high should, authorities believed, take around a month.

McCarthy had watched as Gladys Baker administer her care selflessly, but she turned to him and said 'these boys are now all-in.'[52] McCarthy could not hide his antipathy. 'Brainless lot of buggers!' he exploded at the skeleton-thin and bootless Rod Marsland, 'How can they expect these men to climb mountains!'[53] Of John Keith McCarthy, Frank Holland wrote: 'A man among men, always able to get the best out of others while always giving the best of himself.'[54] Holland failed to write of his own strength of character stamina and resolve, but on 27 March 1942, 21 very grateful men signed a letter of thanks to Frank Holland. His war continued as a Coastwatcher, Z Special Unit Commando and Lieutenant (VX102689). He was awarded a Member of the British Empire medal (MBE).

'Jock' Olney had written to his sister Marion weeks before of how enthralled he was with New Britain: 'Like the tropics you read about, with the beautiful blue waters and lovely cool nights.'[55] For his brother Neil, it seemed a lifetime since they shared a cup of tea. They had enlisted in the 2/22nd together with friend Roy Merrington Earle (VX35581). Neil had become separated from both 'Jock' and Roy – they had probably been captured or worse. 'Jock' Olney and Roy Earle both died on 1 July 1942.

Between 23 January and 14 May, Neil Olney covered around 900 miles (1448km) by foot, native canoe and a small pinnace.

Breaking through the jungle is a hell of a task at any time, but for starving men and not knowing where you're going makes it much worse.[56]

Neil, left, and 'Jock', right, Olney. Johnson

He was 'ravenously hungry', the water bottles had long been empty and it was agonizing to see coconuts high in the trees but not having the strength to climb. He had to make do with the fermenting coconuts lying below. His immediate superiors Lt Lennox Douglas Henry (VX38976) and Capt Herbert Nathan Silverman (VX129333) had been killed and he had linked up with 11 others, led by Sgt Bert Smith 'who proved himself a very fine and capable leader.'[57] Smith himself became 'very ill and it looked as though he wouldn't pull through but by sheer determination he did.'[58] Olney was too debilitated to travel the final phase of the journey and was humbled by the care he received. Keith McCarthy arrived 'with ten or more police boys, they were really beautiful types of chaps' who supported him to the coast where Rod Marsland, 'a very fine chap ... assisted by two or three capable natives in charge of the pinnace', took him down to the final evacuation point.[59] Marsland and McCarthy had organized a flotilla of canoes to ferry the weakest men to Iboki. He was then placed into the care of Mrs Gladys Baker.

It was like looking at something magic to see her walking up from the little pier. This woman isn't the usual type of person you meet, she has a charming manner, could tell those coons off in the best Aussie fashion, is 100 per cent efficient and above all has the courage which made us all feel mighty proud to have ever been associated with her, and to Gladys Baker wherever she may be good luck from the boys of 2/22nd.[60]

MV Lakatoi. AWM

Olney was grateful, too, for New Guinea residents such as Patrol Officer Gwynne Caleb 'Blue' Harris, who took charge of the boats and others who put their own lives at risk.

> *Typical men of the islands, game as Ned Kelly, keen sense of humour and their many stories kept our spirits high ... their breezy and humorous manner was a real delight and I feel sure that our acquaintance with such men as these has vastly improved our own.*[61]

MV Laurabada. AWM

Food was plentiful at Iboki and the masses of troops now assembled there rested while the final part of McCarthy's west-coast quest was implemented. On 15 March, there was a round-table discussion between military officers and owners/captains of the mosquito fleet boats at Iboki. On 19 March, the entire fleet travelled to Gladys Baker's plantation on Witu Island. On arrival, Marsland was sent to 'arrest' the Lakatoi, the inter-island ship of 250 tons. After initial protests, the ship's master and mate cooperated. Baker and some soldiers killed as many of her livestock as the ship could stock. That night Gladys Baker played poker with the soldiers and lost £11, 'I was holding fours all the time.'[62] On [21] March, loaded with stores, fuel and water, Lakatoi departed with 214 aboard – AIF, NGVR, civilians, native police, European police, native crew and other natives.[63] Gladys Baker piloted from Witu through the Dampier Straits to Umboi Island, without the aid of charts even though the waterway was renowned for its currents and reef outcrops. The following day, the voyage continued. Lincoln Bell, now with the rank of Lt RANVR, chose to remain in New Guinea and was killed on 1 April 1943. Patrol Officer 'Blue' Harris, with the Australian New Guinea Army Unit (ANGAU) rank of Capt (PX98), remained in New Guinea as a Coastwatcher. Harris was captured and executed by the Japanese on 25 March 1944.

The final phase of the rescue operation now depended on a successful evacuation from the east coast. Had the boat MV *Laurabada* arrived before the Japanese? Had those stranded near Palmalmal escaped New Britain and could they rendezvous with Lakatoi to take on the food and water necessary to sail to Australia?

Endnotes

1. McCarthy, J.K. Patrol into Yesterday, Cheshire, 1963, p.183.
2. sites.google.com/site/rpngcnames/ walstab-john accessed 26 October 2016.
3. McCarthy, p.183.
4. Ibid., p.183–184.
5. Ibid., p.183.
6. Nelson H.N., 'McCarthy, John Keith (1905–1976)', Australian Dictionary of Biography, National Centre of Biography, Australian National University, adb.anu.edu.au/ biography/ mccarthy-john-keith-10910/text19375 published first in hardcopy in 2000, accessed online 26 October 2016.
7. McCarthy, p.184.
8. Feldt, The Coastwatchers, p.35.
9. McCarthy, p.184.

10. Feldt, p.35.
11. Ibid.
12. McCarthy, p.200.
13. asopa.typepad.com/asopa_people/2011/01/your-dads-a-hero-bill-harry-rabaul.html accessed 27 October 2016.
14. McCarthy, p.196.
15. Ibid.
16. Ibid.
17. Ibid., p.197.
18. Ibid., p.198. These comments also contained in Cameron H. G. 3DRL/1088, AWM, Canberra.
19. Cameron H.G. 3DRL/1088, AWM, Canberra.
20. McCarthy, p.198.
21. Ibid.
22. Ibid.
23. Ibid.
24. Ibid., p.200.
25. Ibid., p.202.
26. Ibid., p.203.
27. Ibid.
28. McCarthy was told years later that Cameron had gained permission to head to the New Guinea mainland. Cameron was awarded a DSO and while McCarthy agreed Cameron's courage was not in doubt, he questioned his 'judgment' as they 'could certainly have used that boat'. Ibid., p.203
29. Coote, P. 'A daring escape: Gladys Baker', *Una Voce*, June 2002, p.14.
30. Ibid.
31. Ibid.
32. Ibid.
33. Ibid.
34. McCarthy, p.207.
35. Ibid.
36. Ibid.
37. Ibid.
38. Ibid.
39. Wigmore, p.659.
40. Ibid., p.656.
41. Stone, P. (ed.), with Holland, M. and Holland, J. *El Tigre: Frank Holland MBE, Commando, Coastwatcher*, Oceans, 1999, p.22.
42. Ibid., p.38.
43. Ibid., p.44.
44. Ibid., p.46.
45. Ibid.
46. Ibid., p.47.
47. Ibid., p.56.
48. McCarthy, p.207.
49. Stone with Holland, p.69.
50. Ibid., p.70.
51. Ibid.
52. McCarthy, p.211.
53. Stone with Holland, p.70.
54. Ibid., p.77.
55. Johnson, p.36.
56. Olney, J.N. 3DRL 957, AWM.
57. Ibid.
58. Ibid.
59. Ibid.
60. Ibid.
61. Ibid.
62. Coote, P. 'A daring escape: Gladys Baker'.
63. 162 AIF/NGVR; 6 NGAU; 6 European police; 16 civilians; 4 European crew; 18 native crew and 2 'other natives'; Wigmore, p.661.

CHAPTER TWELVE

ANY MEANS OF ESCAPE

*'We were like skeletons, with beards and
long hair and dressed in laplaps.'*

Pte William James 'Bill' Neave

This was not the adventure Gnr Gordon Abel had imagined when he put his age up to enlist; the last three months had been a nightmare. He had been reliant on kind indigenous New Britons to stay alive, grateful for pumpkin and green paw paw because he and his companions otherwise ate 'grass seed stripped and boiled in our tin, occasionally a tree lizard.'[1] He and his mates were 'coastal artillery and militia as well', which meant they 'did not feel at home with the AIF men of the 2/22 Bn ... they were all strangers to us.'[2] The two 18-year-olds were very ill with daily attacks of malaria and they had lost track of how many hundreds of miles they had trudged when they came to Drina River Plantation and found 100 or so soldiers there. They felt unsafe with so many members of *Lark Force* in one place, so Abel and his mate Reg continued down the coast. Three more days and they found they could go no further. A native runner arrived, imploring them to return to Palmalmal Plantation as 'a boat was coming.' It seemed too good to be true but Abel was terribly weak and Reg was 'just about blind.'[3] Dragging Reg with him, Abel hoped the boat would still be there if and when he reached Palmalmal.

War, a teenage adventure, proved to be a nightmare. Left to right: Abel,
Taylor and Bloomfield. Johnson

Like Abel, Gnr Arch Taylor had witnessed things no teenager
should. He had seen men shot dead, he had watched helplessly as *Lark
Force* troops died of disease and hunger. He was bitter:

> *Nothing whatsoever has been done to get us back ... do they*
> *want us again – perhaps we are not of any use now after-all*
> *what's one hundred men ... it was a very depressing thought to*
> *think that we were not wanted.*[4]

He pushed on with his mate Gnr Jack Hart. But then Hart fell down a
steep incline. It took Taylor 15 minutes to reach Hart, whose hands and
face were covered in blood and who had broken a leg. Taylor 'didn't
even know how to bandage a sore finger, let alone fix a broken leg.'[5]
The splint was basic, constructed from sticks and vines. He made Hart
as comfortable as he could before hurrying to the village they had last
seen. In his haste Taylor nearly drowned, as he attempted to swim a
swollen river. He was totally exhausted upon reaching the village to 'beg
for help.'[6] With a terrible sense of guilt for leaving his fellow gunner, he
could move no further. There was relief and gratitude when the villagers
arrived back carrying Hart. They remained for nearly two months.

Two months of hell as we suffered with malaria, dengue,

dysentery, tropical ulcers, abscessed ears and God knows what. We hate the place, hate everything about it – I had no eye for beauty.[7]

Hart developed bed sores. Taylor was grateful for the village's care but the health of both teenagers continued to deteriorate. It was nothing short of a miracle when a message arrived from Lt Bill Owen suggesting that, with the help of the natives and canoes, they should rendezvous at a point south to be rescued by boat.

The day he enlisted, Gnr David Bloomfield had nonchalantly told his mother he wouldn't 'be home for tea tomorrow night Mum.'[8] The 'why?' had caused consternation and threats to have him withdrawn because he was only 17. He now recoiled from the memory of how he had snapped: 'I'll re-join under a different name and you won't know where I am.'[9] His mum had no idea where he was now and he so wished he was back home. It was the middle of February and he seemed to be wandering aimlessly through the jungles of New Britain, 'getting weaker from lack of proper food, malaria and dysentery.'[10] Bloomfield appreciated how fortunate he had been. Unlike fellow gunner 'Smacker' Hazelgrove, he had missed being caught up in the massacre at Tol. On an early hunting expedition with Mr R.C. 'Hutch' Hutchinson, he had an extremely close encounter with a Japanese officer. 'Hutch' was a New Britain-based government agricultural chemist and entomologist – their friendship had been cemented by war. He and Bloomfield went chasing a pig. As they reached the apex of a sharp bend so did a lone Japanese officer. The track was so narrow that Bloomfield had stepped in front of Hutch so the officer could continue walking in the opposite direction. It was bizarre.

My arm brushed against his … I noted almost every detail of his uniform – a khaki net over his steel helmet, gold epaulets on the shoulders of his light khaki jacket, a black leather belt, a sword on his left hip, a pistol in a black holster on his right hip, light khaki riding breeches, black leggings and black boots.[11]

All three men were so startled that they continued on their way without making eye contact. As soon as the Australians turned the next corner, they ran as fast as they could. They heard high-pitched screams and rifle shots behind them but they just kept going, through the Bulus River and into the heavy underbrush on the opposite bank. Japanese soldiers arrived but made no attempt to ford the river. As soldiers died around him, Bloomfield wondered if his luck would hold.

Bloomfield had been an avid reader but his Penguin paperback The Hound of the Baskervilles now had more value as cigarette paper for the bruss, the 'very inferior, locally grown leaf ' he had found drying in native huts.[12] It sometimes eased the hunger pains. He couldn't remember the last time he had eaten proper food but at least he wasn't dead yet. Bloomfield wrote: 'Four men died from malaria, exacerbated by exhaustion, lack of food and no medication.'[13] He had heard George 'The Greek' Harris had died of blackwater fever. Could one death be more tragic than another?

George had been unable to enlist in the AIF because he was not a British citizen. Born in Polamon, Greece, in September 1907 as George

Peter Vamvakaris, Pte Harris (VX30971) may have believed he would be sent to the Middle East to help in the Greek campaign. But George Vamvakaris died of blackwater fever in the mountains of New Britain.

Bloomfield wasn't sure where he found the willpower but he was determined to reach the evacuation point at Drina. He got as far as Wunung but by then was 'suffering attacks of malaria almost daily.'[14] During one attack he lost his sight for 24 hours. The young gunner had begun to lose hope.

Lt Bill Owen (left) and Father Ted Harris. AWM

*I was no longer with the party of civilians whose knowledge of
the coast and folk lore was invaluable and something in which
I took comfort and respected ... We were in fact trapped. We
were no longer a fighting force, having very few weapons and
little ammunition. We were sick, we were tired and we were
hungry and the prospects of our situation improving was [sic]
highly unlikely.*[15]

He wasn't sure how, but he arrived at Palmalmal in Jacquinot Bay and
quickly realized that his survival was greatly enhanced under the care of
the Missionaries of the Sacred Heart priest, Irish-Australian Balmain-
born Father Edward Charles 'Ted' Harris.

Harris had been well provisioned his Mal Mal Mission, until
hundreds of troops in dire need arrived. 'In old trousers, sandshoes,
a white shirt and black priest's hat', Harris tirelessly cared for them,
washing and dressing their wounds, preparing meals and dispensing
his own wardrobe of fresh clothes.[16] The strongest soldiers Harris sent
on to fellow Catholic priest Father William Culhane at his Awul mission.

Pte Billy Cook couldn't believe the attention he received when he
arrived at Mal Mal. Everyone was astonished that Cook had survived.
He was reunited with fellow 2/10 Field Ambulance member Pte John
Maxwell Holah (NX59095). Holah told Cook that no one had given
Cook a chance of 'ever leaving the island, and ... two weeks, at the most,
to live.'[17] As Maj Palmer had said, Cook was a 'tough old bastard.'[18]
Cook defied all odds and, for many who yearned for evacuation, he
defined Australian toughness – a blue-collar worker, the antithesis of
the bronzed Aussie, a 'battler' and a survivor. The humble Cook couldn't
understand the fuss; he just wanted to go home and was fully aware
how very few of the 2/10 Field Ambulance men had that opportunity.
In the interim, he excused himself for accepting the exaltation when it
came in the form of sustenance: 'A plate of hot scones with butter and
a cup of Ovaltine' followed by ' a cigarette – good old Fine Cut – and I
felt like a king.'[19] Word was that a ship was coming – hopefully a navy
destroyer – and Cook desperately wanted this rumour to be true.

Anti-Aircraft CO Lt David Selby was another who was frustrated by the *Lark Force* campaign, which in his mind had been a total debacle from the beginning, and so it continued to be as he sat among a body of more than 100 men. Being on the coast, they continued to be completely at the mercy of any small Japanese landing party. Morale was low and the troops were unarmed, unless you counted the pistols that the officers still wore and Lt Owen's shotgun. There was one soldier who had a Tommy gun but 'it was so rusted it was doubtful if it would work' and there 'were only half a dozen rounds left for it.'[19] Just a dozen enemy soldiers and a machine gun 'would round up the lot of us.'[21] Each new story deepened his despondency – troops were dying of disease, and three young privates trying to retreat across the river estuary at Waterfall Bay had been washed out to sea.

He helped where he could with the men suffering from malaria, who lay in a state of coma, 'their faces yellow, lips parted, noses waxen and pinched and their eyes wide open and staring, staring into space.'[22] The men looked as if they were staring into the sky for Catalina aircraft 'which would never come.'[23] Three more died during the night and Selby struggled for the words he needed to deliver as they were buried. It was impossible not to think of each 'poor fellow and what a miserable end' it was 'to lie there under uncomfortable coral in this pestilent spot.'[24] Selby borrowed a mission prayer book, condensed a short service and acted as officiating clergyman at all subsequent burials. There was respite when the party arrived at Wunung Plantation owned by the German family Yencke. Her husband had been interned, yet Mrs Yencke had willingly cooked meals for *Lark Force* troops.

Selby bonded quickly with Father Harris, a 'wonderfully eloquent ... a delightful Irish Brogue and a frank and infectious smile ... as honest, sincere and generous man' as Selby had ever met.[25] Because of his wireless, the priest relayed all the latest news. It was disheartening to learn of the fall of Singapore, an island fortress that authorities had deemed impregnable. It seemed that authorities had underestimated the Japanese there, too. Selby was himself suffering badly from tropical ulcers, and his ankles and feet were so swollen that he could no longer get his boots on. Standing caused horrible pain. Then it happened to him also – malaria so bad he descended rapidly into delirium. His last conscious thought was how much he prayed that this not be cerebral malaria.

It filled me with a cold fear ... we saw men whom we knew one day to be sane, rational human beings, and next day, smitten by this foul disease, they had become incoherent, raving lunatics ... a man values his sanity more highly than his life, and I was haunted by the dread that overnight I might be converted to one of those pathetic travesties of human beings and worse, live to return home in that state.[26]

Along the eastern seaboard, groups of men desperately attempted to reach Palmalmal. Those who travelled with civilians who understood the terrain were the most fortunate. David Andrew 'Dave' Laws (NGVR) had been working as Rabaul Radio Superintendent. He now found himself leading a small band of Australian Army signallers. It was yet another serious misjudgement that six signal reinforcements had been

No Sunday picnic in the Baining Mountains. Left to right: unknown, Dave Laws, Sig Bill Lord, Sig Dan Thomson, Sig Shorty Barwick; distant three unknown. Photo taken by Sgt Les Robbins. AWM

Fortress Signallers marching through Queenscliff, Victoria. AWM

despatched from Sydney on 9 December 1941 in MV *Malaita*. They had barely arrived before they were under attack and then retreating. Signalman (Sig) William Frederick 'Bill' Lord (SX38290) had been in the army less than 12 months before he was fighting his way up mountain ranges. So, too, South Australian Sig George Bartlett 'Shorty' Barwick (SX28143).Tasmanian Daniel James Thomson (TX16309), at 20, was the baby in the group. Sgt Leslie Ian Hamilton 'Les' Robbins (N14130) had celebrated his 12 months in the army just before they boarded Malaita. Robbins carried his camera and an image of the group taken in the Baining Mountains could have been of a Sunday picnic, not of this desperate escape attempt.

Dave Laws's local knowledge was instrumental in the survival and escape of this group. He then turned back into the jungle to lead more on the harrowing forced march from Drina to Palmalmal.

Members of the Australian Corps of Signals had marched proudly through the streets of Queenscliff, Victoria, to a hero's farewell prior to embarkation for Rabaul. They had been the picture of precision and health. Many never returned. Sig Robert Colin Clack (VX129389) from Ballarat was killed in action on 23 January 1942. Cpl Jack Archibald 'Mac' McLeod (SX38285) was executed at Tol. Sig Leonard Frederick

Auchetti (VX129373), 20, drowned trying to cross the Warangoi River. Sgt Arthur Thomas 'Crash' Bowran (NX191440), 21, died of illness on 23 February 1942 and was buried at Palmalmal Mission. Sgt Douglas Roy Morcom (VX129335), Sig Arnold Claude Scriven (SX38286), L/Cpl Thomas Vernon Price (SX38284), Sig Thomas Stanley Hennessy (VX129364) and Sig Alan James Batchler (TX16308) died on 1 July 1942.

Pte Jack Moyle had joined a party led by Capt McInnes. They walked from one plantation to another, eating whatever and resting whenever they could. Rangarere Plantation owner John McLean had a 28-foot (8.5m) boat with a 30-horsepower engine hidden in an inlet. McInnes argued with him for days, until McLean agreed that the boat was theirs. It took a week to paint the boat green, and gather fuel and supplies for the voyage into the unknown. Confidence rose when some charts were found and, on 13 February, the group pushed off. But the boat remained wedged in the shallows. They waited for another high tide and, with much physical exertion, they pushed the boat into deeper water. They travelled at night; this prevented attacks by enemy aircraft but increased navigation hazards.

Jack Moyle scribbled: 'No one knows much about sailing a boat and the reefs are very bad.'[27] Following the coast seemed logical until they ran into a reef. The boat vibrated badly and their only choice was to beach in another inlet, unload the supplies and straighten the bent propeller blades. The fittest reloaded the boat and carried the weakest back onboard. McLean, the boat's owner, arrived with luggage – the Japanese were not far away and he had decided a reckless journey in a small overloaded boat was his only option.

The soldiers were pleased to have McLean onboard – finally, someone who knew something about boats and navigating these waters. McLean argued that the best option was to travel away from the reefs in the opposite direction, past Rabaul to New Ireland. The dangers of moving past a

Pte Jack Moyle. Moyle

Japanese armada were undeniable but the troops agreed that there was little option. It was Monday 16 February. They travelled by night, then anchored by day and moved ashore to obtain supplies. If Jack Moyle had not been so tired, hungry, wet and ill with malaria fevers, he might have recalled how willingly he had left the family farm at Spring Creek in the gentle temperate district of Tallangatta, Victoria.

Arriving at the southern end of New Ireland, they weighed anchor, camouflaged the boat and moved ashore at Cape St George. Alerted to their presence by natives, former Assistant District Officer at Namatanai, Alan Fairlie 'Bill' Kyle, arrived in a dugout canoe. Kyle had been a Sapper in the 4th Divisional Signal Company during WWI. McInnes decided to travel with Kyle to his hideout to use the teleradio to signal Port Moresby for a rescue. The rest of the group were instructed to load any supplies they could scrounge. For days the men waited, sleeping on the beach, tormented by mosquitoes and sandflies, but neither McInnes nor Kyle returned. 'We have almost given up hope', wrote Moyle. They waited seven days. Natives woke them to report that Japanese boats were close by and then an aircraft flew low overhead – it seemed that the teleradio transmission had alerted the enemy. Japanese search parties landed to find the radio set and its operators, and Kyle's hut was found and destroyed.

Moyle's group had no alternative but to scatter, each man intent on his own survival. McLean decided that it was better not to be found with soldiers and headed inland. McInnes finally managed to rejoin them. The ensuing weeks were accentuated by searching for food and dodging enemy boats and soldiers. By now McInnes was very ill, as was RAAF Warrant Officer Neale Eustace Evans (2281). Moyle had decided in 1940 that there was no place for horses in warfare and had left the Light Horse. In March 1942, on the island of New Ireland, Moyle caught horses and with another soldier, Cpl John Stuart 'Jack' Ballantyne (VX29934), rode up the coast in search of help.

The route was rugged and within two days the horses had foundered and died. The soldiers continued on foot. Ballantyne suffered a bad dose of malaria and Moyle traded his final money to a villager for a small pig, which he skinned with his pocketknife and cooked. Ballantyne recovered well enough to set off for the next village, but then he collapsed again and there was no option but to shelter in a village hut. The following morning, the soldiers woke to discover that the villagers had hastily dispersed.

Approaching loudly was a band of former plantation boys, discontented at being deserted by their European employers. They were heavily armed with spears and knives, and expressed their anger loudly at the two Australians. The soldiers carried a pistol but very little ammunition. Ballantyne struggled to his feet and they angrily waved their pistol, pretending to take aim – the malcontents retreated.

They had travelled for 10 days and they had forged nearly 100 miles (161km) – both men were exhausted. As they hobbled up the track, they noticed two men and four horses approaching. The men were dressed all in white with pith helmets. Were they priests, German or European, friend or foe? It was a great relief to be greeted by Lt Clive Allan McVean (VX19901) and Sgt Douglas Arthur Aplin (VX20231). The two were on their way to rescue the McInnes group. Unfortunately, WO Evans had died two days after Moyle and Ballantyne had departed and several others were now very ill. Moyle and Ballantyne were told to continue on to Muliama Plantation. On 6 April, McVean and Aplin returned with McInnes and the other survivors. There were now nine civilians[28] and eight *Lark Force*.[29]

On 9 April, Moyle and five others departed on a mission to persuade Chin Pak, the Chinese storekeeper on Boang Island, that his boat *Quong Wah* should be liberated to enable the 17 Europeans and Australians the opportunity to escape. After being assured that he would be recompensed after hostilities ended, the merchant agreed and included the engine boy.

The boat proved to be barely seaworthy and its engine cantankerous. Anchoring near one plantation, they offered the owner passage, to which the man answered: 'No thanks, I know that rotten old tub and I wouldn't go anywhere in it, I'll be safer here.' With this reassuring observation, the group of 17 took again to the ocean – it was the night of 28 April. When the engine stopped they drifted; when it could be started, the crammed boat was more able to engage the heavy swell.

The barely seaworthy Quong Wah. Moyle

When they finally landed on the New Guinea mainland at Buna they felt tremendous relief, particularly when they found that Buna was still in Allied hands. It was 6 May and all the food and water had been consumed but 17 men and a very rickety boat had survived 560 miles (901km). 'Our appearance, dirty, unshaven, thin and in ragged clothes, hardly indicated we were white people.'[30] The news was worse than they imagined. Bougainville, Tulgai and Manus Islands were now occupied; Lae, Salamaua and the Markham Vallery, north of Buna, also. Port Moresby had been bombed. They were told that there were only two possible escapes. Either they climbed 100 miles (161km) over the Kokoda Trail, or boarded a small 300-ton boat down the coast to Milne Bay. To them, 300 tons was actually a large boat and they were in no condition to climb any more mountains. On the evening of 29 May, Jack Moyle and his companions boarded another boat at Port Moresby – their fifth. At least the Van Hertz was large, seaworthy, had abundant food and water, and had qualified people doing the driving. Most importantly, it was taking them home to Australia.

Alan Fairlie 'Bill' Kyle and his assistant, Patrol Officer Gregory Wade Benham, both now commissioned in the RANVR, chose to remain in New Ireland as Coastwatchers and report Japanese movements to the Allies. Both Kyle and Benham were captured and executed on 1 September 1942.

Weak radio signals sent from *Lark Force* troops attempting to escape had been received by military personnel in New Guinea and outlying

The route taken by Jack Moyle and his Lark Force *and civilian companions.*
Moyle

islands. Lt Allan Thomas Timperley (PX176), Australian New Guinea Army Unit (ANGAU), a pre-war civil servant originally from Ipswich, north-west of Brisbane, immediately put to sea from the Trobriands to Palmalmal in a launch and arrived on 5 April. Sgt John Henry Marsh (QX42288) was a crew member of the Jean L led by ANGAU Warrant Officer Hylton Edmund Jarrett (PX184), which departed from Port Moresby on a similar rescue mission. The reefs and tides ensured that it was a hazardous journey and, at times, they wondered if there was anyone still alive or if the Japanese occupied the entire island of New Britain. At each stop to take on water and fresh supplies, they felt the

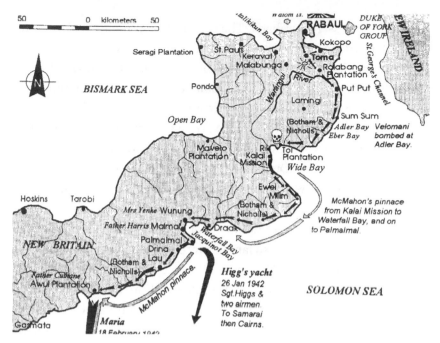

Escaping by any means. Stone/Holland

panic and sense of abandonment within the communities and observed the increasing lawlessness as those who now had nothing looted.

On a boat with a top speed of just eight knots, progress was annoyingly slow and they realized that should they need to escape quickly this was not an option. Spasmodic, weak wireless signals kept them going. It was April, and three days shy of a month on the boat, when they dropped anchor yet again and moved ashore. AA Lt Peter Fisher and his party were overjoyed. It was Easter Sunday and there was no better Easter present. The appearance of the survivors was startling – they were emaciated and ill. As the sick were being brought ashore, Pte Albert Charles Vinnell (VX47739) died. There was no sign of his 22-year-old brother Pte Arthur Raymond Vinnell (VX47742). Warrnambool couple Albert and Ada Vinnell would not hear until 1945 that Arthur too had died, on 1 July 1942.

Sgt Marsh thought it ironic that he and his crew had used a Japanese compass and German charts to evacuate Australian troops from enemy-occupied New Britain. They transferred their wretched, precious cargo to the larger vessel Laurabada. The return trip on their small boat was no less hazardous but the crew were in a lighter mood.

Lt David Selby, at Mal Mal Mission, felt himself coming out of his stupor: 'the mists cleared ... every bone and muscle ached and I was soaked in sweat, but I knew I had fought with death.'[31] The news was heart-warming – a ship was likely to arrive the next day. It was difficult to contain the nervousness and those black thoughts that gnawed at the back of the brain. 'Our minds drove us on with visions of a ship slowly slipping below the horizon.'[32] It didn't seem possible after so many terrible deaths but, this day when they buried their dead, the feelings of sorrow were even deeper because these men had been through so much, travelled so far and were so near rescue yet their lives had been snatched away. There was little sleep that night and, if men's prayers could propel a ship, then it would surely arrive. Selby occupied himself in trying to convince Father Harris into coming with them lest the Japanese carry out their threat of reprisal against those assisting Australian troops. Father Harris simply smiled and said: 'I must stay and look after my children.'[33]

Pte Billy Cook had been hoping for a navy destroyer but the ship that arrived in April in no way resembled a destroyer or any 'ship' he had imagined. Instead, the 150-ton small schooner *Laurabada* berthed at the mission wharf. It made little difference because 'it meant our freedom, it looked like the *Queen Mary*.'[34] *Laurabada* was not intended to carry 156 passengers but no one was being left behind and men occupied any space they could find. Pte Billy Cook was one of the first to climb onboard, followed by Gnr David Bloomfield and his CO Lt Selby.

Gnr Gordon Abel arrived at Palmalmal in a canoe to find *Laurabada* due to sail. He was so weak that he had to be lifted onboard. Abel was assigned six feet (1.8m) of deck space and some 'heavenly soup' – it was 9 April 1942 and his 19th birthday.[35] *Laurabada* was captained by Lt Ivan Champion (RANVR). Champion, who was born in Port Moresby, had been the Assistant Magistrate of New Guinea's Misima Island and his knowledge of the region and its waters gave confidence to the 131 officers and troops, 21 civilians and four members of the RAN who

The overcrowded boat Laurabada. AWM

overloaded the boat. Into rough seas the boat heaved and rocked and
threatened to sink, but those within would have bailed out and paddled
the whole trip if necessary.

While Abel was fortunate to catch the *Laurabada*, Pte William
James 'Bill' Neave (VX24188) arrived too late. On 8 June 1940, Neave
had enlisted in the 2/22nd with his mates George Duncan Coates
(VX24162) and Wilfrid Lancelot 'Lance' Howlett (VX24179), who had
worked together on the Victorian pastoral station, Dergholm. They
had almost been caught by the Japanese at Gasmata. In the ensuing
escape attempt, Howlett was taken prisoner and he died on 1 July 1942.
By the time Neave and Coates reached the village of Tui, 'we were like
skeletons, with beards and long hair and dressed in laplaps.'[36]

Their bodies were consumed by malaria and Neave could go no
further. The villagers allowed Neave and Coates to shelter there for two
weeks, or was it three? Neave watched his mate George Coates die on
26 March 1942. Neave's 5 foot 4 inch (1.62m) frame was wasted to half

his normal weight, to five-and-a-half stone (35kg). He was saved by a fellow soldier arriving with a dose of quinine. A message came from Father Ted Harris that an evacuation was to be made from Jacquinot Bay about 30 miles (48km) away. It them took enormous willpower and four days; they arrived only to hear Father Harris say 'I'm sorry to have to tell you ... the ship has gone and won't be coming back.'[37]

It was again the NGVR's Dave Laws who came to the rescue. Finding Neave and several others, he contacted Port Moresby requesting urgent assistance. None came because Moresby was now under attack. Laws found an 18-foot (5m) boat and a drum of fuel hidden. Unfortunately, the engine was seized. For weeks Law, an excellent mechanic, worked with Neave and others who scrounged and worked with anything they could find. Finally, the boat was running and the party put to sea. For 183 days Neave had 'slogged hundreds of miles through the almost impenetrable jungles and mountains, gorges and rivers.'[38] Now he was stuck in a cramped, barely seaworthy boat with a temperamental engine, little food and water, a dodgy compass and 16 others pushing through 'mountainous' waves 'as high as a house' or drifting miles off course when the engine gave out. 'I was scared. Anyone who says he was not scared is not telling the truth.'[39] Laws wasn't feeling confident either; he might have been a good radio operator and mechanic, but a navigator he wasn't, and the strong south-easterly monsoon was blowing hard.

Neave suffered another bout of malaria and became comatose. His shipmates thought he was dead and were about to throw him overboard when one noticed he was still breathing. Their food supply consisted of coconuts, which went bad. It was six days and nights at sea before they saw lights and land, but the current carried them away as they attempted to land. They despaired. They thought they were at Buna but the winds, currents and Law's wayward navigation meant they were off course by around 200 miles (322km). They were probably off Salamaua or Lae, and both townships were enemy occupied. The next day, they landed at Sio on the Huon Peninsula – on a coral reef half a mile (1km) from the shore from which natives rescued them. The party had half a gallon (2L) of petrol left, no food and no water. Fortunately, they found food in a deserted homestead. Again Law contacted Port Moresby, requesting an urgent air drop of food, medical supplies and petrol. 'They didn't send any food or medical supplies but they dropped some petrol from a plane', said Neave. 'It was aviation petrol – no good for our boat!'[40]

The party set off by boat for Bogadjim, south of Madang, where they hoped they would be picked up and taken overland to Port Moresby. On the way, one spark plug after another broke because of the aviation fuel. Eventually they drifted ashore where, fortunately, they were found by a Coastwatcher who took them to Bogadjim. Neave and his group were spent and with a missionary's care they rested for weeks to regain enough strength for the long walk inland across the Ramu Valley. From Bogadjim, over the Finisterre Ranges and through the Ramu Valley to Bena Bena in central New Guinea – a repetition of their terrible trek through New Britain. By Bena Bena, their number was 13 but they took heart in the care given to them by a warlike tribe with bones through their noses: 'they were really good to us – better than a lot of the more civilized blokes.'[41] His opinion was firmed when an aircraft arrived to rescue six American airmen who had made a forced landing. 'But they wouldn't pick us up.'[42] The Australians were given boots and some supplies and told that 'if we wanted to get to Port Moresby we would have to walk to Wau – about 200 miles [322km] away over the Finisterre Ranges.'[43] It took them three weeks to finish the mountainous trek to Wau from where they were finally flown to Port Moresby.

On his return to Australia on 27 March 1942, Pte Bill Neave found that his army record showed he was 'derelict' in the jungle for 183 days.

Haunted Lark Force. AWM

An emaciated Lt David Selby being interviewed. AWM

After hospitalization for malaria, Neave joined the 2/4 Battalion and fought again in New Guinea. Lt David Andrew Laws (P479) ANGAU returned to the New Guinea jungles as a member of M Special Unit and was killed in action on 5 May 1943. Father Ted Harris was taken by the Japanese from his mission and executed at sea. His body was dumped overboard and eventually washed ashore. The invaders did not permit the natives to bury him. Father William Culhane was also executed by the Japanese.

Having left on 9 April, Laurabada entered the China Straits and pushed up along the Papuan coast. At Port Moresby, a long line of ambulances waited and, as the escapees disembarked on 12 April, onlookers threw packets of cigarettes. It was not until then that they considered the state of their clothes. Moyle recalled:

'Most had no pants just native loin clothes and those who possessed shirts were lucky.'[44] Their appearance was startling for authorities and while the officers were interviewed, the troops were medically examined, fed and given fresh clothes.

It was with mutually agreed haste that *Lark Force* survivors were loaded on the *Macdhui* for a comfortable and rapid trip home.

Awaiting Lt Selby was a war correspondent, eager to learn of adventure. Selby doubted he could tell the story honestly. Asked what inspired him to continue, 'I showed him the brownish smears which were all that was left of the portraits in my wallet ... my wife and child.'[45] As Selby slipped between clean white sheets that night, his thoughts were tinged with sorrow and joy. Tomorrow his wife would learn he was alive but there was sorrow for those 'fin young men of my battery [who] had been misled.'[46]

Endnotes

1. Abel, G. MSS1623.
2. Ibid.
3. Ibid.
4. Taylor, A.G. MSS1533.
5. Ibid.
6. Ibid.
7. Ibid.
8. australiansatwarfilmar hive.unsw.edu. au/archive/1778-david-bloomfield
9. Ibid.
10. Bloomfield, D. *Rabaul Diary*, p.48.
11. Ibid., p.37.
12. Ibid., p.46.
13. Ibid., p.49.
14. Ibid.
15. Ibid., p.52.
16. Dawes, J. *Every man for himself: the life of Father Edward Charles Harris MSC*, The Catholic Newspaper Company, Sydney, 1945.
17. Cook, *Medical Soldiers*, p.114.
18. Ibid., p.108.
19. Ibid., p.112.
20. Selby, *Hell and High Fever*, p.87.
21. Ibid.
22. Ibid., p.100.
23. Ibid., p.101.
24. Ibid., p.140.
25. Ibid., p.111.
26. Ibid., p.149.
27. Moyle, *Escape from Rabaul*, p.25.
28. New Ireland Administrators, J. McDonald and M. Jones; T. Thomas, the New Ireland radio operator; Harry Murray, Kavieng storekeeper and plantation owners, H. Waters, B. Farthing and J. McLean and S. Warrant and L. Dean.
29. Apart from Moyle, McInnes, Ballantyne, McVean and Aplin, the 2/22nd contingent included Sgt Deric Hawthorne Pitts (VX29262), Pte Herbert Graeme Parsons (VX29259) and L/Cpl Norman John Burgell (VX46453).
30. Moyle, Escape from Rabaul, p.43.
31. Selby, Hell and High Fever, p.152.
32. Ibid., p.186.
33. Ibid., p.191.
34. Cook, Medical Soldiers, p.115.
35. Abel, G. MSS1623
36. Coleman, R. 'When home was a trip through hell', in *Una Voce, Journal of the Papua New Guinea Association of Australia*, No.4, December 2014, pp.53–54.
37. Ibid.
38. Ibid.
39. Ibid.
40. Ibid.
41. Ibid.
42. Ibid.
43. Ibid.
44. Cook, Medical Soldiers, p.118.
45. Selby, *Hell and High Fever*, p.196.
46. Ibid.

CHAPTER THIRTEEN

PRISONERS-OF-WAR

*'Why was no real organisation made
for the civilian population?'*

Kenneth Ryall

Civilians who chose to remain in New Britain did so for a variety of reasons. Administrative staff were reluctant to leave their posts because their Australian superiors, in their wisdom, had neither given permission nor organized evacuation. Some residents believed that the plantations they and their families had hewed from the jungle could be saved and that they had a responsibility to the indigenous families who depended on the plantations for survival. Older citizens knew the terrain well and realized they were beyond the hardships of any escape route. As with the Australian military, some may have underestimated the enemy, believing that the invaders might be benevolent – even grateful – for plantation production. None could have realized the total contempt held for any non-Japanese by the invaders, or their brutal nature. Australian civilian administration ended in New Britain on 23 January 1942 and ceased in Papua on 14 February. A harsh reality faced those who remained in occupied New Britain and surrounding islands. Over the ensuing years, they were subjected to inhuman treatment and most died.

In Rabaul, civilians had withdrawn to 'Refuge Gully' off Namanula Road. Along with plantation owner Kenneth William Ryall, they were left to lament 'Why was no real organisation made for the civilian population?'[1] Although the gully shelters were well roofed and clean with adequate food, cooking appliances and bedding, their homes had been mosquito-proofed and now the lack of netting caused discomfort. Nonetheless, mosquitoes were soon the least of their distress. They had no way of knowing how the battle had proceeded and there was nothing they could do as gunfire intensified on 23 and 24 January and explosions reverberated around the gully.

Prior to his retreat, Deputy Administrator Harold Page had appointed architect and civil engineer Robert Leeuwin 'Nobby' Clark, a member of the Legislative Council and

Gordon Thomas in pre-war Rabaul. Rabaul Historical Society

President of the Returned Service League (RSL), as Chief Civil Warden. Clark, a WWI Australian Flying Corps officer and long-time Rabaul resident, was immediately concerned as aircraft overhead, emblazoned with the rising sun, indiscriminately raked hillsides and gullies with machine-gun fire. A morning of relative calm saw Clark bravely walk into Rabaul, carrying a white flag to surrender those sheltering in Refuge Gully. He was accompanied by the senior government officer present, Hector E. Robinson, and Gordon Thomas, editor of the *Rabaul Times*. Thomas was another with first-hand experience of war. As a member of the AIF 19th Battalion in WWI, he had been gassed and wounded, and had been a POW. History was repeating itself. As the three men walked tentatively into town, they were dismayed at the

The Japanese build-up was remarkably rapid. Marching through Rabaul streets, LEFT, *and Zero fighters on the airfield,* RIGHT. NGVR Museum

destruction to the proud and beautiful Rabaul. The roof of Anzac House had collapsed and the windows shattered. Malaguna Avenue was now full of craters and the once-beautiful canopy of trees were grotesque in their destruction, giant roots now protruding from the mud.[2] Small, dishevelled soldiers moved swiftly from building to building, looting shops and once-majestic homes at will, wantonly destroying and strewing personal belongings throughout the streets.

Thousands of books from the Agnes Wisdom library and government offices were placed in a pile and set alight.[3]

It was surreal as the men walked down the road; initially ignored by the invaders, they were soon surrounded and jostled. Thomas was hit on the arm with a rifle and the three were stripped of their watches and other valuables. Ordered to carry soldier packs, they drew level with the New Guinea Club, where just days before they had drunk with a jovial crowd. Now from the flagpole flew a Japanese naval ensign. The Australians were left under guard to stand in the sun and contemplate this bitter change of circumstances.

Japanese soldiers arrived at Refuge Gully. They were abusive as they pushed and shoved residents to the baseball field. Armed guards were posted and Gordon Thomas reported that civilians were 'subjected to many indignities and insults'[4] as they were then herded into Kuomintang Hall in Chinatown. Thomas wrote:

> *Tens of thousands of Nip soldiers were spoiling and moiling*
> *the town; entering our houses, ransacking our wardrobes,*

*destroying our little household goods, our books and papers;
and gloating over our women-folk with their slotty-sexy eyes,
mentally raping them.*[5]

In one room, a small party of *Lark Force* prisoners were kept apart from the civilians.

The following day, trucks arrived and civilian men were taken to the wharves to unload the contents of an ever-increasing convoy of Japanese transports – a routine followed as more and more civilians and soldiers were brought in from outlying areas. The Japanese build-up of Rabaul was rapid and extensive, with an estimated 100,000 Japanese troops and thousands of Chinese and Indians brought to Rabaul as slave labour. Rabaul was divided into two separate sections, military and naval, as the town soon doubled in size with hastily erected buildings. Hundreds of auxiliary ships arrived, carrying troops and supplies, and Japanese nurses and secretaries. For a further 3,000 Asian women, Rabaul was a bleak destination. Transported in as 'comfort women', they were placed into brothels for Japanese troops.

As the freedoms and quality of life for New Britain's Europeans diminished, so too did those of other residents. The Australian Government had evacuated most European women and children,

The popular Rabaul hotel established by Chin Ah Chee. www.chm.com.pg

but had done nothing for Asian, mixed race and indigenous families. Rabaul, and the wider New Britain area, had been home to them for generations but they had been treated with disregard by Australian bureaucracy regardless of their initiative, industry and loyalty. The large Chinese community was left to fend for itself against an enemy that had proven ruthless since their invasion of China in 1937.

Chin Ah Chee's family migrated from Hannan, China, and, in keeping with Hannan custom, Chin Ah Chee had entered the hotel and restaurant business by establishing the Ah Chee Hotel on Casuarina Avenue. The hotel soon became an institution within the growing capital of New Britain and the family prospered. A main street was named in his honour.[6] With Ah Chee's premature death, his son Chin Hoi Meen commenced work at age 16. After some low-paid positions, the teenage Chin Hoi Meen secured employment as a clerk and weather observer with the Department of Agriculture. Aged 19, in 1936 he married June Lan Wan. With the escalation of the Australian military presence in New Britain, Chinese residents were willing to enlist but, because they were not British citizens, enlistment in the Australian Army or NGVR was not permitted. In 1941, Chin Hoi Meen joined in the only capacity allowed – the ambulance detachment of the NGVR. Immiediately after the invasion, members provided first aid to wounded Australian soldiers but were then instructed to discard their uniforms and seek safety for their families.

During January 1942, most Chinese set up bush camps outside Rabaul and elsewhere in the Gazelle Peninsula. Chu Leong decided to go up river but, before doing so, he 'had sawn his trading vessel in half so that it could not be of any use to the invaders.'[7] To discourage dissent, the Japanese

Chin Hoi Meen being awarded the King's Medal. www.chm.com.pg

beheaded 10 Chinese residents and 'leaders of the Rabaul Chinese community were subsequently shot in cold blood near the Wunawutung Hotel on the north coast of Rabaul.'[8] While their non-interventionist policy saved them from wholesale massacre, the Chinese population suffered badly under the Japanese regime and many perished from disease and ill treatment.

Chin Hoi Meen had sent his wife, then pregnant with their second child, and three-year-old son Larry to Adler Bay with other fleeing families, while he remained in Rabaul.

Taken captive, he was made to unload ships and dig waterholes.'[9]

Chin Hoi Meen applied for permission to go to Sum Sum plantation at Adler Bay, 70 miles (113km) from Rabaul, to join his wife and family. Permits were issued for him and two friends to proceed through the various checkpoints from Rabaul to the Warangoi River. One of the men drowned trying to cross the river but Chin Hoi Meen was determined to continue, and four days later he walked into the plantation only to find Japanese soldiers camped there. Chinese families had been living 'with the daily fear of knowing that they could be killed any time.'[10] From 1943 Allied aircraft attacks increased, making the situation even more dangerous, particularly when Allied pilots failed to determine Chinese from Japanese.

Leo Kam On. Downs

In 1943 two New Guineans crept into Chin Hoi Meen's house and gave him a note from a Coastwatcher, requesting his assistance in providing vital information on Japanese forces in New Britain. Chin Hoi Meen agreed and commenced years of obtaining intelligence and sketching maps of Japanese troop positions, ammunition dumps and fortifications – information that proved vital to Allied Command. Due to his fast thinking, two American airmen shot down in New Britain were brought to safety and collected by an Allied submarine.

By 1944, the Japanese imposed greater restrictions on the Chinese community and they were taken to a prison camp near Kokopo. Chin Hoi Meen and his family survived the war and, in 1949, he was awarded

Vunapope Mission complex south of Rabaul. Bowman

the King's Medal for courage and service in the cause of freedom. In Australia during 1954, Chin Hoi Meen was presented to the Queen as a war hero.

It took a special man, who was abandoned by the government and the powers that be to risk his and his family's lives by helping Australians fight the apanese.[11]

Leo Kam On was another who saw active service as a member of the ambulance detachment and helped with surgery on wounded Australian troops. He, too, became involved in coastwatching activities to assist in the Allied re-occupation of New Britain.

Years of Australian Commonwealth paternalism within the territory, and their predominantly peaceful nature, had left the indigenous people particularly ill prepared for the invasion. They were subjected to terrible deprivation and crimes. Wagirama of Masini had been employed at the Roman Catholic mission at Malagunan. He was now placed in the Rabaul jail and sent to work on airfield extensions at Lakunai: 'I was not paid, poorly fed and not allowed to wash.'[12]

Aposa of Bumbuk, Warisi, had been a very good student at the Roman Catholic school at Taliligap. He and others were whipped and jailed for taking food from the native garden to give to priests. He was then sent to work in Ah Song's store, which had been converted into a Japanese eating house. Chinese girls were made to work as waitresses there, though he was not sure if they had been used also as 'harlots'.[13]

Another indigenous statement indicated the degree of confusion and grief felt:

> When the fighting came the white people went and the sisters were taken by the Japanese and some white men too. And our land was confused by ways of the Japanese and some of the war came to us in our district ... they tore our books and they stole our clothes and our little bit of money.[14]

Villagers were cruelly tied and led with vines 'on the way like horses' for days, the vines cutting 'very hard on our arms.'[15] Placed on barges, they were taken to Rabaul and the men were thrown into prison. The women vanished into soldier quarters.

> Our enemy lectured us strongly about the work that we would do and our stance in front of the officer ... some of us cut the grass of the compound and some dug pits and some cut kunai for houses and some chopped wood and some drew water and some filled drums and some mixed cement. There was no rest from hurt and it was a state of confusion and our state of fear of the airplanes and the food we ate was not good food as it was like food for the pigs. The beatings were not to my way of think [sic].[16]

Throughout New Britain, beleaguered communities grasped to life any way they could.

Vunapope was the headquarters of the Sacred Heart Mission, which extended over New Britain, New Ireland and Manus Island, with 60 priests attending the spiritual needs of an estimated 60,000 Catholics.[17] Vunapope was a substantial complex with numerous institutions, workshops, hospitals, the seminary and a teacher-training college. It boasted its own printing and bookbinding department, which provided books in 32 different languages. A cathedral dominated the enclave, which included a generous residence for Bishop Leo Scharmach. The three-storey building housed five priests, 35 brothers and the convents for three sisterhoods and 45 native sisters.

Those who lived at and had taken refuge in Vunapope could do little but wait as gunfire came closer and closer – they didn't know what to expect. As Japanese soldiers arrived, native labourers were shot. Bishop Scharmach's first impression, when confronted, was that the enemy 'were rather small. Their uniforms looked strange to us and their military caps funny.'[18] The bishop was a proud, resourceful and confident man, his natural arrogance reinforced by his strong faith.

Bishop Leo Scharmach. Scharmach

As prisoners of the Japanese, provided we remained obedient and did not meddle in military matters, our lives and property would be guaranteed.[19]

But 'meddling' and the sanctity of life were often in conflict, particularly when the jailers demonstrated a blatant disregard for the latter. An AIF officer was tied to a tree in front of the bishop's house, tortured and butchered. Priests were killed for the slightest suspicion of administering aid to *Lark Force* troops or intervening in the abuse and killing of parishioners. Scharmach struggled with 'the Japanese treatment of prisoners, their disregard of human life and their ruthless confiscation of our property.'[20] It remained a balancing act with an erratic jailer.

One of the bishop's biggest challenges was the safety of the nuns and sisters in his charge. Sister M. Berenice of Our Lady of the Sacred Heart Convent was housed with a group of sisters in one of the mission

Vunapope sisters with students. Bowman

buildings. They were not allowed to have any contact with the people from any other building. Sister Bernice was the eighth of 11 children born at Tumbulgum, near Murwillumbah, Queensland. She attended boarding school in the Tweed Valley near Mount Warning and was posted to New Britain as a teacher.[21]

> *At first the Japanese were menacing. At night they would come knocking on our door. Of course we never opened it but they would go around and around outside ... It was terrible until the Bishop really got control. Every day we were searched, we were called to order and counted. And we were warned: Never let a Japanese soldier find you alone.*[22]

The nuns were anxious for the safety of the indigenous sisters, their students and parishioners but also for the flood of Australian soldiers, injured and sick, who had arrived at the Vunapope hospital. Sister Bernice believed that the *Lark Force* garrison had been abandoned and sacrificed by their government.

It was too late to do anything to save Rabaul, they said let's
forget about it, it never happened. So they sacrificed over a
thousand men ... that is the hurtful truth.[23]

Just prior to the invasion, the bishop and his staff had been given permission by the manager of Burns Philp and Carters, who had sought refuge at the mission, to salvage the company's stores. 'The Bishop had told us to take anything of value, any clothing, anything else, and to put it away.'[24] Trying to keep the stores hidden in various caches in and around the mission was a challenge. The nuns were constantly lined up, taunted, attempts made to tear their veils off and searched. There was a particular room in which the nuns had hidden food. Every time the Japanese attempted to enter this room, the nuns shouted: '"Malaria in there. Malaria!" ... [Because] we knew the Japanese were terrified of malaria and of TB.'[25] Those supplies lasted around six months.

The Australian Army and civilian nursing sisters had been left at the mission with the wounded in the charge of Australian Army Padre John May, when Australian army medical staff attempted their escape from New Britain. Their safety following the invasion was extremely precarious. After the end of the war, this was described in the following manner:

At the time they were dumbfounded and shocked at their
abandonment by the doctors, and the bitterness at being left
in such a hopeless situation has not been erased by subsequent
knowledge of the doctors' activities in the field [26]

Now small figures in khaki scurried towards the hospital, their netted helmets heavily camouflaged with twigs and leaves. They entered the hospital with an air of arrogance and 'jabbered shrilly and proceeded to make themselves objectionable', related Sister Alice Bowman. Padre May and Australian Army Nursing Senior Sister, Lt Kay Parker, surrendered the hospital and 100 patients. All were immediately intimidated. The army sisters were told that, because there were no doctors present, they could not be nurses. Lt Daisy 'Tootie' Keast described how they were

Slapping Australian Army nurses required standing on a stool but became a regular sport. Bowman

then told that 'we were for the use of the troops.' Machine guns were poked into their bodies and 'we had to stand there with our arms up surrendering for an eternity.'[27] Patients were pushed, screamed at and their food eaten by the enemy soldiers, who shoved nurses away when they attempted to resume medical treatment. Keast was given a 'most fearful whack and I was knocked down and got a few kicks because I didn't bow deep enough.'[28] The Japanese continued to assault and rampage, and as soon as they concerned themselves more with plunder than prisoners, the nursing staff did what they could to make patients more comfortable before returning to their own quarters. Their stretchers were smashed and their bedding was torn and thrown aside. Food tins were 'strewn everywhere and the contents trampled into the sheets.'[29] The few prized possessions, mostly of sentimental value, that the nurses had been allowed to bring with them were either stolen or smashed. With glum expressions they regarded each other and one said softly, 'we are prisoners of war now.'[30] Lt Kay Parker had stood defiantly in front of the sisters. Her determined look and her exceptional height of six feet (1.8m) antagonized the enemy.

One stood on a stool to look Parker earnestly in the face. This became a regular ritual, except in future it was accompanied by a slap.

Each day brought its own challenges, as the nurses struggled to maintain their dignity and safety, and that of their patients. Keast described how:

Many's the time they chased us trying to urinate on us while the rest of them just stayed back and screamed with laughter. It was nothing for them to take their trousers off.[31]

Lt Daisy Keast, left, and Lt Marjory 'Jean' Anderson, right

Lt Kay Parker, left, and Lt Mavis Cullen, right. AWM

When their fear heightened, they slept in the hospital ward under the beds of patients. The troops were in no condition to come to the aid of the nurses but it was a comfort to be in the company of male Australians. Lt Mavis Cullen was also comforted by the 'last resort' – if things 'got too bad and we felt we couldn't cope', they each intended to self-administer the 'tube of morphine in our uniform pocket.'[32]

The nurses felt helpless as patients were dragged away and not seen again – one day every it was fifth patient, another day 'twenty of the patients were taken away, executed and buried in a mass grave.'[33] On another occasion, the nurses were pulled out to see patients tied and standing over their own graves. Civilian nurse Alice Bowman wrote: 'Our days now became filled with the plodding of army boots and gravel paths and the unnecessary bellow of "Tenko".'[34] As they mustered to be counted and re-counted, 'accompanied by grunts in an effort to make an impact – presumably to back up their lack of stature' and with 'fired bayonets swinging dangerously about', the nurses tried to balance determination with subservience. Any sign of resentment resulted in a

While there was comparative safety when the nurses moved into the convent food, became scarcer. Sister Alice Bowman called this sketch 'Dinner arrives'.
Bowman

beating but they were determined not to show weakness or cry in front of the enemy.[35]

Relief came when they were moved into the convent with the nuns and, to their surprise, joined by Methodist missionary nurses Mavis Green, Dora Wilson, Jean Christopher and Dorothy Beale, Dorothy Maye from Kavieng, as well as Rabaul plantation owner Mrs Kathleen Bignell. The women named their quarters 'Australia House'. There was strength in numbers should an enemy soldier attempt to molest them. Food became scarcer and scarcer but there was reasonable stability over the next couple of months, according to Sister Bowman — but a stability that 'lulled us into a false sense of security.'[36]

The nurses were dismayed and powerless as the remaining patients were pushed into trucks and taken north to a POW camp in Rabaul. Within days, the non-convent women were ordered to pack and told they would need little, as they were being taken to 'Paradise'. This

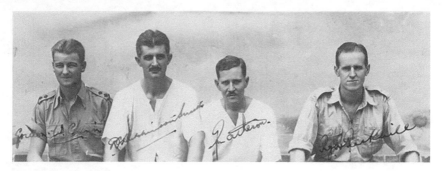

Lark Force *17 Anti-tank Battery officers now POW. Left to right: Lt Gordon Chinn, Capt David Hutchinson-Smith, Maj Gwynne Matheson and Lt Robert Parkhill.* AWM

sounded ominous and the nuns were distressed as they watched their Australian companions being driven away.

In March 1942, Capt David Hutchinson-Smith struggled with his new reality. As an officer he had been spared death, while *Lark Force* troops had been ruthlessly bayoneted.

Taken by launch back to Rabaul, he was ushered none too gently into the presence of a diminutive unshaven Japanese officer 'clad only in riding breeches, with a small cloth peak cap on the back of his cropped head.'[37] It was laughable that this Japanese officer accused the Australians of 'Outraging the terms of international law in relation to the waging of the war.'[38] Hutchinson-Smith was asked 'if he wished to die.'[39] Hutchinson-Smith was unaware that, on 27 January 1942, Maj Richard Erskine Travers (VX44162) had been similarly interrogated as to the whereabouts of the CO of *Lark Force*. Travers did not divulge the information, probably because he had no real idea of where Col Scanlan had retreated. Travers was executed.

Hutchinson-Smith was fortunate. After a great deal of shouting and intimidation, he was informed that he was now a prisoner-of-war (POW). As he was pushed further into the occupied town, he observed the might of the invading force. In the harbour there was a huge concentration of ships: destroyers, cruisers, tankers, transports, repair ships and submarine mother ships with 'their ugly, black brood' of midget submarines.[40] The skies were full of Zero fighters. Japanese officers 'complete with magnificent swords, white gloves and acres of service and other ribbons' strolled about Rabaul.[41] How had it come to this?

When the number of civilian and military POWs became too large for the Kuomintang Hall, they were moved to the Malaguna Road army camp, yet another ironic twist. Each day they continued to be trucked out on work details. Each day was worse than the last, as more *Lark Force* troops succumbed to malnutrition and disease, or were taken away never to return. AA Gnr Ormond Merton Gilmore Preece (NX191467), 18, died on 6 March. Fellow Gnr William Charles Shields (VX32338), 42, died on 25 March. L/Cpl Bernard Edward Luggate Cox (VX13226)

had served with 2nd Pioneer Battalion in WWI. He died of illness aged 45 in Rabaul on 27 March. AA Gnr Maurice Ogilvie (NX191452), 19, died of illness on 29 March 1942. Pte Alan Leslie Hutchins (VX41293), 24, died of illness on 31 March 1942. Bdr Lloyd Prossier Cockerill-Smith (SX11452), 28, died on 19 April. Pte Ernest James Stevenson (VX24013), 21, died on 1 May. In May 1942, the Japanese collated nominal rolls of all the POWs as jurisdiction changed from the Japanese army to the Japanese navy. At this time, POWs were allowed to write letters home. The brief and highly censored letters were loaded into mailbags, which were dropped in an early raid on Port Moresby airfield. It proved to be another cruel blow for relatives, providing hope that

Thirty-two-year-old Pte Eric George Oxnam (VX34445), left, died on 30 April and 2/22nd and former Salvation Army Bandsman, 21-year-old Pte Frederick John 'Peter' Meyer (VX37940), right, died on 27 April 1942.

their son, husband or father was cared for and likely to return home as soon as the Allies liberated Rabaul.

Western Australia's Alice Dennis was heartened to receive a letter from her son L/Cpl William Eric Rule Dennis (WX8167) of 1 Independent Company:

I am a prisoner of war and am being held at Rabaul under the Japanese. I am quite well, and the Japanese are treating us very well. I will write every opportunity and will be looking forward to receiving mail. Will you let Daphne know at once please and send her my love. There is no need to worry, we are being well looked after, Love to all Eric.[42]

But they were not being treated at all well, deprived of food, medical supplies and freedom, and used as forced labour.

News that Rabaul had been attacked featured prominently in media headlines and the Australian Government acted predictably, with a statement intended to settle panic but lacking truth. A Western Australian headline declared 'Enemy at Rabaul' but assured readers that the Australian War Cabinet statement 'did not mention any sign of fighting.'[43] Deputy Prime Minister and Minister for the Army, Francis 'Frank' Forde, announced that, while it was known Japan had landed forces, this 'did not suggest that a battle was in progress', and he assured the Australian people that 'every possible step was being taken to safeguard Australian lives and property.'[44] On 29 January 1942, Sydney newspaper The Sun reported military sources as stating: 'The armed forces defending Rabaul would be able to hold out for several weeks'; that the very terrain of New Britain lent itself to the advantage of Australian defenders.[45]

The initial burst of news was followed by a total news blackout. Concerned families besieged their parliamentary representatives and, on 6 February 1942, Frank Forde felt it necessary to warn Prime Minister John Curtin:

The attitudes of those with near relatives in our Garrison at

Rabaul is becoming bitter and hostile at the lack of news of their sons, brothers and husbands, and of the feeling that is being created that although something could be done to assist them, nothing is being attempted.[46]

But nothing could be done, the Australian Government had long lost the initiative and, through procrastination and inertia and deference to other powers, the fate of those who remained in New Britain was grim. The discomfiture deteriorated further as the trickle of escapees became a flood and the suppression of their stories and the truth more difficult.

Having rendezvoused with the Laurabada to offload the necessary supplies for that boat to continue to Port Moresby, the Lakatoi, under

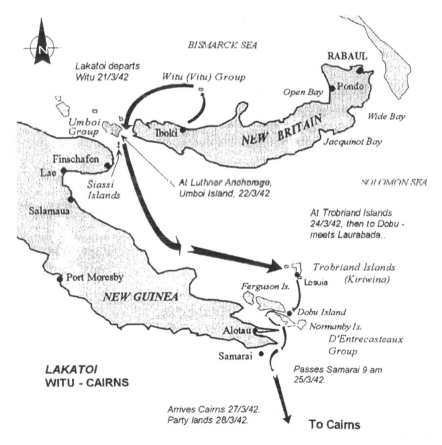

The voyage of Lakatoi 21–27 March 1942. Stone/Holland

Capt H. Coe, with 214 AIF, NGVR, civilians, native police, European police, native crew, the indomitable Keith McCarthy, Frank Holland and Gladys Baker onboard, continued south towards Australia. The voyage was daring and treacherous but, when given the option of going to Port Moresby or voyaging south, the decision was unanimous. Orders from military headquarters mattered not, they just wanted to put as many sea miles between them and New Guinea as they could – they just wanted to go home. They sailed at night and pulled in close to shore during the day, camouflaging the boat with palm fronds.

It took six days but the Australian mainland was the most wonderful sight imaginable. As Cairns appeared on the horizon, the most hardened warrior cried with relief. Smiles spread across haggard faces and some broke into song, but it seemed that authorities were neither prepared for nor overjoyed by their arrival, and the Lakatoi was ordered to remain off the coast. Frank Holland wrote in his diary:

27 March 1942. Can see the mainland of Australia and about 3pm we drop anchor outside of Cairns and wait for the pilot to come out to take us in ... 28 March 1942 still waiting for the pilot, and saw him coming about 10am.[47]

Why the delay? It was just one more frustration for people who had suffered too many. Troops onboard were ordered to shave their beards and to throw their few possessions overboard. Invariably, this consisted of a copra sack containing a bowl made out of a half coconut shell, a prized book, half a blanket and perhaps a bush knife. The men were ordered to line up and were examined by a doctor. It seemed that the authorities were more worried about the nation's quarantine than the ragged, bearded scarecrows who wished to place their feet on home soil; after their ordeal, they were left to languish for more than 18 hours on a barely seaworthy and highly unsanitary boat.

Military authorities had been in conversation with the Mayor of Cairns but the wheels turned slowly. The mayor contacted the Very Rev T. Hunt, Vicar of the Diocese of Cairns, who agreed to offer a school as accommodation. The escapees were expected to sleep on the floor.

When Rev Hunt discovered the condition of the men, he was greatly embarrassed and expressed the opinion that the best hotel in town should have been given over for the men.[48] It was only when the Red Cross arrived that the arrivals were lavished with food and clothing. As news spread, Cairns residents arrived to do what they could. Once ashore telegrams were dispatched to their families, who had no idea the troops were safely in Australia.

Sgt Bert Smith welcomed home by his wife, Liliane Smith, and his mother, Margaret Smith. AWM

The military authorities struggled to adapt and cope. One soldier was told that, according to his army record, he was guilty of dereliction of duty. Another received a bill for his lost uniform. Tol plantation survivor Pte Billy Cook went ashore with fellow Field Ambulance member Pte Jack Holah. Jack was allowed to draw a small amount of money through his army pay book. Billy Cook tried to explain that his pay book had been taken by the Japanese: 'Billy Cook was not allowed any money ... if you don't have a pay book, you don't get any money!'[49] In less than two weeks, Gnr Gordon Abel was to turn 19. He had left Australia as an optimistic and robust 17-year-old, and was now a frail and disillusioned man. He sent a telegram to his brother: 'Arrived Cairns yesterday, broke please wire fiver, love Gordon'.[50] It was not until he arrived in Sydney that he was given clothes to replace his hospital pyjamas; he was also handed a bill 'for lost rifles and other gear.'[51]

> *I was so hurt by this action I swore that I would not talk to another officer ... and I never did.*[52]

Finally, a special train arrived to take the troops south for reunions with their grateful families.

At a brief early-morning stopover at Albury, Pte Jack Moyle was delighted to be greeted by his parents, Jack and Mary, before continuing on to Victoria and respite at Heidelberg Hospital. He was desperate to return to Tallangatta and the family farm – it had been 16 months. George Cardwell and Jack Sutherland were there ahead of him, they too with escape stories: 'we had a long talk about our mostly bad experiences of the Rabaul disaster.'[53] For most of the 323 *Lark Force* troops who had escaped, the immediate future meant months in hospital and rehabilitation centres.

Initially, the media approached the story in a triumphant propaganda tone. *The Sydney Morning Herald* of 7 April 1942 and its article 'THE STORY OF RABAUL' featured glowing prose.

At last the veil has been lifted on the sombre but splendid story of Rabaul. It is a story to fill Australia with sadness and pride – sadness for the men who fell facing 'fearful odds', and pride in the courage and endurance of this garrison of young Australians who stood undaunted against an overwhelming Japanese invasion force, strongly supported by warships and aircraft. Their country, alas! asked the impossible of them, but they did not flinch from the ordeal or dream of surrender. Their job was to hold, as long as it could be held, what they knew to be the bulwark of their homeland, and to inflict the maximum of damage on the Invaders. This job they did superlatively well.[54]

But it became increasingly obvious to the Australian people that, while the 'STORY OF RABAUL' was one of the bravery of soldiers such as Sgt Bert Smith, the story of *Lark Force* and the occupation of Rabaul was one of the grimmest chapters in their nation's history. Furthermore, on 1 July 1942, the story would conclude with the worst maritime disaster in Australia's history.

Endnotes

1. A5954 532/1, National Archives, Canberra.
2. Bowman, A. p.36.
3. Wigmore, p.678.
4. Downs, p.67.
5. Thomas, G. 'Rabaul 1942–45', manuscript, Pacific Manuscripts Bureau microfilm 36, p.18.
6. www.chm.com.pg
7. Noble, R. 'Chu Leong' in *Una Voce*, No.3, September 2014, p.53.
8. www.chm.com.pg
9. Ibid.
10. Ibid.
11. Ibid.
12. Testimonies held by NGVR Museum, Brisbane.
13. Ibid.
14. MSS1968 *Ure Kaveve Kini ta ra pal na banubat aro Rabaul – About our stay in the prison in Rabaul (during the war)*, AWM, Canberra.
15. Ibid.
16. Ibid.
17. Scharmach, L. *This Crowd Beats Us All*, Catholic Press, 1960, p.3.
18. Ibid., p.6.
19. Ibid., p.21.
20. Ibid., p.22.
21. www.angellpro.com.au/mission.htm
22. Ibid.
23. Ibid.
24. Ibid.
25. Ibid.
26. Kenny, C. *Captives: Australian Army Nurses in Japanese Prison Camps*, University of Q, 1986, p.27.
27. Nelson, H. *Prisoners of War: Australians under Nippon*, ABC books, 1985, p.77.
28. Ibid.
29. Bowman, p.53.
30. Nelson, p.77.
31. Ibid.
32. Ibid.
33. Ibid., p.76.
34. Bowman, p.54.
35. Nelson, p.77.
36. Bowman, p.84.
37. Hutchinson-Smith, D.C. MSS1534.
38. Ibid.
39. Ibid.
40. Ibid.
41. Ibid.
42. Wigmore, p.674.
43. *The Daily News*, 24 January 1942
44. Ibid.
45. *The Sun*, 29 July 1942.
46. A2684/3 749, National Archives, Canberra.
47. Stone with Holland, p.74.
48. Ibid., p.76.
49. Cook, *Medical Soldiers*, p.127.
50. Abel, G. MSS1623.
51. Ibid.
52. Ibid.
53. Moyle, p.46.
54. *The Sydney Morning Herald*, 7 April 1942.

CHAPTER FOURTEEN

DOWN TO THE SEA IN SHIPS

*'There was no church service to honour our father,
no funeral, no good-bye.'*

Margaret Ruxton

The telegram caused tears. 'Homeward bound awfully sorry long period anxiety, hope all well you can reply care Burns Philip Cairns'.[1] Barbara Selby read the 17 words from her husband over and over. There was another telegram, this one from the 'Minister for the Army', which read:

It is with pleasure that I have to inform you that Lieut David Mayer Selby has arrived safely at an Australian port.[2]

On 4 February 1942, Sydney's *The Daily Telegraph* announced to readers that Selby was returning to Sydney, and wrote how this mild-mannered officer and his 'Australian anti-aircraft battery in Rabaul' had astonished the Japanese when they opened fire and attacking aircraft had 'scattered in all directions.'[3] In the name of national morale, journalists were liberal with the truth.

The faces of the four *Lark Force* officers upon their arrival in Cairns reflected an array of emotions, but not the media's adulation. They had been placed in an unenviable position by their superiors and had

Left to right: Maj Palmer, Lt Selby, Maj Owen, Capt Goodman. AWM

watched men die senselessly. Maj Edward Charles Palmer (NX35096), CO of 2/10 Field Ambulance, had cared for many during the escape. Yet his decision to leave the nurses behind was a questionable one and, of his 24-man detachment, only he and four others had escaped. Palmer was awarded an Officer of the Order of the British Empire (OBE), was promoted to Lt Col and continued to serve with the Field Ambulance until June 1946. Capt Christopher Ernest Goodman (VX44904) and Maj Bill Owen (VX45223) were members of 2/22nd. Goodman was discharged the following year. Bill Owen joined the 39th Battalion and was promoted to Lt Col. On 29 July 1942, Owen was killed while throwing grenades in close-quarter fighting with the Japanese on the Kokoda Track, New Guinea. He was posthumously awarded an American Distinguished Service Cross for gallant and distinguished service – the first Australian so awarded.

The eyes of Lt David Mayer Selby (NX142851) betrayed his ordeal and the emotion of losing so many young militia gunners. He received no awards. He was promoted to Captain and remained in the military

POW camp, Rabaul. Rabaul Historical Society

until the end of the war. Selby returned to the law, was appointed a Queen's Counsel in 1960, and served in Papua New Guinea as an acting judge of its Supreme Court. In 1962, he was appointed to the Supreme Court of NSW. He was known as a 'great' and 'compassionate' judge. In 1991, Sydney University awarded him an honorary doctorate.[4] Selby said he lived life to the full, perhaps because 'of my men who became prisoners of war, I saw none again.'[5] He died in 2002.

Back in New Britain, by June 1942, Capt David Hutchinson-Smith was familiar with the POW routine, at least as familiar as anyone could be with such unpredictable jailers. Officers were kept in a hut separate from the troops but the Japanese regime demanded that all ranks follow orders immediately and make no eye contact. Still, there was irrational behaviour and terrible cruelty. Australian POWs were beaten for even imagined slights. Capt Stewart Nottage kept a diary but there were only grim entries. Bombardier Lloyd Prossier Cockerill-Smith (SX11452) died on 19 April and was buried in the cemetery beside the graves of four soldiers and two civilians. L/Bdr Fitzroy Alexander Campbell (SX11418) was accused of some infraction and disappeared on 16 May;

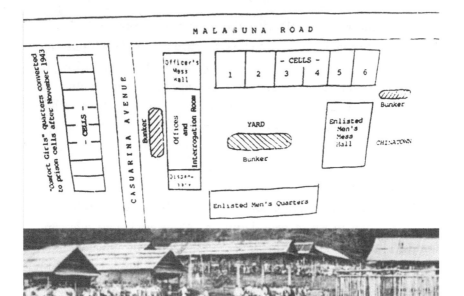

Rabaul POW camp and layout sketch. Rabaul Historical Society

he was 22. On the same day, Gnr Joseph Quinlan (VX129414), 20, was taken away and never returned.[6]

One of the most disturbing incidents occurred on 31 May 1942. Alfred 'Ted' Harvey was the manager of Kau Kau Plantation at Lassul Bay. His wife, Marion, had an 11-year-old son, Richard, by a previous marriage. Also at the plantation was Marion Harvey's brother, James Samuel Manson, and planter William Henry Parker. Ted Harvey had transmitted messages via his plantation wireless as the Japanese invaded. After an informer revealed the family's whereabouts, they were arrested. The guards were observed kicking a soccer ball with Richard, while the adults were tried for spying and communicating with the Allies. On 31 May, the four adults and 11-year-old Richard were lined up and shot by a firing squad. The Australian Government chose not to bring war crime charges against those responsible for these executions after WWII, instead accepting that the Japanese court martial and executions had not violated the code of war. It was one of many bewildering decisions made in the name of diplomacy.

Captain John Finch Akeroyd (VX18194) was 2/22nd Regimental

Medical Officer (RMO). During the escape attempts, he had treated bullet and shrapnel wounds and tropical diseases, and set broken limbs with scant medical resources. Dr Akeroyd chose to remain with troops who were too infirm to escape, even though this meant capture. As a POW, Dr Akeroyd could ask for medical supplies – but was rebuked and hit for his pleas. The Australian civilian and military POWs grew weaker as the minimal food allowance diminished. The POWs were ordered to join celebrations for the Japanese Emperor's birthday, on 29 April. For them, the highlight was the issue of bread.

One rumour circulating camp was that POWs were to be moved to Japan. The prospect was daunting. At around 4.30 a.m. on 22 June 1942, *Lark Force* officers were awakened by unusual activity. Capt Hutchinson-Smith pulled himself from his bunk at the sounds of 'shouting and stomping and we could hear the men and civilians moving about and talking.'[7] He and several other officers attempted to leave their hut but found light machine guns directed at the doorways and 'the Japanese made it unmistakeably clear that we were to remain inside.'[8]

The officers could only watch the sad progression of POWs, supporting each other and carrying their pathetic few possessions, as they were herded away in groups of 50 by angry guards. Dr Akeroyd was helpless to stop wounded and ill troops being carried away on improvised stretchers and old doors. Capt Stewart Nottage asked that officers be allowed to join their soldiers, only to be shoved further back into the hut. Padre John May led prayers through the hut's open side and read the psalm for the day, which for Hutchinson-Smith 'was singularly appropriate.'[9] While some of the soldiers attempted cheerful banter, the sad procession of young and old, civilians and non-civilians, sick and upright, made for a very sad spectacle. With their departure, Hutchinson-Smith wrote how a 'strange mantle of quiet and desolation descended on the place.'[10]

Rudolph Joseph 'Rudy' Buckley was of Irish and Tolai descent. Schooled at the Malaguna Road Roman Catholic mission, his life in Rabaul had been carefree. On 23 January 1942, his world descended into chaos. His father William Reuben Buckley, a mechanic, was forced

Rudy Buckley, Army issue handkerchief and VX19523 B. O'Neil. NGVR Museum

to work at the Japanese navy workshop, in the former Burns Philp garage opposite Colyer Watsons. Although only 12, Rudy was made to work 9 or 10 hours a day on menial duties by the Japanese military, for which he was given one small bag of rice a week. Rudy was one of those little kids with a large toothy grin who had delighted Australian troops. He had enjoyed watching and laughing with them; they were friendly and often handed out treats or a few coins. The Australian soldiers were no longer happy; they were thinner, their clothes were in tatters and their guns had gone. The POW camp where they were kept was cramped and their jailers were harsh.

Rudy was working near the Colyer Watson wharf, close to the Shell wharf depot, when he looked up to see long lines of people, some in civilian clothes, more in uniform remnants but still wearing slouch hats. Guards with rifles and long bayonets prodded and screamed. Curious, he risked the wrath of Japanese soldiers to edge closer. The POWs were forced onto a ship. Unbeknown to the youngster, the ship was named *Montevideo Maru*. One soldier smiled at Rudy and, as the attention of guards was distracted, threw him an army-issue handkerchief. Rudy returned that evening to Ratongor, 20 miles (32km) from Rabaul, where his family was kept captive. Before placing the handkerchief in his tin box of Australian army badges, he examined the khaki cloth. In smudged black ink was written 'V.X.19523 B. O'Neil'. Knowing the consequences of being found with Australian Army memorabilia, Rudy buried his treasure box.

The following year his father, William, was accused of deliberately

MV Montevideo Maru. Montevideo Maru Association

delaying vehicle repairs. Attempting to explain the unavailability of spare parts, he was viciously bashed with a crank handle. William Buckley died four days later. Rudy survived the occupation and returned to school, before being employed by the Commonwealth Department of Works and the Department of Civil Aviation. Granted Australian citizenship in 1964, he served with the Papua New Guinea Volunteer Rifles at Rabaul, until moving to Australia in 1975. It was not until 2004 that a discussion with a fellow member of the NG & PNG Volunteer Rifles Ex Members Association alerted Rudy to the significance of the khaki handkerchief, and he learnt more of 'V.X.19523 B. O'Neil'.[11]

The Australian military tradition had been important to Pte Barry Richard David O'Neil (VX19523). His father, William Barry O'Neil (VP7545), retired a Major. It was of no surprise that, at 19, Barry enlisted in the militia as soon as war was declared, and then transferred to the 2/22nd AIF. His sister, Mahala Eleanor O'Neil (VF345079), joined the Australian Women's Army Service in 1942 and was demobilized as a Warrant Officer in 1946.

Gordon Thomas realized how fortunate he was, though 'fortunate' was perhaps too praiseworthy a word when you were undertaking duties set by the enemy. On 22 January, another Australian civilian technician who had been undertaking pump repairs in the POW camp arrived and 'breathlessly informed us that all prisoners from the camp, except the officers' had been 'marched out and placed onboard a ship for Japan.'[12] Later, this was confirmed by indigenous labourers and Chinese cooks in Japanese messes. The contingent had included most of the male

Gnr Keith Trigg
(alias Eric Triggs).

George Thornton. AWM

European civilian population, his friends.

The 7,266-ton, twin-screw diesel Motor Vessel (MV) *Montevideo Maru*, was a Japanese passenger ship constructed in Nagasaki in 1926 and operated by the Osaka Shosen Kaisha Shipping Line between Japan and South America. Requisitioned by the Imperial Japanese Navy, the *Montevideo Maru* was used to transport troops and supplies. On 22 June 1942, the ship's cargo was 1,053 Rabaul POWs destined for Japan as slave labour, but the ship carried no distinguishing symbols to identify this human cargo.

The three Turner brothers had always been inseparable, and Sid and Dudley were particularly protective of the youngest brother Daryl. When, in 1940, Sid and Dud decided to enlist, Daryl was barely 17 and had just left school.[13] There was no way they were going to leave Daryl behind, so with some falsifying of birthdates they were inducted together, selected for 1 Independent Company and embarked for New Ireland together. Their attempted escape in the *Induna Star* had been thwarted but they were alive and still together, and Sid and Dud were as determined as ever to keep Daryl safe. Now they were being shoved into the putrid, stifling, unventilated hold of a Japanese transport.

Men sick with malaria and dysentery, and some now seasick, were pushed up against others with no room to move. All suffered identical conditions, including men of authority and privilege such as the Deputy Administrator Harold Page and eight other heads of Rabaul government departments. They included NobbyClark, MLC, Chief Civil Warden; Harry Orton Townsend, Treasurer NG Administration; Crown Law Officer Gerald Hogan; Harry Holland, the manager of AWA; Charles

Hector Roderick MacLean, the Manager of WRC, Rabaul; and Philip Coote, Manager of Burns Philip, Rabaul.

Medical doctors and assistants were helpless in relieving the misery, and the prayers of missionaries could scarcely be heard above the ship's engines. Hotel managers such as Alfred Ernest Dickenson Banks, and other members of the Rabaul community who had hosted *Lark Force* troops, now shared their misfortune.

Sgt Arthur Gullidge. Cox

The bright and proud faces of troops who had arrived a year ago such as Eric Triggs and George Thornton were now devoid of hope. Triggs from Tuggerah, NSW, wrote on his enlistment paper that he was nearly 23. Only he was really Keith Trigg and 17. George Thornton was another who pretended to be 23 with previous artillery training, but was only 17.

Hans Teien had been the motorman of MS *Herstein*. Swedish Steward, Karl Thorsell, was killed when their ship was bombed. Their Captain, Gottfred M. Gundersen, had escaped New Britain but Teien and the rest of the Norwegian crew listened to the familiar sounds of engine revolutions and a ship's hull

NGVR Staff Sgt Horace Plummer. Downs

driving through ocean, but in very unfamiliar surroundings.

NGVR Staff Sgt Horace Oswald Plummer (NGX478) counted the 36 NGVR members stuck in this dreadful ship. Being only part-time soldiers made no difference to the Japanese.

Sgt Francis Ryan was a schoolteacher; Sgt Charles MacLean was a dentist; Rifleman (Rfn) Bernard O'Connor was an entomologist; Rfn William Reynolds was a Commonwealth Bank employee; Cpl Robert Allan Bird was a Customs Department official and Victor Florance a solicitor. Plantation manager Charles William Booth Houghton (NGX510) had changed civilian clothes for those of NGVR just two days before the invasion, as had the recently married Lionel Stephen Dix (NGX504). S/Sgt Plummer realized how ridiculous his own situation was as he sat in this ghastly, unhygienic space – he was the Rabaul Health Inspector.

Sgt Arthur Gullidge had suffered life's hardships first-hand. He was a child when his father, William, was killed in a Broken Hill mine cave-in. His mother Emily, a Salvation Army officer, shifted the family with each new appointment. Arthur matured in a world of Christian ethics and bands, and emerged the nation's most prolific composer of brass band music. He had been Bandmaster of the Brunswick Citadel Band and it was largely due to his encouragement that Salvation Army musicians enlisted to create the band of the 2/22nd. Of the 23 musicians, several had been executed or died of disease. Pte Fred Kollmorgen had not been seen since the invasion but the rest of the Gullidge band of talented musicians now suffered a very uncertain future.

Brothers and brothers-in-arms continued to support each other as best they could, as day and night merged into one. Ptes Basil and Rex Whyte, 23, were the twin sons of Albert and Sarah Ann Wythe of Hamilton, Victoria, and had enlisted in the 2/22nd. Gunners Gerald John McShane and John Eshott Carr were born a week apart and enlisted together at 19. The POWs estimated they had been about eight days at sea; how many more before this nightmare finished?

The crew of the Salmon-class United States submarine USS *Sturgeon* were refreshed from rest and relaxation in Fremantle, Western Australia. Their ship had been given a refit so when the submarine headed into the waters west of Manila, Philippines, both crew and boat were combat ready. On 25 June 1942, a nine-ship Japanese convoy was sighted and the Sturgeon's Commanding Officer Lt Commander William L 'Bull' Wright (USN) ordered the release of three torpedoes at the largest ship. The ensuing explosions signified success and Sturgeon was immediately subjected to 21 depth charges. Both Wright and his crew knew that they had been fortunate to escape with a few broken gauges. Sturgeon took up a patrol north-west of Bojeador, Philippines. Before midnight on 30 June, Wright roused from his cabin; the officer of the watch had sighted a darkened Japanese auxiliary ship. Wright observed the ship heading westward at high speed, probably for the island of Hainan, China. Though the transport was zigzagging, it was alone – every submariner's dream, an unescorted motor vessel.

Wright ordered all engines worked up to full power in an attempt to get ahead of the enemy transport. In the Sturgeon log, Wright wrote:

For an hour and a half we couldn't make a nickel. This fellow was really going, making at least 17 knots [31km/h], and probably a bit more.[14]

Gerald McShane, left, and John Carr, right. AWM

USS Sturgeon. ww2today.com/1st-july-1942-australian-tragedy-uss-sturgeon-sinks-montevideo-maru

The enemy ship was at a range of 18,000 yards (16km) but Sturgeon continued the pursuit, in the hope that the auxiliary would slow or change course in their direction. As a new day began, off Luzon, Philippines, the ship slowed to 12 knots (22km/h). Wright wrote in the log that 'after that it was easy. Proceeding to intercept target.'[15]

Unbeknown to the Sturgeon crew, their target was waiting for destroyer escorts. Wright ordered a course change and at 0146 came the order to 'dive'. Once in periscope range Wright was pleased to see that the unmarked ship was larger than initially thought. The submarine stealthily closed to within 4,000 yards (3.7km). At 0225, Sturgeon fired a four-torpedo spread from the after tubes and, four minutes later, an explosion was heard and observed. Sturgeon surfaced as the ship's bow was 'well up' and the *Montevideo Maru* slipped stern-first beneath the horizon [16]

The 88 Japanese crew and guards were ordered to abandon ship but time and lack of inclination meant no effort was made to release the POWs from the holds. Of the 88 Japanese, 17 survived the sinking and subsequent march through the Philippines jungle, and returned to their homeland. Of the 208 civilian and 845 military Rabaul POWs onboard the *Montevideo Maru*, none survived.

In 1944, *The Herald and Weekly Times* published a 96-page bold and splendid 'Pictorial Record of the Battle for Australia' magazine entitled:

JUNGLE VICTORY: Outline of Military Events in New Guinea and Papua with over 150 photographs.[17]

The war in the Pacific was not yet won and the emphasis was on nationalism and victorious endeavour. The inside front and back covers celebrated the firm

Patriotic advertisements in the 1944 Jungle Victory.

relationship between the media, industry and banking sectors, and the war effort, offering congratulations to 'our fighting men' and 'Australia's fighting forces by the 9,000 men and women working in the factories of General Motors-Holden's Limited.'[18] The back cover featured an iconic bush image from one of the world's most urbanized nations – denoting Australia as 'The land of Freedom' from the 'The State Savings Bank of Victoria'.[19]

The magazine purported to tell the story of 'the military events' of the New Guinea war. Photographs vividly portrayed a hard-fought campaign from an Allied victorious perspective. Death and misery, bodies and mayhem, were evidenced predominantly in pictures of defeated enemy soldiers.

What must have been disturbing for the families and friends of *Lark Force* troops was the complete denial surrounding the invasion of New Britain and adjacent islands, and the battle for Rabaul. Any service and sacrifice of civilians and military personnel, and their subsequent disappearance, were not alluded to. The magazine's map depicted New Britain and New Ireland in pristine white, as islands unsullied by the war. Under the banner words 'The Battle for Australia', was written:

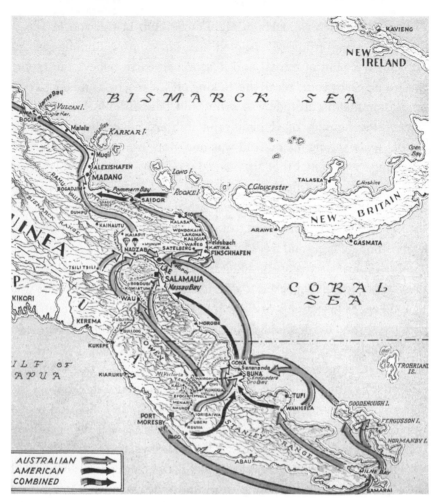

The map of New Guinea battles in 1944's Jungle Victory.

'no campaign has been more important to the people of Australia than the various battles in New Guinea.'[20] The chapter titled '1st Phase: Retirement', reported that 'the invasion of New Guinea ... found the Allies largely unprepared' and that the first enemy landing was at Lae.[21]

According to the popular and widely distributed magazine, there had been merely 'spasmodic air raids' on New Guinea prior to a Japanese invasion of Lae and Salamaua on 8 March 1942. It also announced that civilians had been evacuated prior to the invasion and a 'scorched earth policy' had then been conducted to deny the Japanese infrastructure.[22]

For survivors such as Lt Hugh MacKenzie, Sub Lt Gill and Lt David Selby, who had fruitlessly cajoled the *Lark Force* Commander to implement a plan of retreat and a 'scorched earth policy', the report was ironic. Selby could recall the 'ticking off' he received and the strong accusation that his attitude was wrong and 'defeatist'.[23]

For the families of civilians and military alike, the publication *Jungle Victory* rang hollow and was one more example of the mire of subterfuge and denial that they faced. Only the vaguest information was made public, partly due to the desire of Australian authorities to maintain secrecy about the debacle in New Britain, and partly due to the lack of official confirmation from an unwilling enemy. The weight of supposition, of hope and trepidation, was hard to bear.

Cyril John Gascoigne was a Rabaul auctioneer. On Boxing Day 1941, the Gascoigne family packed to evacuate. Ivor Norman Gascoigne was 15 and begged his parents to allow him to remain in Rabaul because he had just started his first job, as an office boy at Amalgamated Wireless. His entreaties were heartfelt, as was the argument that he would be safe with his father. It was agreed that Ivor could remain in Rabaul. His sister Betty recalled how she, her mother and brother watched from the decks of the evacuation ship, as the figures of the father and brother she would never see again grew smaller and smaller. 'It was the beginning of an almost unbearable silence that would last years.'[24]

Families clung to the slightest hope. Letters and parcels continued to be posted. The Groat family were not unusual in continuing their one-sided conversation with a son. They had received a postcard from Pte John George Groat (VX23647).

Dear Mother,
I am a prisoner of war and being cared
for by the Japanese. I am in good health,
please do not worry. Let all my friends
know. Now and all Lots of love from your
loving son, Jack.[25]

Jack was a country lad, a notable horseman   *Pte Jack Groat* Nisbet

268

and horse breaker, and the family believed that this would ensure he survived. But it was difficult as the years and silence continued.

The waiting and trying to find out what was going on, writing and keeping the letters as cheerful as possible, and even sending radio messages via a lady from Toorak, kept us going.[26]

Jack's father Tom felt the strain and died in July 1944 at 61, not knowing that Jack had died in the hold of the *Montevideo Maru* on 1 July 1942.

Family hopes and fears were further kindled when letters were received from Rabaul POWs in Japan. It was in the first week of July 1942 that the Australian Army and civilian nurses and Mrs Kathleen Bignell were removed from Vunapope Mission. They had been ordered to pack little because they were off to 'Paradise'. As their lorry travelled the coast road, they were amazed at the changes:

Littering this once beautiful beachfront were untidy huts surrounded by garbage and uprooted trees entangled in barbed wire; newly erected wharves and landing stages jutted out into the sea. This was the once delightful Blue Lagoon area, where swimming parties took tea under the palm trees. Such happy memories ...[27]

The 18 women were led up the lurching gangway of the *Naruto Maru* and ordered to descend into the hold. There was a commotion above but it was voices, male English-speaking voices. As the new passengers climbed down into the hold, 'shrieks of joy and relief greeted the astonished men.'[28] The joyful reunion was shared by the 60 *Lark Force*, NGVR officers and civilians with everyone seemingly speaking at once. The unmarked transport cast its lines on 5 July. Kathleen Bignell described how arduous the sea voyage was: 'insufferably hot hold, except for 20 minutes on deck three times a day' and a cup of water every two days, but at least they were oblivious to the fate of those who had set off on the same journey on 22 June.[29]

Sister 'Tootie' Keast and other Rabaul nurses on their way to Australia, Keast savouring her first tinned meat in three years. AWM

On 14 July, the *Naruto Maru* POWs were offloaded at Yokohama, Japan. They carried their few belongings along a road lined with 'jeering Japs'.[30] The women were placed in the Yokohama Yacht Club. Perhaps it had once been a grand seafront establishment but from 1942 onwards for the Australian Army nurses and women civilians it was hellish. They received so little food that they collected seaweed, rotten carrots and other refuse from close to shore, using a bamboo pole with a prong of wire attached.

They were ordered to manufacture small bags for soldiers to carry their religious tokens, as well as folding and gluing envelopes. They became so hungry that they 'stole the stinking brown glue when guards weren't looking and ate it.'[31] The Australian women looked forward to the eighth day of each month, named 'Degradation Day' by their jailers. After they knelt and bowed in the direction of the Emperor's palace, they were permitted to 'rake out' vegetables thrown into a cesspit.[32] The women urged each other on and a poem titled 'The Spirit of Australia' was written:

Their cruelty cannot hurt me, Their boasting cannot irk me,
No jot care I; my pride rides high, And hope will ne'er desert me.[33]

For years the women suffered degradation and physical punishment, as Kathleen Bignell's diary attested:

December 24 1943: ordered to cart ashes ... Guard hit [Sister]
McGowan so hard she fell on top of me. January 7 1944: Called
'Goshe (Australian) Pigs' ... cleaning roads
... frozen ... lined up and screamed at for hour. January 9:
[Sister] Bowie thrown and kicked. [Sisters] Goss and Kay
Parker struck. January 19: seaweed for lunch.
Starving. Stole half wheatmeal biscuit from guard ...[Sister]
McGowan had sword jabbed against stomach. Myself bashed
... Cleaned out sewer septic tank.[34]

Sister 'Tootie' Keast fully appreciated how important the solidarity of this band of women was to her own survival, and her admiration for her fellow Australian Army nurses was fundamental to surviving this ghastly existence. They were determined not to cry or beg in front of guards, even when ordered to shovel paths of snow for guards in knee-high boots while they were barefooted. Sister Eileen Callaghan became ill and it was apparent that it was tuberculosis. Sister Kay Parker isolated Callaghan and took complete responsibility for her care.[35] They were cut off from the world.

In August 1945, Kay Parker was ordered to front Japanese POW camp officials. She was told that the Americans had dropped a bomb on Hiroshima and it had caused much damage. Because of this, the nurses 'had three days to live ... All prisoners-of-war in Japan were going to be killed within three days.'[36] The news was devastating. 'Tootie' Keast remembered the dread she felt when, a couple of nights later, Parker was ordered to face the authorities again. 'They told her that another bomb had been dropped at Nagasaki.'[37] Japan was surrendering and, although she could appreciate the terrible damage inflicted, 'Tootie' Keast also realized the second bomb had 'saved the lives' of all POWs.

Male POWs from Rabaul faced a similar ordeal, following their internment in the Zentsuji POW camp, on Shikoku Island in southern Japan. An estimated 205 Allied POWs were held at Zentsuji. Commonly, officers were not worked as hard as other ranks but they all faced malnutrition, lack of medical care, inadequate clothing and heating to combat the bitter winters, and physical abuse. POWs at Zentsuji faced additional psychological abuse because the camp was used for propaganda purposes. In 1942 in one occasion of many, film crews recorded a friendly address to the POWs by Japanese Camp Commandant Major General Mizuhara, after which warmly dressed prisoners were handed fruit, packets of cigarettes and other food. The POWs were then immediately removed from camera range and all gifts confiscated. As in other POW camps, Red Cross supplies and medical supplies were looted and never delivered. Upon surrender, tons of unused Red Cross supplies and medical supplies were found in POW camps throughout Japan.

The letters from Zentsuji were few and heavily censored but for families it meant great relief. *Lark Force* heavy battery Captain, Stewart Nottage, managed to get a letter through to his wife in 1943. 'Tell Helen

Pure propaganda – well-fed and clothed POWs at Zentsuji.[38]

ABOVE: *Lark Force officers at Zentsuji POW Camp. Left to right: Lt Kenneth Robertson, Capt Stewart Nottage, Maj James Clark, Lt Stanley Cooper, Lt Albert Chandler.* AWM RIGHT: *Left to right: Col Joseph Scanlan and Lt Raymond Tyrell.* AWM

that Daddy extends to her Birthday Greetings on June 16 also yourself on July 13th.'[39] Lt Hutchinson-Smith managed to post a letter to his wife, after cooperating with camp censors.

> *Enjoying the best of health, and looking as fit as a fiddle ...*
> *Studying, food is good ... we go for a walk through the fields,*
> *hills and villages and it is quite enjoyable ... we have warm*
> *clothing and there is a concert every Sunday.*[40]

Hutchinson-Smith was 'anxious' to receive news from Australia. Because of his falsified account of life at Zentsuji, he was given stockpiled letters from home and could now write 'my proudest possession are the two photographs' of his family.[41]

For the Australians it was three more years of physically and mentally debilitating internment. Dr Akeroyd had been taken to work in a hospital at Ichioka in Osaka, known as a place of cruelty, starvation and death. There was no anaesthetic and sterilizing of the most basic instruments was done in water in which rice had been boiled. Although

Jubilant celebrations for the end of the war against the Japanese. SMH

ill himself, Akeroyd reported the theft of patient food by guards. Akeroyd was beaten badly and watched as his patients were also. He developed tuberculosis and barely survived life as a POW. He was awarded an MBE in 1947 and an Australia Medal in 1978. Capt John Finch Akeroyd died in December 1982. On 16 September 1945, Capt Hutchinson-Smith was overjoyed in a letter to his wife:

> *I am still finding it hard to believe. Just think of it in just a short time I shall be with you all once again. We have been saying 'home for Christmas' for a few years now, and at last it is to come true. So excited I feel about five years old, heard a white woman's voice after 3 years. She was an American nurse.*[42]

On 15 August 1945, Australian Prime Minister Ben Chifley announced to the Australian people that the war against Japan had ended.

During the following weeks throughout Asia and the Pacific, Japanese forces gradually surrendered and, on the deck of the USS Missouri in Tokyo Bay, an official surrender ceremony took place on 2 September. The Australian people were ecstatic and the celebrations throughout cities and towns were memorable. But for families whose men and women had been killed in the war in Europe and against the Japanese, there was no celebration, nor for the thousands of families who had received official telegrams with the words 'Missing' or 'believed to be a Prisoner of War'.

Margaret McGregor was sitting down to high-school examinations when these were disrupted with the news. A holiday was declared. 'The trains were chaotic. Drivers disregarded timetables. There was a lot of tooting and whistle blowing.'[43] Her life had been dominated by the war and there was a youthful 'speculation, excitement and apprehension about a change in our lives.'[44] Her mother, Elinor Marjorie 'Madge' McGregor, had told Margaret and her sisters how she had joined the celebrations at the end of the previous war.

How she had been caught up in the jubilant, dancing crowds, even kissed soundly by complete strangers – it all sounded pretty weird to me. So what would happen now?[45]

But this time Madge's husband, their father, Pte Sydney McGregor, 2/22nd AIF, had not been heard from for years. When Margaret and her sister arrived home, her mother declared that they were to go to a family celebration. 'We didn't want to go. None of us wanted to go.'[46] At the station:

Pte Sydney McGregor.
Ruxton

We sat on, isolated in our collective misery. We weren't excited or jubilant; we were conscious of the telegrams on the mantelpiece. The first one had said 'Missing, believed prisoner of war'. The latest one read 'Missing, believed killed' … 'Why don't we just go home?' Our Mum gave a great sigh of

General Imamura of the Japanese Rabaul forces.

The surrender ceremony onboard HMS Glory. AWM

hopelessness 'We've got to go, the family expects us to be there'
... She screwed up her face, 'Why are they making me go ...
what have I got to celebrate?'[47]

Two months later, the family learnt that Sydney McGregor, husband and father, had perished when the *Montevideo Maru* was sunk in July 1942. 'My mother was heartbroken.'[48] So, too, were Sydney McGregor's three daughters but there was no encouragement in 1945 to openly mourn and this was compounded because 'there was no church service to honour our father, no funeral, no good-bye.'[49]

The long-wished -for newspaper headline finally appeared in bold black print: 'Rabaul Surrender on Thursday ... General Imamura of the Japanese Rabaul forces ... scheduled to take place.'[50] The surrender of 'at least 86,000 Japs will be involved' onboard the British aircraft carrier Glory.[51] On the morning of 10 September 1945, HMA Ships *Vendetta*, *Manoora* and *Katoomba*, and numerous small craft sailed into Simpson Harbour. In echoes of the descriptions written in letters by *Lark Force* troops, a special correspondent onboard wrote of the breathtaking physical beauty of Rabaul:

The scenic beauty of Simpson Harbour unfolded as we made our way slowly to our anchorage. Matupi had been active, and wisps of steam were rising from the crater ... Vulcan looked quite serene.[52]

The reality of Rabaul in September 1945, and the testimony of survivors, quickly dispelled the vision of serenity and beauty. Rabaul in no way reflected the gracious pre-war town. The shore of the harbour was littered with bombed, gutted and burned-out ships, their masts and funnel tops mournful testimony to the destruction of war. The once-proud shipping wharves were now battered and broken. Concrete foundations were a tragic reminder of the grand homes and resilient society. The only sign of life was in the expansive vegetable gardens for Japanese-only tables. There was an eerie stillness in this land whose dark secrets would soon be revealed. It was unimaginable that thousands of *Lark Force* troops, civilians, Asian and indigenous people had simply vanished. Each story and each grave revealed inhumanity on a scale that none of the Australian soldiers who purposefully strode ashore could anticipate or could ever comprehend.

Endnotes

1. Selby, D. PR00199, AWM, Canberra.
2. Ibid.
3. Ibid.
4. *The Sydney Morning Herald*, 3 October 2002.
5. Selby, *Hell and High Fever*, p.197.
6. Nottage, S.G PR83/189.
7. Hutchinson-Smith, D.C. MSS1534.
8. Ibid.
9. Ibid.
10. Ibid.
11. Hayes, M.R 'Rudy Buckley and the *Montevideo Maru*', www.pngaa.net/ Library/ RudyBuckley.htm accessed 25 November 2016.
12. Thomas, G. 'Rabaul 1942–45' manuscript.
13. Dale, M. Email, 6 and 9 September 2016.
14. *USS Sturgeon* Log, NGVR Museum, Brisbane.
15. Ibid.
16. Ibid.
17. *Jungle Victory: Outline of Military Events in New Guinea and Papua with over 150 photographs,* A Sun publication, Herald and Weekly Press, 1944.
18. Ibid.
19. Ibid.
20. Ibid., p.2.
21. Ibid., p.4.
22. Ibid., p.5.
23. Selby, p.24.
24. Muller, B. *Una Voce*, No 3, Sept 2014. Betty Muller died on 4 August 2014.
25. Nisbet, A. www.jje.info/lostlives/people/ groatjg.html accessed 15 October 2016.
26. Ibid.
27. Bowman, A. p.89.
28. Ibid., p.91.
29. *The Sun*, 30 September 1945.
30. Ibid.
31. Ibid.
32. Ibid.
33. Ibid.
34. Ibid.
35. Bassett, Guns and Brooches, p.147.
36. Nelson, *Prisoners of War: Australians under Nippon*, p.195.
37. Ibid.
38. www.us-japandialogueonpows.org/ Photo%20album%20of%20Zentsuji%20 POW%20 camp.htm accessed 8 December 2016.
39. Nottage, S.G.
40. Hutchinson-Smith.
41. Ibid.
42. Ibid.
43. Ruxton, M www.jje.info/lostlives/ people/mcgregors.html
44. Ibid.
45. Ibid.
46. Ibid.
47. Ibid.
48. Ibid.
49. Ibid.
50. *Advocate*, 3 September 1945.
51. Ibid.
52. *The Argus,* 12 September 1945.

CHAPTER FIFTEEN

SUBTERFUGE AND DENIAL

*'When you start realising the impact on
so many people ... it is powerful.'*

Andrea Williams

Australians had weathered a horrible six years. They had convinced themselves that nothing could shock them; they had read and seen so much. They were or knew families who had suffered grief with the knowledge that loved ones were not returning. Peace had come, the war in Europe and the war in the Pacific were finally over – they wanted only good news and the opportunity to heal – but the bad news was far from over and for thousands of families the agonizing wait continued.

At 9.35 a.m. on 10 September 1945, the Australian flag was raised once more at Rabaul, a town with a ghostly aura. A journalist who came ashore with Australian forces wrote:

*In the peace before this peace Rabaul was something of a
tropical paradise ... But Rabaul today is shorn of its glamour
and in its desolation is neither pretty nor impressive ... we
walked through the so-called town area where literally no stone
remains upon stone. What the Japs did not despoil, our bombers
flattened and made the Japs turn tail and live like rats in caves.*[1]

Australians coming ashore at Rabaul. AWM

Slowly, traumatized and starving people began to nervously emerge, trying to believe that they were finally free from the terror and misery. At the beginning of 1942, it was believed there were more than 30,000 local Tolai people. It was found now there were around 24,000.[2] ANGAU personnel were recognized and by the third day the re-occupying forces had made contact with thousands of indigenous New Britons, whose delight was no better demonstrated than by the small boy who stood by the roadside all day to salute. Cpl Ronald Broinowski (TX5789) was a member of the 101 Australian Field Security Section, tasked with others to secure Rabaul. More and more indigenous people crept from the jungle. It was clear to Broinowski that they 'had not had an easy time.'[3] Their smiles were 'ready and charming as ever' but 'they were rickety, and had many sores.'[4] They sang quietly at first and then louder and louder, 'God save the King' in pidgin, followed by songs they had dared not sing since the Japanese invaded. With confidence, the 'natives were

A small boy stood all day saluting reoccupation troops. NGVR Museum

280

Australian Army nurses arriving in Rabaul and their welcoming party. AWM

becoming increasingly angry' and the 'Japanese remained impassive.'[5] The first Australian Army nurses to alight from boats were mobbed by the welcoming and curious – the youngest children never before having seen a European woman.

Four pale, very thin European civilians appeared: former Public Works engineer, R.A.D. Greswick; G. McKechine, who had been an engineer at Pondo Plantation; Electrical Contractor, J. Ellis; and former *Rabaul Times* editor Gordon Thomas. The men had been detailed technical duties, and later Thomas as chef to Japanese officers. The men were surprised they had not been shipped out in July 1942 and knew of another party of Europeans found hiding on Raniolo plantation, which Thomas was 'almost positive were executed.'[6] They could now finally tell military authorities that the bulk of the POWs had been observed boarding the *Montevideo Maru* and that later, Japanese military had freely confirmed to them that the ship had sunk. 'They didn't mind telling us because it was not their fault – but our own allies!'[7] Thomas repeated the truth countless times when implored for information by evacuated Rabaul families. Invariably, the truth was too hard to bear and he was dismissed with 'well, I just feel that he is still somewhere, and that he did not go on that boat.'[8]

The Chinese Rabaul community had been forced to take shelter

Four Europeans remained captive in Rabaul throughout the Japanese occupation. Left to right: Greswick, Thomas, McKechine and Ellis. AWM

in camps outside their town. *Lark Force* Major, Edmunds-Wilson, testified that following the invasion Rabaul was a city in crisis and that the 'atrocities during the first few days were indescribable', as drunken invading soldiers 'went from house to house raping, looting and killing.' The Chinese community was treated with 'fearful cruelty'.[9] Of the estimated 1,200 Chinese living in Rabaul in 1942, it was believed

Chinese citizens in a valley outside Rabaul. AWM

Left and right: Liberated members of the Rabaul Chinese community show their delight. AWM

that around 850 survived. After each raid, reprisals were taken against indigenous and Chinese citizens.

Australian soldiers needed to capture and disarm all Japanese but they also desperately wanted to do more for the people. Cpl Broinowski tried to remain dispassionate but it was increasingly difficult. As the Chinese community appeared from ramshackle shacks, 'what a sight they were, dressed in their ragged best for our benefit covered with

Allied bombing resulted in civilian deaths. At Vunapope Mission, shelters were dug into the hillside. AWM

tropical ulcers. Deprivation and brutality.'[10] Individuals spoke of being kicked and beaten for failing to salute 'their conquerors' and worse. The Vunapope Mission Sacred Heart nuns had been saddened when the Australian Army nurses and other female companions were abruptly removed in 1942. Had it not been for the intervention of Bishop Scharmach, this would have been their fate also. Life in Japanese-occupied New Britain was gruelling but the nuns kept busy caring for the priests and mixed-race and orphan children

For 18 months, the mission commune was forced to live in Ramale Valley. AWM

under their care. More missionaries were brought to the mission. Their ethnic origins were as diverse as their religious beliefs but now there was no shortage of language classes to occupy the time.

When the Allied bombing intensified, the priests dug shelters in the hills but these became increasingly crowded. People struggled to breathe, disease spread and missionaries died. All were gradually starving. Indigenous sisters foraged for food to assist the commune but they were invariably caught and tortured. Suddenly, in June 1944 they were taken to the Ramale Valley, a sheer uninhabited ravine, and brusquely ordered to descend. Hundreds slid and slipped down the sheer precipice into the dank, dark gorge.

The watercourse flowing through was solely for the use of Japanese soldiers downstream, so digging a well was an immediate task. Pig weed was the stable diet supplemented with 'grubs, larvae and snake.'[11] Sister Berenice Twohill admitted that, although rats were a problem, the commune 'ate feral cats.'[12]

Guard platforms were built high above and surrounding the gorge. Eventually, the missionaries were permitted to establish vegetable and fruit gardens, but guards stole the precious produce. To remind missionaries of the punishment for non-compliance, indigenous locals

Sacred Heart nuns being evacuated. AWM

were tortured in front of them. On 16 September 1945, their prayers were finally answered with a loud call of 'Cooee'. They cried 'Cooee' in reply and offered thanks as Australian soldiers, led by a Redemptist missionary, materialized. It took little time before the grateful missionaries were evacuated to the safety of an RAN ship.

Australian military investigations revealed proof of Japanese brutality and harrowing testimonies detailed rape, execution and cannibalism. An estimated 600 British-Indian soldiers taken prisoner in Singapore, and an additional 1,504 Chinese soldiers, had been shipped to New Britain as slave labour to build a 350-mile (563km) tunnel complex for Japanese soldiers and supply storage. Their treatment was appalling. Of the Chinese soldiers, half were executed or died. Of the Indian soldiers, only 18 survived. As the Allies closed in on Rabaul, the tunnels took on a more sinister purpose – not only to imprison POWs but, had the Allied advance not been so rapid, to bury POWs and remove evidence of war crimes.

Identifying war criminals. AWM

Australian investigators were overwhelmed with reports of grievous criminal acts and mass graves bore witness to the reality of life and death under Japanese occupation. Re-occupation forces were warned about what they might find, but nothing could have prepared them for what they found when they arrived at Tol and Waitavalo Plantations and at Gasmata. Hardened soldiers wept at the sight of exposed bones, torn Red Cross armbands and once-proudly worn AIF uniforms.

Indigenous sisters identify torturers. AWM

TOP AND BOTTOM: *Tol Plantation 1945.* NGVR Museum

For three soldiers, it was particularly poignant to land on Rabaul shores. Sgt Bruce Webster, Cpl Hugh 'Nipper' Webster and Sgt Arch Taylor waded into the shallows and felt the familiar New Britain humidity soak their uniforms with sweat. They were much stronger since last here – fit, well fed and not suffering malaria fevers – but nonetheless their stomachs churned and emotions were edgy. Each man had his own demons to combat but they needed to do this for their mates, to ensure that fellow *Lark Force* troops were not forgotten, and they needed to forgive themselves for obeying Col Scanlan's order 'everyman for himself ' and successfully escaping.

For Webster, a name was important. He had enlisted with childhood friends, the brothers Les and Walter Whittle, and Norm Walkley – 'the four W's'. On 4 February 1942, the four had been marched to Waitavolo and shot. When the wounded Webster stirred, the Japanese were gone and Les and Walter Whittle were dead. Walkley was barely alive and did not survive. 'Nipper' spoke little of his war experiences but gave his son Tony the middle names of Walter, Leslie and Norman.

Survivor guilt was an ongoing challenge. How could the living make sense of death and the unanswerable question, why him and not me? Pte Bill Neave had escaped but:

*In the long, lonely hours of the night the memories still come
flooding back ... they are still raw and painful; they still bring
tears. There are still ghosts that haunt.*[13]

Gnr Gordon Abel was 18 when he witnessed the Tol Massacre. In 1994,
52 years later he wrote:

*I can no longer sustain the hatred of Japan that I had then,
and no longer want to kill all Japanese, but I still can't forget
or fully forgive and for these feelings I offer no apologies.*[14]

No one knew better than Pte Billy Cook about near-death experiences
and the fickleness of fate. How he had survived 11 bayonet wounds
no one could understand, least of all Cook. The physical wounds
mended faster than the emotional ones: 'I've got a lot of memories that
sometimes wake me in the night, cold with sweat.'[15] Unfortunately
for Cook, life continued to be traumatic. In 1951, while employed on
railway maintenance, he was knocked down and run over by a train. He
survived but lost both legs.

Fred Kollmorgen's parents were Salvationists and he was
accomplished on the euphonium, tenor horn and trombone, but he was
not a member of the Salvation Army Brunswick Citadel Band. Arthur
Gullidge recognized his musical talent and agreed that Kollmorgen
should join the 2/22nd band. He admired Gullidge and enjoyed
the band, but continued to feel like an outsider. When the Japanese
air raids increased, the musicians trained as medical orderlies were
needed in the hospital. Kollmorgen had been working as a water truck
driver with the 2/22nd and felt more comfortable in that company. He
convinced military authorities that he should continue those duties. Pte
Fred Kollmorgen was the only member of the 2/22nd band to return to
Australia.

The photographs faded with age but the memories remained. The
Anti-Aircraft Battery officers and non-commissioned officers who had
cast their eyes over Rabaul Harbour from Frisbee Ridge back in January
1942 could never have predicted their futures.

Left to right: Sgt Bruce Perkins, Cpl 'Nipper' Webster and Sgt Arch Taylor. AWM

Sgts Gilchrist, Green and Peters drowned on 1 July 1942. Lts Fisher and Selby escaped but lived with the memory of the 46 of their battery who did not. Of the 40 Tasmanians who eagerly enlisted in the Anti-Aircraft Battery in February 1941, half still too young to vote, only two returned to Australia. Staff Sgt Bill Warhurst, given the giant task of training these very raw, over-enthusiastic recruits, remained with them on the *Montevideo Maru*.

Chaplain John May was strengthened by his faith, although this faith was severely tested by events in Rabaul and during POW internment in Japan. In a letter to the Reverend G. Johnson, he wrote of how helpless he felt as his troops were marched away on 22 June 1942. When informed by a Japanese camp official that their ship had been sunk, it was 'a grievous shock', especially after 'so long a period of anxiety and uncertainty preceding it'. John Lovett May returned to Tasmania and died in January 2010, aged 96.[16]

Some families were faced with the emotional challenge of the return of one or two sons from active duty but not another. The Olney family needed to welcome back Neil but not Jock. Cpl Leonard Harold Dickenson (VX36539) had escaped but brother Pte George Dickenson (VX27624) perished. The Yench boys were barely distinguishable as men, let alone brothers, when they arrived back in Australia onboard

Gnr Arch Taylor needed to return to New Britain to say a proper goodbye. AWM

the overcrowded Laurabada, dirty, dishevelled, emaciated, sick and barely alive. Henry half-carried Ray down the gangway. A nurse who cared for them in Victoria's Heidelberg Hospital believed that she had 'never seen men in such a condition and survive.'[17] The sons of Christian and Grace had been caught up in the promise of a shared adventure and enlisted in the 2/22nd. They were hoping to catch up with another brother, Alfred, already in the Middle East. Instead, they became part of *Lark Force*. As they retreated from Rabaul, the three brothers became separated – George was massacred at Tol.

During their escape ordeal, the ill and exhausted Ray begged to be left but Henry prevailed with the statement: 'Mum's lost one son she is not going to lose another.'[18] There was gratitude within the Yench household but the empty seat at the table caused anger: 'They were trained for the desert and sent to rot in the jungle.'[19]

As the investigations in Rabaul continued, Maj Harold Stannett Williams (VX890003) of the Australian War Crimes Section was attached to General Douglas MacArthur's headquarters with the Occupation Forces in Tokyo. Although he had studied medicine, his preference was the business world, and he resided in and ran a company in pre-war Japan. His local knowledge and fluent Japanese proved invaluable as he searched through bundles of cards and files

L/Cpl Ernest Keith Ghiggoli. AWM

to uncover the fate of Australian Japanese POWs, determined to ease the anguish of families even if confirmation would surely result in more sadness.

Williams' contacts with the Japanese Navy and Army Departments, Foreign Office and Prisoner of War Information Bureau (PWIB) were frustrating.

Although the PWIB insisted that no information was available, he continued his search and discovered the following letter from the Japanese Navy. Dated 6 January 1943, it stated that 845 POW and 208 civilians embarked at Rabaul on *Montevideo Maru* on 22 June 1942, and had died when the transport was torpedoed off Luzon on 1 July 1942. Attached to the letter was a 48-page roll of names.[20] Translation proved difficult but it was definitive proof of the men killed in Australia's worst maritime disaster.

Telegrams flooded homes the length and breadth of Australia, with profound and enduring consequences. For Beverly Jeffrey, it was her 'worst memory': 'After saying '"bring him home safely" in our prayers every night for the past 3–4 years, it was a bitter blow' when told that her father Pte Joseph William Jeffrey (VX29427) 'wouldn't be coming home.'[21] With news of the death of his brother, Pte Vincent Arthur Lyons (VX38403), adolescent Frank Lyons was unable 'to console my mother.' He was perplexed because nobody came, just the telegram; 'when a death occurs, people come and help, don't they?' It was the longest night of his life. 'Nobody came ... the whole night, just myself, my mum and dad and two young sisters.'[22] Edith Lyons never overcame the bitterness in which she held Australian authorities. 'One dreadful day my brother's medals arrived ... I never saw them. She [my mother] threw them out.'[23] Frank raced to the rubbish bin to retrieve them but 'the garbage truck had already been.'[24]

For Arthur and Amy Ghiggoli of Mangoplah, NSW, the black words on yellow paper were impossible to truly comprehend. Their handsome

23-year-old son L/Cpl Ernest Keith Ghiggioli (NX36559) was dead. The fair-haired L/ Cpl Kevin Victor Geyer (NX47935), 24, was with him when the *Montevideo Maru* sank. Kevin had been an above-average cricket, tennis and rugby league player. The Geyer family had fielded their own cricket team and now they could no longer. The Tenterfield community rallied behind the family and commissioned a memorial plaque. 'Presented to Mr and Mrs G.W. Geyer by Homestead Friends in Memory of Kevin. Loved By All.'[25]

L/Cpl Kevin Geyer. AWM

(Spr) John Mervyn Render (VX129387) of the Royal Australian Engineers (RAE) was attached to the Fortress Engineers. In 1931, he married Doris Fleming. By 1941 the couple had two daughters, Joan and Jennifer, and had purchased a small weatherboard house in the Victorian seaside town of Frankston. Jack had enjoyed growing prize-winning flowers. Now Doris was left to raise their daughters alone.

Laurie and Maggie Lambton migrated from England to ensure greater opportunities for sons Richard and Lawrence. Life was difficult but hard work enabled them to enjoy modest circumstances. War came and their boys enlisted in the 2/22nd. The years of silence took their toll on Laurie and, although he had never been ill, he developed pneumonia and died without knowing what had happened to his sons. In 1945, Maggie received two telegrams and her 'whole world collapsed.'[26]

Mabel Sibraa inserted a memorial notice in *The Sydney Morning Herald* on 24 November 1945, announcing that her son had been 'Presumed Lost at sea.' The word 'presumed' was not yet fully accepted. She still hoped, even believed, that her commando son, Pte Lloyd Sylvester Sibraa (NX34251) was still alive. Lloyd had always been a most enterprizing youth and if anyone survived it was going to be Lloydie. In 1947, Mabel finally conceded that her son was not coming home and, on the anniversary of the sinking of the *Montevideo Maru*, inserted her small poem in the same newspaper.

At night when the shadows are falling
And I am all alone
There comes that longing Lloydie.[27]

For the women of Mabel's generation, their lives were defined by loss. Many were widows too soon, with the sacrifice of husbands on WWI battlefields or the premature death of veteran husbands carrying destructive injuries of mind and body. They were comforted as they watched sons grow; then another war and their sons did not return.

The six Queensland Keid brothers had enlisted in WWI. Four were killed; Harry the eldest was wounded but returned home, as did his youngest brother Guy. The Australian Government awarded a brooch to Mary Keid with a star for each son killed.

Her son Leonard, killed on the Western Front, had been married to Eliza. When Eliza fell into a deep depression, she was committed to hospital for shock treatment. Mary Keid now needed to care for Leonard and Eliza's small children and played a pivotal role in the upbringing of the eldest, Les. Mary was a polite and caring woman, and only once was a flash of her deep grief revealed. When collectors knocked at the door asking for donations to build a local war memorial she replied:

An ordinary family caught up in war; Richard, Laurie, Lawrence and Maggie Lambton. Weightman

Dudley, Daryl and Sid Turner. Dale

'Sorry, not me. I already gave four sons.'[28] Her grandson Les did an apprenticeship on Brisbane trams while supporting his mother Eliza and sisters as best he could. He reassured Mary and Eliza that, because he was attached to *Lark Force* Ordnance, he was well behind the front line. Eliza continued to write and send parcels to her son in Rabaul throughout the war 'unshaken in her belief that he would return safe and well.'[29] Cpl Norman Leslie Keid drowned on 1 July 1942 somewhere off Luzon, the Philippines.

> *Eliza's hair turned white within a couple of days of learning the truth. War had robbed her of her husband and now her son. She was poor, nearly sixty and not in good health.*[30]

For three and a half years the Turner family 'went into a kind of suspended animation, praying for the best but fearing the worst.'[31] In early October 1945, Salvation Army officers arrived to tell Jesse and Mark that their three sons had died with the sinking of a Japanese transport. Four weeks later, they were officially informed. It was of the smallest comfort to know that Sidney and Dudley kept their promise to stay together and watch over their young brother Daryl, but life left the Turner household in Sydney. Mark Turner quietly withdrew from society. The husband of the Turner's elder daughter, Alexis, died of war injuries and Alexis became a recluse while living next door to her parents. Ona, the youngest of the five children, never married and continued to live with her parents. Jesse Turner received her government-issue small silver badge with three stars, one for each son killed, and wore it every day until she died.

For the families grief was personal and a path each needed to travel in their own way, but the grief deeply affected towns and communities, as new names were etched on weathered war memorials. Lang Lang, 47 miles (76km) from Melbourne, served an extensive dairying and pastoral district. The Lang Lang butter factory, owned by Albert and Ada Vinnell, was at the centre of the business district. Post-war, the Lang Lang butter factory began to fail. Perhaps it was the impact of a changing economy, or perhaps it was caused by a loss of heart when the Vinnell family received advice that son Pte Albert Vinnell, aged 30, had died of illness on 6 April 1942 while attempting to escape New Britain, and Pte Arthur Vinnell, 22, was 'presumed drowned'.

Just when the nation was ready to move on, it was dragged into hell with the return of ill and emaciated Japanese POWs from Japan, Thailand, Malaya and Singapore. Country and city newspaper headlines highlighted the same words: 'Atrocities, torture and extreme privation.'[32] The outrage was universal on news of the death of 32 missionaries. Now 'among the heroes and martyrs of the Faith ... blood of the martyrs is the seed of the Church', stated The West Australian on 15 November 1945. A clergyman held 'the West' to blame, because the west had taught the Japanese the 'art of industry, economics, and militarism, but not Christ.'[33] Recriminations strengthened: 'Two Hundred Civilians in Rabaul in 1942 Could Have Been Saved'[34]; 'Failure to Evacuate from Rabaul'[35]; 'The story of what happened inside Rabaul ... indicates a long series of atrocities and horrors.'[36]

The Bitapaka Cemetery, New Britain, is one more beautifully revered cemetery to war, but with only 57 known graves there are more names here than graves. Perfectly symmetrical walls stand tall, as did the soldiers they represent. An avenue of stone pylons bearing line after line of bronze plaques dominate the green space, 31 miles (50km) south of Rabaul. A central stone lectern describes how 'the fortunes of war denied the known and honoured burial given to their comrades in death.' The avenue leads to the cross of sacrifice and in this there is a strong connection. The memorial that dominates bears the names of 1,225 members of the Australian Army, New Guinea and Papuan local forces and constabulary, and the RAAF, who have no known graves. This is a Commonwealth war cemetery, so the names of the civilians with no known grave or who drowned with *Lark Force* troops on 1 July 1942 are not recorded here.

Between 1942 and 1945, so many New Britain and New Ireland civilians simply disappeared – the nucleus of an entire community. William and Bessie Huntley were not seen after 19 August 1942. David Topal of Tereri Plantation, New Ireland, was only 14 when killed with his father Henry. Mrs Phebe Clothilde Parkinson was 78 when she disappeared from Namatanai on 27 May 1944. Government administrators; planters such as Stanley Ashby; hotel manager Alfred Banks; agricultural inspector John Titchener; Rabaul Postmaster James Smith; medical assistant Thomas Evans and telephone technician Hedley Turnbull also disappeared. Adolf 'Ardie' Schmidt was the dedicated head teacher of native schools in Rabaul. Albert Herron was a Commonwealth Bank officer when he and Barbara married in Rabaul – they were expecting their first child. Septimus Filan had been an audit clerk. Thomas Evans was Senior Technical Officer at the Medical Experimental Station and had resided in the territory for 15 years. He and Grace had a two-year-old son, Thomas David, and were expecting their second child.

Henry Fulton, crippled with childhood polio and thus unable to enlist with his brothers in the AIF, had moved to Rabaul to work for Burns Philip for his own adventure. Henry's three brothers survived active service in WWII; Henry died.

For their evacuated families, the anguish was prolonged and they were unable to truly move on. This was exacerbated by at first official denial then protracted formalities. Just before Christmas 1945, Violet Houghton signed for an innocuous-looking letter with the government stamp of the Queensland Echelon and Records Office. The first sentence sent hills through her body.

It is with deep regret that I have to advise you on behalf of the
Minister for the Army that it would appear from information
given hereunder that your husband, Charles William Booth
Houghton, lost his life at sea whilst a civilian prisoner of the
Japanese on board a transport named 'Montevideo Maru'.[37]

Charles Houghton. AWM

The letter informed her that, 'although an allotment and dependant allowance is being paid to you by District Finance Office, Brisbane', she was not so entitled because her husband was not serving with the NGVR when captured. Violet Houghton was requested to refund immediately any monetary sums she had received. Money was of major concern to the young family; Violet applied for her husband's death certificat to entitle her to her husband's life insurance. The death certificate did not arrive, just a note that there were delays 'due to the officer who was attending to such matters was recently transferred abroad'.[38]

Violet Houghton maintained that Charles was indeed enlisted in the NGVR. A solicitor on her behalf continued the battle and, as more and more months passed, asked why there had not even been 'the courtesy of a reply'? 'The widow is unable to collect insurance moneys ... kindly treat this matter as urgent.'[39] In 1951, the national trustees wrote to Army Records Melbourne asking again for a certificate of death. A scribble on an External Affairs file declared 'no trace of him' and referred the file back to the Department of Army.[40] In March 1952, a letter from the Australian Government to the Public Trustee, Sydney, acknowledged that Charles Houghton was Rifleman NGX510 and advised that Army Northern Command, Brisbane, be contacted concerning his will. In June 1953, Violet Houghton was awarded her husband's 1939/45 Star, Pacific Star and War Medal. They were unclaimed and returned.

In 1945, the Australian Government announced that 'dependants of civilians who lost their lives on the *Montevideo Maru* would receive pensions and benefits on the same lines as the service pensions.' These pensions were to be backdated to 1 July 1942.

Furthermore, death duties were waivered.[41] For families evacuated from Rabaul by the same government, this was wonderful news. Walter James Ryan had been Rabaul's British Petroleum manager. His wife Frances and their two children were evacuated to Sydney. The family were living in one room in a boarding house and, although Frances was working, their finances were dire, particularly as 'death duties were unjustly imposed by the Government of the State of New South Wales on my husband's estate.'[42] She was 'deeply dismayed and distressed' but found the fortitude to write to PM Ben Chifley on behalf of 'we women who were kept in ignorance of our men's fate far too long' and for the 'years of anxiety, loneliness and sadness' this caused.[43] The angst escalated for Frances Ryan when the Australian Government, which boasted of standing 'for honesty and fair play', reneged on the promise of the pensions and benefits announced in the House of Representatives.[44] Frances Ryan's letter was jockeyed between the Prime Minister's Office and the Secretary of the Dept of External Affairs, then forwarded to the Department of External Territories, which sent the file to Treasury. The following year, a memo found its way back to the PM's office recommending that Frances Ryan register 'any claim for compensation' with the office of the Controller of Enemy Property, Dept of Treasury. The memo emphasized that any such claim did not mean 'that any responsibility is accepted by the Commonwealth Government.'[45] The endless paper trail facing aggrieved relatives continued and, as anticipated, many ceased the fight through sheer exhaustion.

A three-volume report tabled in 1942 by the Army Minister Frank Forde came with his recommendation that an independent enquiry be made into all aspects of the fall of Rabaul and *Lark Force*. In 1945 Frances Ryan wrote to her Prime Minister, asking that an enquiry be held into 'the tragedy of Rabaul'. PM John Curtin believed this enquiry should be delayed until the return of Australian POWs. The 14th Prime Minister of Australia died unexpectedly in office in July 1945. In June 1946, the matter was debated further and PM Ben Chifley believed that the country needed to heal and that an enquiry should only be held if leaders had been 'corrupt or treasonous rather than fallible or mistaken.'[46] In a rare agreement, Opposition Leader Robert Menzies commented that he did not 'personally agree' to 'post-mortems'.[47] In 1949, Menzies assumed the mantle of Prime Minister of Australia, a position he held for a record 18 years until 1966.

The questions of who, when, where and why remained. The nominal roll of Australian POWs onboard the *Montevideo Maru*, brought home by Maj Williams in 1945, went missing for 65 years. The official Australian Government report on the Tol massacre was not released until 1988. POW cards were offered by the Japanese Government following the war. Whereas other countries, including the United States and Great Britain, soon accepted, the Australian Government did not until 2012. Each begrudging revelation resulted from the dogged determination of descendants to extract the truth from an Australian Government reluctant to accept responsibility and public admonishment for the debacle of Rabaul, *Lark Force* and the *Montevideo Maru*.

Formed into associations such as the Rabaul & *Montevideo Maru*

Bitapaka war Cemetery, New Britain.

Society, *Montevideo Maru* Foundation and the *Montevideo Maru* Memorial Committee, they continued to fight for recognition of the service and sacrifice of their relatives. In 1955, a tablet was erected on the wall of a missionary training institute in Haberfield, Sydney, honouring the 10 Methodist missionaries and two lay workers killed in WWII. On 16 September 1993, the Rabaul 1942–45 Memorial was unveiled on the shores of Simpson Harbour, close to where the men boarded the *Montevideo Maru*. On 6 November 1993, the NGVR & PNGVR ex-members associations erected a memorial plaque in the Hall of Memories at the Brisbane Cenotaph in honour of the 34 NGVR men lost on the *Montevideo Maru*. On 4 July 2002, a plaque bearing the names of 97 named civilians executed by the Japanese at Kavieng, New Ireland, on 18 February 1942 was unveiled. The Australian Capital Territory Memorial dedicated on 10 August 2006, honouring ACT men and women killed in WWII, recognized those who died on the *Montevideo Maru*. Not until 21 June 2010 did the Australian Government, through its Minister for Veterans' Affairs, formally recognize and offer an apology.

As we stand here today, I would like to formally mark the great loss of the Montevideo Maru *and honour those who died. Australia is forever grateful for their service in defence of our nation during the Second World War. I would especially like to acknowledge the great emotional suffering of the families and friends they left behind. These people endured many long and painful years waiting for news of their loved ones and they deserve to be remembered.*[48]

The missing nominal roll was found and, in July 2012, a national memorial was dedicated in the grounds of the Australian War Memorial to the 1,053 troops and civilians who died on the *Montevideo Maru* on 1 July 1942.

In 1942, Prime Minister Robert Gordon Menzies and his defence chiefs too-hastily deployed battalions in an arc across Australia's north, at Timor, Ambon and New Britain. Justified at the time as protecting the

Australian territory of New Guinea and airfields linking Australia with Allies in south-east Asia, the strategy was ill conceived and motivated by the desire to appease and succour favour with the British, Americans and the Dutch. Racial prejudice led to a severe underestimation of the Japanese military.

Named prophetically after small, non-predatory birds: Sparrow Force on Timor, Gull Force on Ambon and *Lark Force* on New Britain, the garrison forces were poorly trained and equipped. Six weeks prior to the Japanese invasion of Rabaul, the Australian Cabinet and Chiefs of Staff accepted that *Lark Force* personnel were 'hostages to fortune'. The failure to publicly accept flawed strategic policy and the humiliation of evacuating the Bird Forces meant that thousands were abandoned and sacrificed.

Decades of subterfuge under successive conservative governments ensured that the reputation of Australia's longest-serving Prime Minister remained untarnished. As the 1960s became the 1970s and 1980s, trade and commerce eclipsed historical veracity and political correctness ensured that the truth remained hidden.

Endnotes

1.   1 Nelson, H. 'Rabaul' in Lal, B.V. (ed) *Pacific Places, Pacific Histories: Essays in Honor of Robert C. Kiste*, University of Hawai'I Press, 2004, p.169. 2

2.   Ibid., p.171.

3.   Broinowski, R.L. MSS0824, AWM.

4.   Ibid.

5.   Ibid.

6.   www.jje.info/lostlives/transcripts/D00056.html

7.   Ibid.

8.   Ibid.

9.   *Pacific Islands Monthly*, October, 1945.

10. Broinowski, R.L. MSS0824, AWM.

11. Scharmach, L. *This Crowd Beats Us All*, p.211.

12. www.angellpro.com.au/mission.htm

13. Coleman, R. 'When home was a trip through hell', in *Una Voce*.

14. Abel, MSS1623.

15. Cook, AWM54 607/9/1.

16. Jackson K. & Friends. 'PNG Attitude: Past times: *Montevideo Maru*', accessed 1 April 2016 asopa.typepad.com/asopa_people/montevideo-maru

17. Yench, L. Conversation 28 May 2016.

18. Ibid.

19. Ibid.

20. AWM 54 779/1/1 Report on Investigation in Manila and Japan Re Aust. POW and Civilians By Maj H.S.Williams.

21. Jardine, B. www.jje.info/lostlives/people/jefferyjw.html

22. Reeson, M. *A Very Long War: The Families Who Waited*, p. 62.

23. Ibid., p.95.

24. Ibid.

25. Geyer, I. Conversation 3 October 2016; email 6 and 9 October 2016

26. Weightman. L. www.jje.info/lostlives/people/lambtonr.html

27. *The Sydney Morning Herald* on 1 July 1947.

28. Jackson K. & Friends. 'PNG Attitude: Past times: *Montevideo Maru*', accessed 1 April 2016 asopa.typepad.com/asopa_people/montevideo-maru/

29. Hampson, C. *The Brothers Keid*, p.94.

30. Ibid., p.95.

31. Dale, M. Email, 6 and 9 September 2016.

32. *Queensland Times*, 10 September 1945.

33. *Pacific Islands Monthly*, October, 1945.

34. *Cairns Post,* 17 Oct 1945.

35. *The Mercury*, 24 June 1946.

36. *The Mercury*, 25 June 1947.

37. A1066, 45/55/3/19. Dept of External Affairs 'Internees –Australians abroad: Civilians reported lost on board SS *Montevideo Maru*', National Archives, Canberra.

38. Ibid.

39. Ibid.

40. Ibid.

41. Ibid.

42. Ibid.

43. Ibid.

44. Ibid.

45. Ibid.

46. 'Submission to the Commonwealth Government', p.18.

47. Ibid.

48. www.aph.gov.au/About_Parliament/Parliamentary_Departments/Parliamentary_ Library/pubs/BN/1011/MontevideoMaru

BIBLIOGRAPHY

Australian War Memorial

AWM54 607/1/1A, '[New Britain] *Lark Force*, New Britain, 1942 – Casualty returns, evacuations, nominal rolls, escapes, etc.

AWM54 607/8/1, AWM54 607/8/1 'New Britain – Evacuation: Evacuation Scheme – Report on withdrawal of troops from New Britain, January 1942, by Capt J.K. McCarthy OC NGAU New Britain, and individual reports by Sgt F. Holland, A.L. Robinson NGVR, Drv W.D. Collins, G.P. Brown, Sgt R.T. Bruce and R.W. Feetum, on their escape from the Japanese and their account of the Toll massacre.'

AWM54 607/9/1, 'I'll Remember Rabaul – Cook.'

AWM54 779/1/1, 'POW – Maj Williams Report.'

AWM54 779/1/5A, 'POW *Montevideo Maru*.'

AWM54 779/1/5B, 'POW *Montevideo Maru*.'

AWM54 779/1/26B, 'POW and Internees, *Montevideo Maru*, sinking.'

AWM54 779/4/11, 'Prisoners of War and Internees – Treatment by Enemy. Report on American, Australian and European POW's and internees, by Col T. Takahasi, Senior Staff Officer SE apanese Forces ('Those prisoners captured in Solomons, New Guinea, New Britain and New Ireland area) (Oct 1945).'

AWM54 1010/1/30, '[War Crimes and Trials – General:] *Montevideo Maru* – List of passengers believed to have left New Britain on above ship, compiled by A. Creswick and G. Thomas, recovered Prisoners of War.'

AWM68 3DRL 8052/122 Part 4, 'Executions on Kavieng South Wharf.'

AWM83 251, 'USA versus Hiroshi Tamura.'

AWM315 271/004/002, 'Correspondence Ministerial.'

AWM315 271/004/013, 'Correspondence Ministerial.'

Abel, G. MSS1623

Ballantyne, J. PR04958

Bensley, R.S. PR82/026

Botham, W.G. PR04594

Broinowski, R.L. MSS0824

Brown, P.H. PR87/011

Cameron, A.G. 3DRL/1088

Cook, W. PR90/053

Crocker, W. PR83/093

Dennis, W.E.R. PR04700

Dore, A.V. PR01835

Fisher, P.W. PR89/040

Ghiggioli family. PR04738

Greenwood, C.F. PR02055

Hannah, R.B. PR04517

Holmes, H.W. PR90/023

Hutchinson-Smith, D.C. MSS1534

Japanese War History – Naval Operations, MSS0708

Larkin, W.H. PR03444

Lerew, J.M. EXDOC168.

Malasaet People. 'About our Stay in the Prison in Rabaul', MSS1968 MSS1968 *Ure Kaveve Kini ta ra pal na banubat aro Rabaul* – About our stay in the prison in Rabaul (during the war).

McCallum, J.T. PR88/056

New Guinea Women's Club, 3DRL/6199 Nottage, S.G. PR83/189

Oldroyd-Harris, J.D. PR87/228 Olney, J.N. 3DRL/0957

Palmer, J.P. MSS2155

Robb, R.P. PR01219

Selby, D.M. MSS0704

Selby, D.M. PR00109

Taylor, A.G. MSS1533

Turner, V.H. PR01469

Vasey, F.S. PR04644

Walsh, T.R. PR05259

Yeowart, R.A. PR91/073

National Archives

A461, AF420/1/1 Part 1, 'Enemy breaches of all the rules of warfare (including Japanese atrocities) Part One.'

A518 GR16/2/1 Defence General Information of deaths for persons lost on *Montevideo Maru*

A1066 IC45/55/319 Internees – Australians abroad. Civilians reported lost on *Montevideo Maru*

A2670 333/1941 War Cabinet Agendum No90/1942 Australian Defence Forces at Rabaul

A2671 90/1942 War Cabinet Agendum No90/1942 Australian Defence Forces at Rabaul

A2671 333/1941 War Cabinet Agendum No333/1941 Defence of Rabaul

A2700 1014 Territory of New Guinea – pension payments to dependants of officers and residents of New Guinea

A7030 13 List of members of New Guinea Volunteers on fulltime duty reported to have been onboard *Montevideo Maru*

A14143 1 *Montevideo Maru* serial name list of POW and Internees who perished B883 series service records

B3856 144/1/362 Part 1 and Part 2 *Montevideo Maru*

B6121 182P sinking of Japanese Prison Ship *Montevideo Maru* MP727/1
GP25/334 Rabaul Garrison lost in *Montevideo Maru* MP742/1 336/1/1614
War Crimes
WWII Army Series personnel file

Books, newspapers and Journals

Advocate, 3 September 1945.

Aplin, D.A. Rabaul 1942, 2/22nd Battalion AIF *Lark Force* Association, McCarron Bird, 1980.

Australian Dictionary of Biography, National Centre of Biography, Australian National University.

Bassett, J. *Guns and Brooches: Australian Army Nursing from the Boer War to the Gulf War*, Oxford, 1992.

Bloomfield, *Rabaul diary: escaping captivity in 1942*, Australian Military History Publications, 2001.

Bowman, A.M. *Not now tomorrow: Ima nai ashita*, Daisy, 1996.

Connolly, R. and Wilson B. (eds) *Medical Soldiers: 2/10 Australian Field Ambulance 8 Div., 1940–45*, 2/10 Australian Field Ambulance Association, 1985.

Cox, L. *Brave and True: From Blue to Khaki – the Band of the 2/22nd Battalion*, The Salvation Army, Australia Southern Territory, Archives & Museum, Melbourne, 2003.

Dale, M. Email, 6 and 9 September 2016.

Dawes, J. *Every man for himself: the life of Father Edward Charles Harris, MSC, 'Martyr' of Mal Mal, the man who would not retreat*, The Catholic Newspaper Company, 1945.

Downs, I. *The New Guinea Volunteer Rifles NGVR 1939–1943: A history*, Pacific Press, 1999.

Feldt, E. *The Coastwatchers*, Melbourne, Oxford University Press, 1946.

Gamble, B. *Darkest Hour: The true story of Lark Force at Rabaul*, Zenith, 2006.

Geyer, I. Conversation 3 October 2016; email 6 and 9 October 2016.

Gill, J.C.H. 'The last days of Rabaul: (December 13, 1941 to January 23, 1942)' *Journal of the Royal Historical Society of Queensland*, vol 6, 1961, Royal Historical Society of Queensland.

Gillison, D. *Australia in the War of 1939–1945*, Series 3 (Air), *Royal Australian Air Force 1939–1945*, Canberra, 1962.

Hall, T. *New Guinea 1942–44*, Methuen, 1981.

Hampson, C. *The Brothers Keid*, self-published, 2005.

Hasluck, P. *The Government and the People 1942–45*, Griffin Press, 1970.

Henderson, M.L. *Yours sincerely, Tom: A Lost child of the Empire*, self-published, 2000.

Horner, D. *The Gunners: A History of Australian Artillery*, Allen & Unwin, 1995.

Horner, D. *SAS: Phantoms of the Jungle—A History of the Australian Special Air Service*, Allen & Unwin, 1989.

Johnson, C. *Little hell: the story of the 2/22nd Battalion and Lark Force*, History House, 2004.

Johnson, R.W., and Threlfall, N.A. *Volcano Town: the 1937–43 eruptions at Rabaul*, Robert Brown, 1985.

Jungle Victory: Outline of Military Events in New Guinea and Papua with over 150 photographs, A Sun publication, Herald and Weekly Press, 1944.

Kenny, C. *Captives: Australian army nurses in Japanese prison camps*, Uni of Q, 1986.

Kettle, E. *That they might live*, Leonard, 1979.

Lal, B.V. (ed) *Pacific Places, Pacific Histories: Essays in Honor of Robert C. Kiste*, University of Hawai'i Press, 2004

McCarthy, D. *South-West Pacific Area – First Year: Kokoda to Wau. Australia in the War of 1949–1945*, Official War History Series. Series 1—Army, AWM, 1959.

McCarthy, J.K. *Patrol into Yesterday*, Cheshire, 1963.

McCosker, A. *Masked Eden: a history of the Australians in New Guinea*, Matala, 1998.

McNab, S. *We were the first: the Unit history of no 1 Independent company*, Australian Military History Publications, 1998.

Mitchell, R. *One Bloke's Story 1937 to 1946: Henry Mitchell's MM Escape from Rabaul*, Development and Advisory Publications Australia, 1998.

Montevideo Maru Memorial Committee, 'The Tragedy of the *Montevideo Maru*', Submission to the Commonwealth Government, 2009.

Moyle, J.T. *Escape from Rabaul and The Moyles of Spring Creek*, self-published, 1999.

Nelson, H. *POW, Prisoners of war: Australians under Nippon*, ABC Books, 1985.

Nikakis, G. *He's Not Coming Home*, Lothian, 2005.

Reeson, M. *A Very Long War: the families who waited*, Melbourne University Press, 2000.

Reeson, M. *Where Abouts Unknown*, Albatross, 1993.

Scharmach, L. *This Crowd Beats Us All*, Catholic Press, 1960.

Selby, D.M. *Hell and High Fever*, Currawong, 1956.

Spurling, K. *The Mystery of AE1: Australia's Lost Submarine and Crew*, Missing Pages Books, 2014.

Stephens, A. *The Royal Australian Air Force*, Australian Centenary History of Defence, Vol II, Oxford, 2001.

Stone, P. *Hostages to Freedom the fall of Rabaul*, Oceans, 1994.

Stone, P. Holland, M. and Holland, J. *El Tigre Frank Holland MBE, Commando, Coastwatcher*, Oceans, 1999.

The Argus, 12 September 1945.

The Sun, 30 September 1945.

The Sydney Morning Herald, 4 December 1939.

The Sydney Morning Herald, 7 April 1942.

The Sydney Morning Herald, 3 October 2002.

Una Voce, Journal of the Papua New Guinea Association of Australia.

USS Sturgeon Log, NGVR Museum, Brisbane.

Wall, D. *Heroes at sea,* self-published, 1991.

Watters, D.A.K. *Stitches in Time: Two Centuries of Surgery in Papua New Guinea,* Xlibris, 2011.

Webb, W. *Report on Japanese Atrocities and Breaches of Rules of Warfare,* AWM, 1944.

West, F.J. *Hubert Murray: The Australian Pro-consul,* Oxford University Press, 1968.

Wigmore, L. *The Japanese Thrust, Australia in the War of 1939–1945,* Series 1 (Army), Vol IV, AWM, 1957.

Williams, H.S. *Report re Japanese steamer Montevideo Maru,* Australian Army, 1942.

Winter, C. 'A Good-Will Ship: The Light Cruiser Koln Visits Rabaul (1933)'. *Australian Journal of Politics and History,* 54(1), 44–54, 2008.

Winterbotham, J. *Papua New Guinea Volunteer Rifles: Nominal Roll,* self-published, 2012.

Yench, L. Conversation 28 May 2016.

Websites

adb.anu.edu.au/biography/mccarthy-john-keith-10910/text19375

www.angellpro.com.au/mission.htm

aph.gov.au/About_Parliament/Parliamentary_Departments/Parliamentary_Library/pub s/BN/1011/MontevideoMaru

asopa.typepad.com/asopa_people/montevideo-maru

australian-pow-ww2.com/index.html

australiansatwarfilmar hive.unsw.edu.au/

www.chm.com.pg/about-us/history/

www.jje.info/lostlives/exhib/rabaulmemorial

www.jje.info/lostlives/people

www.jje.info/lostlives/transcripts/D00056.html

montevideomaru.naa.gov.au/contributions/images.aspx?row=50

www.naa.gov.au

www.pngaa.net espace.library.uq.edu.au

www.ww2roll.gov.au

ACKNOWLEDGEMENTS

A number of years ago I was honoured to be guest speaker at the POW memorial commemoration ceremony in Ballarat, Victoria. A man whose name I never knew pushed a DVD into my hand said 'this needs to be written about' and disappeared into the throng of people as fast as he had materialized. The DVD introduced me to the sinking of the *Montevideo Maru*, Australia's worst maritime disaster. During ensuing years I met descendants of the some of the 1,053 Australians who died onboard that Japanese POW transport on 1 July 1942.

In September 2014 I travelled to Rabaul, New Britain, to commemorate the centenary of the loss of Australia's first submarine and the subject of my book *The Mystery of AE1: Australia's lost submarine and crew*. New Britain had a profound affect – it is that kind of place – a place that captures the imagination. I realized *Abandoned and Sacrificed: the Tragedy of the Montevideo Maru* must be written and a return trip to Rabaul confirmed this sentiment.

Andrea Williams and John Holland were encouraging forces. John Holland's family has a proud New Britain history. It was easy to feature his father Frank Holland, a truly fearless man, as a hero. John has dedicated his life to the preservation of wartime New Britain, New Guinea Volunteer Rifles (NGVR) and kindred organizations, memorabilia and archives. The museum he has established in Wacol, Brisbane is inspiring.

Andrea Williams few would argue knows a great deal about New Britain, New Ireland and outlying islands. Her family were prominent plantation owners and businessmen. Her grandfather Philip Coote, company manager of Burns Philp Rabaul, was a passenger onboard the *Montevideo Maru*. Andrea grew up in the Witu Islands and in Rabaul and spent much of her working life in Papua New Guinea with the travel industry. Andrea had a founding role in establishing what became the Rabaul and *Montevideo Maru* Society. The society's memorial sculpture was dedicated at the Australian War Memorial, Canberra in

2012. Currently the President of the Papua New Guinea Association of Australia, Andrea was previously the publisher and editor of Una Voce, the quarterly journal of PNGAA from 2004 to 2012.

I am honoured to have a foreword written by the ACT Minister, Gordon Ramsay, MLA. Minister Ramsay was raised within the Uniting Church. After studying law at Sydney University and a career as an attorney, he was ordained as a Uniting Church minister. His first congregation was in Kingsgrove, Sydney and in 1997 he was appointed to Kippax Uniting Church in Canberra. In 2016 he was elected to the ACT seat of Brindabella and appointed ACT Attorney General, Minister for Regulatory Services, Minister for the Arts and Community Events and Minister for Veterans and Seniors.

There have been many others who have encouraged and whose knowledge and experience were crucial and much appreciated. As always Elizabeth Van Der Hor has patiently navigated my manuscript through comma and 'would' attacks. Thank you Liz. For historians it has become increasingly difficult to find a publisher willing to commit to books which enrich knowledge. I hope this is one such book. I know that New Holland is one such publisher and I am most grateful for their belief and support.

Thanks also to my family. Being an author is not always conducive to being the best mother, grandmother and friend and I am grateful for your understanding.

– Kathryn Spurling

ABOUT THE AUTHOR

Kathryn Spurling served with the Women's Royal Australian Naval Service (WRANS). She completed an honours degree in history at the Australian National University (ANU); a Master of History Degree (Hons) and a PhD in military history at University of New South Wales (UNSW).

Between 1996 and 2011 Kathryn was attached to the School of History, and then the School of Humanities and Social Sciences, UNSW, Australian Defence Force Academy, Canberra, where she tutored history and strategic studies. In 1999 she initiated the *Women in Uniform: Perceptions and Pathways* Conference and co-edited the book of the same name. Dr Spurling has lectured and published extensively within Australia and internationally on military history, peacekeepers and women in the military. She was the first Australian invited to speak at NATO in Brussels on women in the military and was the first Australian appointed as a Summer History Fellow, at the United States Military Academy (West Point).

As part of the RAN submarine centenary commemorations on ANZAC Day 2014, Dr Spurling gave the commemorative address in Rabaul, New Britain, in August 2014.

Dr Spurling was appointed to the ACT Veterans Council by the ACT Chief Minister, the Hon. Katy Gallagher, MLA, in 2011, and continues to serve on this committee for the ACT Chief Minister the Hon. Andrew Barr, MLA.

During 2012 and 2013 Dr Spurling was Visiting Scholar, School of History, Australian National University. In 2014 she was appointed Adjunct Research Associate, School of Education and Humanities, Flinders University.

Other books by the author published by New Holland Publishers:

A Grave Too Far Away: A Tribute to Australians in Bomber Command Europe, 2012.

Cruel Conflict: The Triumph and Tragedy of HMAS Perth I, 2008.

HMAS Canberra: Casualty of Circumstance, 2008.